Gender and Domestic Life

Also by Tony Chapman

Ideal Homes? Social Change and Domestic Life
(co-edited with Jenny Hockey)

Gender and Domestic Life

Changing Practices in Families and Households

Tony Chapman

© Tony Chapman 2004

First published 2004 by
PALGRAVE MACMILLAN
Houndmills, Basingstoke, Hampshire RG21 6XS and
175 Fifth Avenue, New York, N.Y. 10010
Companies and representatives throughout the world

PALGRAVE MACMILLAN is the global academic imprint of the Palgrave Macmillan division of St. Martin's Press, LLC and of Palgrave Macmillan Ltd. Macmillan® is a registered trademark in the United States, United Kingdom and other countries. Palgrave is a registered trademark in the European Union and other countries.

ISBN 0–333–92437–1 hardback
ISBN 0–333–92438–X paperback

This book is printed on paper suitable for recycling and made from fully managed and sustained forest sources.

A catalogue record for this book is available from the British Library.

A catalog record for this book is available from the Library of Congress.

10   9   8   7   6   5   4   3   2   1
13 12 11 10 09 08 07 06 05 04

Printed in China

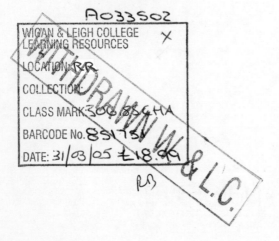

For Jenny

Contents

List of Tables

Acknowledgements

I would like to thank my students and colleagues at the University of Teesside whose interest and encouragement has been invaluable in the preparation of this text. I would particularly like to thank my editor, Catherine Gray at Palgrave Macmillan, for her encouragement, patience and sound advice; and to thank Diane Nutt for providing me with invaluable leads in the literature. Steve Taylor, Martin Wood, Robert MacDonald, George Reid, Barbara Hull, Jenny Hockey, Mark Cieslik, Andrea Abbas and Robin Haggart have also been extremely supportive throughout this project in various ways. Most of all, I want to thank my wife, Jenny, and my children, Michael, Jamie and Edward for putting up with me while writing this book.

TONY CHAPMAN

The author and publishers wish to thank those who have kindly given permission for use of copyright material in this volume: *Basil Blackwell Publishing Ltd* for Table 3.2; *British Sociological Association Publications* for Tables 6.3 and 10.2; *Cambridge University Press* for Tables 10.1 and 10.3; *The Controller of Her Majesty's Stationary Office and the Queen's Printer for Scotland* for Table 6.2; *Sage Publications Ltd* for Tables 1.1, 1.2, 1.3, 1.4; and *the Editorial Board of The Sociological Review* for Table 6.4.

1

Introduction

Why study gender and domestic life?

The aim of this book is to provide sociological explanations for the way that men's and women's experiences of and expectations about domestic roles, responsibilities and relationships have developed and continue to change over time. In so doing the book offers insights into women's and men's potential to challenge traditional notions about gendered practices in the domestic sphere in the future. Rather than using the term 'gender roles' in this book which suggests that activities are fixed and inflexible and non-negotiable, I intend to adopt the term 'domestic practices'. Following the lead of Morgan (1996) I use this term to highlight the point that the pattern of domestic life is strongly affected by wider cultural, economic and political circumstances. But at the same time, such practices are identified, defined and executed according to the unique circumstances that characterise each and every household.

Morgan also recognises that practices are both regularised and routinised to some extent, whilst also being subject to change over time. Change occurs as people move through the life course (by getting married, having children, moving house, getting a new job, getting divorced or retiring) or as external factors impinge on their choices and opportunities (such as economic, technological, political, socio-legal, cultural and environmental change). Consequently, domestic practices are fluid and require constant renegotiation. In this book, domestic practices are defined in the broadest sense to embrace a wide range of activities that take place both within and outside the home including: housework, childcare, leisure, providing income and wealth, strategic planning, managing and spending money and maintaining relationships through caring.

1

The emphasis placed upon gendered expectations about domestic practices, rather than concentrating solely on who does what in and outside the household, underlines the point that very few, if any, domestic practices could (or should) only be performed by one sex. But as this book shows, cultural values may justify the existence of different gendered practices in society in general and the domestic sphere in particular. As a consequence men and women may under particular social and historical circumstances accept these practices relatively uncritically. Indeed, cultural ideas about gendered practices in the domestic sphere may become so deeply embedded that women and men hang on to them with some tenacity (even if, ultimately, rigid adherence to such practices may not always be in their best interests). A key thrust of this analysis is to show that the allocation and acceptance of gendered practices reflects, implicitly or explicitly, gendered power relationships in society.

Sociology, as a discipline, has much to offer in explaining how gendered practices have become established and how they are sustained or changed over time. This is because sociologists are centrally concerned with the way that societal power relationships structure patterns of social behaviour. In some circumstances in the domestic sphere, power is exercised in an absolute sense: that is, by bullying, emotional blackmail, or even using physical force to ensure compliance. But the principal exploratory focus in this book rests on the more subtle and sophisticated ways that power is employed to get women and men to comply with societal expectations of the 'appropriate' way to perform tasks inside and outside the home; and in turn, how men and women often simultaneously resist social convention and each other's wishes, and thereby produce change.

There is, of course, already a very substantial sociological literature on gender and family life, which begs the question, why do we need another one? The answer to this question is both simple and also, one hopes, persuasive. Much of the emphasis in previous texts on gender and domestic life has, for the most part, been concerned with the challenging problems that face families. This book has a much broader scope as it deals with the whole range of households including single person households, nuclear families, gay and lesbian households and communal households. As importantly, this book brings men's experiences of and expectations about domestic life to centre stage. Previously, men have either been regarded as 'off-stage' actors in the sociological literature because it is assumed that they are principally concerned with the public world of work; or conversely, when they are considered, they are portrayed as problematic members of the household.

It is commonplace, when people think and talk about men's and women's domestic roles, expectations and experiences, for them to draw upon stereotypical ideas. Even when such views do not match closely with their own personal experiences, many people seem to feel almost duty bound to run out the old adages about fundamental differences in men's and women's attitudes, attributes and behaviour. Hence the popularity of simplistic self-help books which claim that, for example, *Men are from Mars and Women are from Venus* (Gray, 1992). Sociologists, too, can get into the routine of explaining patterned social behaviour in predictable ways which sometimes means that their research agendas are led by outdated theoretical ideas on what goes on in households rather than grounding their ideas in discrete studies of peoples' actual expectations and experiences.

In the 1950s and early 1960s, for example, many sociologists subscribed to what has become known as the 'cereal box' model of the white, Western nuclear family. Such families, comprising a male breadwinner and female homemaker, were considered to be relatively egalitarian institutions where men and women shared the same goals and distributed resources fairly and equally. The nuclear family household was regarded as one of the key building blocks of society. Indeed, up until the early 1970s, government statisticians and social scientists rarely drew on the idea of gender divisions or differences when studying households and families because it was assumed that the nuclear family was a cohesive and harmonious social unit. The only kinds of households that were regarded as problematic were those which did not match up to the cereal box model of the breadwinner/homemaker household. Such families included highly socially stigmatised 'unmarried mothers', the relatively small number of divorcees, the dispossessed homeless and the chronically poor.

By the late 1960s, a new wave of feminism began to emerge which produced radical attacks on men's power in society in general (Greer, 1970; Firestone, 1970; Millet, 1970; Mitchell, 1975) and upon the constraining institution of the nuclear family in particular (Oakley, 1974; Delphy, [1970] 1977). While feminist writing on the family at this time was characterised by its diversity in terms of its political and theoretical orientation and its empirical focus (see J. Somerville, 2000) one unifying theme that emerged towards the 1970s and into the early 1980s was the exploration of a distinction between the public and private arenas of social life. Indeed, this also amounted to a critique of sociology itself which had largely ignored women in society by concentrating on issues that were presumed only to concern men's experiences in employment, politics and the economy (Acker, 1973; R. Brown, 1976; Stacey, 1991). The debates that ensued hinged on the idea that: 'society is defined by the public sphere of male activities, institutions, hierarchies and conflicts. The family, which perches uneasily between the social and the non-social, is a subsidiary, supporting institution with no independent or determining role' (Gamarnikow *et al.*, 1983: 3).

A new research agenda emerged in sociology and social history which sought to explore the experiences of women who crossed the divide between the private world of the home and moved into the public world of work (see, for example, West, 1982; John, 1986; Bradley, 1989 for British studies; Kahn-Hut, Kaplan Daniels and Colvard, 1982; Stromberg and Harkess, 1988 for American studies). These studies demonstrated, in relation to a variety of types of industry and occupations, that gendered inequalities at work were produced by direct and indirect forms of sex discrimination against women. This, in turn, led to further research on (and campaigning for) equal opportunities at work through the development of family friendly employment policies. In sum, feminists cast doubt on what was then the conventional sociological view of family life as harmonious and egalitarian, and instead argued that the home was a site of women's oppression because their passage to the public life of work, careers, politics and leisure was blocked by discrimination and the demanding burden of motherhood and housewifery.

The emphasis on negative aspects of domestic life led to a third strand of research, often referred to in text books as the 'dark side' of family life. In a similar vein to early feminist writing on the home, researchers challenged the popular notion that the home is necessarily a safe haven for children, older people, or for cohabiting women and men. Such studies have explored a range of issues including domestic violence, child abuse, divorce, widowhood, mental and physical health problems, poverty and homelessness (see Dallos and McLaughlin, 1993, for a general review of this literature).

While I accept that the domestic sphere is often the site of serious economic, social and interpersonal problems, this book takes a generally more positive standpoint. It may be the case that at some point in most people's lives, home life can be experienced as lonely, confining, stifling, exhausting or even as a frightening place. But I believe that it is wrong to give the impression that domestic life is, in general terms, a miserable existence. If this were so, women and men would not invest so much of their money, time, energy and imagination in creating a place that they can call home. There would not be such massive markets for home improvement products and services, for home-based leisure and entertainment, and also the vast range of television shows, newspaper features, books and magazines that give advice and instruction on how to make home life better. Not all couples manage to achieve their aims first time round, but the idea of establishing a happy home life is culturally resilient, and the majority of people try again.

Books on the sociology of the family tend to steer clear of in-depth analysis of the physical place where gendered practices are played out. Instead, they look at couple relationships as the unit of analysis and pay only scant attention to the location of home. By foregrounding relationships, sociologists have tended to underestimate the importance of the domestic sphere as the place where people can achieve their personal, social and economic aspirations, use their imagination, be creative, enjoy their leisure and – perhaps most importantly for many women and men – escape the strictures of the working environment. This problem is especially acute in the field of men's studies which has practically no domestic dimension beyond a few references to the importance of achieving equality in relation to housework. Instead, their texts reveal a strong preoccupation with sexuality, the body and male violence; politics, work, careers and unemployment; socialisation, childhood experiences, dysfunctional relationships, mental health and therapy; and anti-sexism and pro-feminism (see, for example: Brod, 1987; Hearn, 1987; Kimmel, 1987a; R. Chapman, 1988; Seidler, 1991, 1992; Christian, 1994; Mac an Ghaill, 1994, 1996; MacInnes, 1998). Where men's studies directly addresses issues surrounding home life, it is usually in the context of households in crisis: after divorce, separation of fathers from their children, or in response to other crises of masculinity such as downward social mobility or retirement.

In one recent literature review of men's studies in ten European countries, the authors emphasised the importance of the study of men's experiences and expectations about home, but were hard pressed to find much evidence of empirical analysis of men's domestic values and practices beyond studies on gender differences in time spent on domestic work (Hearn *et al.*, 2002). In light of this absence, Hearn *et al.* make the following plea:

> Further exploration of the complex dynamics surrounding negotiations between women and men in relationships regarding housework, parenting and emotion work would be welcome. It would be interesting to see how and when, if ever, women and men form coalitions through a politics of reconciliation, and how gender constellations at 'work' and in the 'private' sphere influence each other. It would be important to further research couples who experience difficult labour market conditions, so, for instance, making the female partner the main earner in the long term or forcing them to accept working times that do not allow traditional housework distribution. (2002: 399)

The omission of the study of home life from most studies of men and masculinity is a serious flaw which has done little to persuade many feminists to test the argument that home is a place where men expect service from women so that they can get on with their own lives in the public world of work, politics, the academy and leisure. This text draws together those studies which have considered men's position in the domestic sphere, the majority of which is written by feminists and women sociologists and social historians, but recognises that there is much room for further analysis. I will elaborate upon these possible lines of inquiry in the concluding chapter of this book.

Changing households and changing practices

Exploring the way that gendered domestic practices change is made complicated in the early twenty-first century by the variety of family values and forms that now exist in most Western nations (see Hantrais and Letablier, 1996; Jagger and Wright, 1999; McKie, Bowlby and Gregory, 1999; Erera, 2001). In the case of the USA, as Stacey has argued:

> Like postmodern culture, contemporary family arrangements are diverse, fluid and unresolved...No longer is there a single culturally dominant family pattern to which the majority of Americans conform and most of the rest aspire. Instead, Americans today have crafted a multiplicity of family and household arrangements that we inhabit uneasily and reconstitute frequently in response to changing personal and occupational circumstances. (1991: 17)

There is much statistical evidence to support these assertions from census data that have been collected across the Western world. For the present, I will confine myself to recent evidence drawn from the USA to demonstrate the point that the traditional nuclear family can no longer be regarded as a universal family form. Table 1.1 shows that the number of households with two parents and children has declined by nearly 20 per cent between 1960 and 1998. And indeed, these data underestimate the extent of family diversity as many of the families that appear to be conventional nuclear families are reconstituted families after divorce and remarriage. Contrary to the cereal box image, the majority of households do not have children in them, as Table 1.2 shows, sometimes because they have grown up and left home, or because couples have chosen not to or cannot have children, or because couples have not yet had children. This table also demonstrates that ethnicity is a significant factor in describing family forms. Black American children, the table shows, are much more likely to be brought up in single parent households (see also Engram, 1982; Davis, 1993; Logan, 1996; Toliver, 1998; Staples, 1999). Hispanics are more likely to conform to the traditional model of the

Table 1.1   *US households with children*

Year	Number of households (millions)	Married couple (%)	Single mother (%)	Single father (%)
1960	25,689	90.9	8.2	0.9
1980	31,022	80.5	17.6	2.0
1998	34,760	72.7	22.1	5.2

Source: adapted from Casper and Bianchi (2002: 11), Table 1.1.

Table 1.2   *Household composition in the USA (%)*

Marital status	White	Black	Hispanic
Married with children	24.2	16.4	36.3
Married no children	31.5	14.9	19.6
Single women with children	5.0	20.5	13.1
Single women no children	15.9	16.0	7.2
Single man with children	1.7	1.7	2.7
Single man no children	10.8	12.9	7.3

Source: adapted from Casper and Bianchi (2002: 15), Table 1.2.

nuclear family, while white couples are increasingly likely to live in households without children. The number of children living in single parent households in the USA has grown dramatically since the 1950s. In 1950, only 6 per cent of children lived with their mother and 1 per cent with their father while 93 per cent lived in a conventional family. By 1998 only 73 per cent lived in a (now not so conventional) nuclear family, 22 per cent lived with their mother and 5 per cent with their father (Casper and Bianchi, 2002: 99).

Changes in marriage and fertility patterns are also particularly pronounced in the USA over the last 40 years. As Table 1.3 shows, average ages of first marriage have increased substantially. In 1960 only about 10 per cent of women and 20 per cent of men remained unmarried beyond the age of 25, but by 1998 this had increased to nearly 40 per cent of women and around 50 per cent of men. This does not mean that all of these men and women were living alone or with their parents. Instead, cohabiting has become much more popular. In 1978 only 3 per cent of women and 4 per cent of men were recorded as cohabitees in census statistics, but by 1998 these percentages had risen to 9 per cent of women and 12 per cent of men (Casper and Bianchi, 2002: 42).

These data signify changing attitudes and behaviour on a grand scale and the purpose of this book is to demonstrate how and why these changes have come about and to assess what impact they have had on gendered domestic practices. For the present I will confine myself to one example to illustrate the magnitude of change in social attitudes. Table 1.4 shows how many American men and women

Table 1.3 *Percentage of women and men in the USA who have never married by age*

Age	1960		1980		1998	
	Women	*Men*	*Women*	*Men*	*Women*	*Men*
15–19	83.9	96.1	91.2	97.2	96.8	98.6
20–24	28.4	53.1	51.2	68.2	70.3	83.4
25–29	10.5	20.8	21.6	32.1	38.6	51.0
30–34	6.9	11.9	10.6	14.9	21.6	29.2
35 +	7.2	7.8	5.7	6.3	7.7	10.6
Median age of first marriage	20.3	23.2	22.0	26.1	25.0	26.7

Source: adapted from Casper and Bianchi (2002: 19), Table 1.3.

Table 1.4 *Changing attitudes about husbands' and wives' domestic and work practices*

	1977		1994	
	Men	*Women*	*Men*	*Women*
Percentage who disapprove of wife working if husband can support her	32.3	34.8	18.9	18.9
Percentage who think it is more important for a wife to support her husband's career	52.7	60.7	22.2	21.1
Percentage who believe that men achieve most outside the home while women achieve most at home	68.9	63.2	38.4	32.8
Percentage who think that working women cannot have as warm and secure relationship with their children	58.4	44.9	39.2	24.2

Source: adapted from Casper and Bianchi (2002: 295), Table 10.2.

adhered to conventional attitudes about breadwinner and homemaker practices in 1978 and 1994. This table shows that in a period of only 27 years, the percentages of men and women who think that married women should not take paid work has almost halved. Even fewer women and men now think that wives should support their husband's careers. The table also shows that the supposed public/private divide between home and work has begun to collapse. In 1977 nearly 70 per cent of men and 63 per cent of women believed that men achieved success outside the home while women achieved this at home. These percentages had fallen to less than 40 per cent of men and only 32 per cent of women by 1998. Furthermore, the once commonly held attitude that working women cannot be good mothers has also declined since the late 1970s. In 1977, 58 per cent of men and 45 per cent of women shared this view, but by 1998, only 39 per cent of men and 24 per cent of women believed that working mothers could not have warm and secure relationships with their children. While these data show that attitudes and behaviour have changed dramatically in a very short period of time, it is also clear that traditional domestic practices have not yet been abandoned completely. This is simply demonstrated. On average, men still earn about 30 per cent more than women across Western nations and women continue to do about 70 per cent of the housework (Coltrane, 2002).

A surface analysis of the range of household types gives the impression that the 'traditional' family is in decline and that almost anything is possible and acceptable now; but, at a deeper level of analysis (as this book shows), a study of the origins of the 'ideas' underlying gendered domestic practices demonstrates that a culturally dominant paradigm of what constitutes a proper home continues to have a pervasive influence over many aspects of contemporary domestic life, even when alternative household forms are established.

Defining home

As this book is concerned with domestic life, it is important at the outset to define what is understood by the term 'home'. Home can be defined in several ways: as a secure, private, physical retreat from the outside world; as an economic asset and future investment; as a representation of self-identity; as a type of relationship; and finally as a cultural object. As it is difficult to discuss each of these definitions separately because they are all closely intertwined, in this section I will simplify the discussion first by briefly considering the home as a physical entity and the advantages this brings to people in terms of security, privacy, status and economic well being. Following this, I will explore the definition of home as a cultural object which can reveal clues about commonly held ideas on what constitutes home life and how this, in turn, may reinforce and sustain established gendered domestic practices.

Home, when defined as a physical place, represents a relatively secure and private retreat. Consequently, householders in the West tend to guard their homes from outsiders by putting up physical defences such as strong doors, locked windows and burglar alarms. They also defend their territory symbolically with, for example, low garden walls and important looking entrances. Furthermore, householders know how to defend their own space and respect other people's through more or less subtle behavioural strategies on the boundary between the public world of the street and the privacy of home. The strong emphasis that is now placed on personal privacy and security has been enhanced by the growing numbers of households that own their own home. Owning a home is often the most important financial investment people make. In the English-speaking Western nations, with which this book is principally concerned, a strong premium is placed on personal ownership of the home with around 60 to 70 per cent of households being privately owned in the UK, the USA and Canada, New Zealand and Australia. The fact that home ownership is so prevalent means that non-ownership is also a significant social marker. This has led some writers to assert that home ownership provides people with 'ontological security' (Saunders, and Williams, 1988; Saunders, 1990). This means that a sense of individual self-worth and indeed a sense of citizenship is closely associated with the privileges, status and security that having a home – or, better still, owning a home – can bring. While such arguments have proved to be contentious because access to the private housing market is limited by issues such as class, gender and ethnicity (see P. Somerville, 1989), private or public rented accommodation is often associated with a lower social status than ownership (Dowling, 1998; Boal, 2000; Rohe, Zante and McCarthy, 2002). Consequently, those people who buy their rented houses often signal their shift into private ownership by making visual alterations to their houses (Dolon, 1999). When people fall on hard times economically – due to, for example, divorce, unemployment or long-term illness – there is a risk that they may lose their homes, which can produce serious personal and psychological consequences (Hamnett, 1999). Homelessness – that is, not owning or renting a permanent home – can have many serious impacts on life chances because of discrimination by, for example, prospective employers against people in that situation (Kennett and Marsh, 1999).

To define the home purely in physical terms, as bricks and mortar, is clearly inadequate for our present purposes. This is because the home as a private place, a secure place or as a principal financial investment is meaningful in the sense that it impacts on the way that householders construct their sense of self-identity. The privacy that the home affords householders is also a crucial defining element. The home represents a relatively private retreat from the public gaze and a place where people can, on the one hand, relax and be themselves whilst, on the other, it can be used as a platform upon which to display identity to significant others. These factors encourage people to think of their home as a highly individualistic expression of their own taste and identity. But, from a sociological point of view, it is also clear that definitions of home are strongly affected by external social, cultural and economic forces.

Sociologists, until relatively recently, tended to pay little attention to the cultural significance of the physical space of homes, and instead concentrated attention on relationships in families. Consequently, there has been a tendency to conflate the terms 'home', 'household' and 'family' or to use them interchangeably. This sociological emphasis on relationships has produced enormously important insights into the way that domestic life is lived, but by paying only scant attention to the physical construction of homes as places and the symbolic meanings attached to them, many of the more subtle meanings of home life were underresearched. Over the last decade many sociologists have shifted their research emphasis to embrace definitions of home as a place, a type of relationship and as an idea. In so doing, they have incorporated methodologies from other social scientific traditions.

Anthropologists, architectural historians and archaeologists also recognise the importance of defining households in terms of the kind of relationships they embody. But they are also interested in studying the home as a cultural object. Archaeologists, for example, attempt to understand how society was lived in the past by interpreting the physical record of what was left behind by a society that has either disappeared, or has been transformed almost beyond recognition over time (Johnson, 1993, 1999). Similarly, anthropologists make sense of societies by observing roles and rituals in their physical context. As Birdwell-Pheasant and Lawrence-Zúñiga show:

> Anthropologists have generally tended to treat houses as a backdrop, a setting with props where presumably more interesting and important aspects of the drama of human cultural and social life are played out. The implicit definition of 'house'...that emerges from the anthropological and archaeological literature refers to a built form where people sleep, eat, socialize and engage in a variety of economic, symbolic, and other activities that sustain the people who use it. The house shelters from the elements both people and their resources, including equipment, furnishings, food stores, and animals, as well as sacred paraphernalia and symbolic goods. (1999: 1)

While anthropologists recognise that individual homes in all societies are unique to some extent, it is also demonstrated that home exteriors and interiors in any given culture tend to be remarkably similar in important ways (see Rapoport, 1969; Kent, 1990; Oliver, 1997; Birdwell-Pheasant and Lawrence-Zúñiga, 1999). In Western countries too, home interiors reveal distinct similarities in domestic practices. For example, it is commonplace to see the same types of furniture face in the same directions in particular types of rooms. The functions of rooms such as kitchens and bathrooms are identifiable by the installation of similar appliances, services and decorative features. Homes have spaces which are clearly distinguishable as family rooms, children's rooms, or adults' rooms. Houses and apartments also have external doors that separate private spaces from the public world, and internal doors which separate householders from each other; almost everybody who is brought up in that culture seems to understand how to behave at these social thresholds (Goffman, 1969; Brown and Altman, 1983; Korosec-Serfaty, 1984, 1986).

Similarities in the physical appearance of homes suggests a degree of cultural conformity in patterns of domestic life. This does not mean that people cannot enjoy a measure of privacy in their own home, and neither does it suggest that people cannot express their individuality through the decorative schemes they choose and the furniture they buy. What it does reveal, however, is that in making choices, householders are very much aware of the potential reaction of significant others to the way that they behave. In this sense, homes can be conceptualised as stage sets, upon which men and women attempt to communicate positive messages to the outside world in order to show that they are successful, respectable, fashionable and socially desirable (T. Chapman, 1999a, 1999c). By definition, if these attributes are communicated successfully, it also signals that people are conforming to social expectations to some degree. Indeed, the key to eliciting and maintaining the social respect of family, friends and neighbours is the ability to match more or less their behaviour rather than breaking the rules by, for example, showing off wealth ostentatiously, or by not conforming to the rules of propriety. Resisting cultural conformity in the community is a risky business and as a consequence cultural conservatism tends to predominate. As Veblen points out:

> Those neighbours of the community who fall short of [a] somewhat indefinite, normal degree of prowess or of property suffer in the esteem of their fellow-men; and consequently they also suffer in their own esteem, since the usual basis of self-respect is the respect accorded by one's neighbours. Only individuals with an aberrant temperament can in the long run retain their self-esteem in the face of the disesteem or their fellows. (in Coser, 1977: 268)

Veblen's notion of an 'aberrant temperament' is interesting, in that he highlights the fact that individuals who do not pull themselves into line with social expectations may feel the weight of social disapproval.

It is now becoming more generally accepted in sociology that studying the home as a cultural object, as well as a kind of social relationship, can reveal much about the way that patterns of behaviour in the domestic sphere are socially reproduced (see Chapman and Hockey, 1999). In this book I will use many examples to emphasise the importance of studying the home as a cultural object by drawing attention to the way that domestic artefacts, technologies and the organisation of domestic space itself symbolically represent and reinforce established practices. Household objects, for example, can embody cultural values about masculinity and femininity in their design (see, for example, Csikszentmihalyi and Rochberg-Halton, 1981; Forty, 1986; Schwartz-Cowan, 1989; Cockburn and Ormrod, 1993).

Power tools were once designed by manufacturers with rugged plastic moulding and 'workmanlike' colours so that men would buy them to do household jobs (or their wives would buy them for their partners). This is changing as women have become more interested in do-it-yourself (DIY). Companies have responded to changing demand and have produced a range of smaller, friendly coloured, flexible or multi-facility craft-oriented power tools to appeal to this market. This suggests that manufacturers have no explicit interest in reproducing domestic gendered practices. On the contrary, it reveals that when men's and women's domestic practices change, manufacturers are quick to capitalise on a new market niche. For example, the current fashion for expansive stainless steel cooking ranges that resemble professional kitchen equipment reflect men's increased interest in home cooking. By the same token, such designs are popular with many women too, because they want to be like glamorous and successful television chefs rather than homely wives and dutiful mothers.

Men and women actively participate in the process of gendering domestic space. Parents, for example, often make explicitly gendered choices about the way to decorate and furnish boys' and girls' bedrooms. Married or cohabiting couples similarly have debates on how their garage, kitchen, bedroom and bathroom should be decorated, furnished and designed to provide an appropriately masculine or feminine impression. In so doing, men and women symbolically represent their influence and control over defined domestic spaces. While it is clear that cultural values have an enormous impact on the decisions men and women make about how a home should be organised, decorated and so on, it is also crucially important to recognise that, in every home, the pattern of negotiation will vary according to individual circumstances. This is because men and women bring to domestic relationships a range of resources, including 'economic power', 'socialised skills', 'physical capabilities' and most importantly 'sets of ideas'. Such resources strongly affect the way that practices and relationships are negotiated. *Economic resources* can include property, a private income, money from paid work, and career potential which may enhance income. *Socialised skills* can include the confidence to build a career or to carry out domestic work and childcare competently. Different *physical capabilities*, such as strength, are virtually irrelevant to most domestic activities with one crucial exception which is pregnancy and childbirth; this, in turn, has a significant impact on roles outside the home and especially in relation to paid work. Finally, and perhaps most importantly, there are *sets of ideas* that women and men internalise about what is 'possible' or 'desirable' for them to do in their adult domestic lives.

Plan of the book

The first step in this analysis of home life begins in Chapter 2 where domestic practices in families and households are defined in two ways. First, I invite the reader temporarily to set aside commonly held gendered assumptions about home life in order to think socio-logically about domestic practices in both practical and cultural terms. Second, this chapter explores the way that power relationships in wider society impact on gender relationships. It will be argued that patriarchy and capitalism continue to impact on the way that domestic practices are defined in the home; but it will also be shown that domestic practices are subject to constant renegotiation by women and men. This argument reflects a more general theoretical shift in sociology to identify the home as a key social institution which both responds to and produces social change.

Chapter 3 explores how the forces of patriarchy and capitalism combined in the nineteenth century to produce an ideology of separate spheres for men as breadwinners and women as home-makers. It will be argued that patriarchal ideology, in tandem with capitalism, had a very significant impact on power relationships in marriage and conceptions of 'masculinity' and 'femininity'. While it will be shown that this separation was never complete in middle- or working-class households, the ideology of separate spheres continues to influence ideas about home life. The two chapters that follow examine the development of breadwinner and homemaker roles in the twentieth century. Chapter 4 will focus on two extended case studies, the first of which will concentrate on the experiences of British working-class men in the mining and fishing industries which produced particularly polarised gendered relationships in the home and community in the first half of the twentieth century. The second study, by contrast, will focus on the link between masculinity, employment and the imperative to succeed in the USA from the early to mid-twentieth century. This analysis will demonstrate the potentially catastrophic impact of career failure on perceptions of masculinity. The chapter concludes with an assessment of the benefits of marriage to men in career terms.

Chapter 5 considers the experience of homemaking in the twentieth century by studying how middle-class households were transformed in response to the loss of servant labour in the first half of the twentieth century. While changing house design, new technology and scientific management techniques all contributed to the transformation of gendered domestic practices in middle-class homes, it will be shown that women's domestic workload increased. While society was successful in persuading women to adapt homemaker roles, the chapter shows that there were fundamental challenges to the homemaker role from the 1960s onwards which were encouraged by feminist thinking. This analysis concludes that attitudes to homemaking and breadwinning have changed substantially but many women continue to support men's career development as a life-style strategy. In so doing, as Chapter 6 explains, women do not necessarily lose the power to negotiate over domestic practices. The analysis in this chapter centres on the negotiation of everyday gendered domestic practices by considering time use in households, patterns of spending and financial planning and, finally, the approach couples take to negotiating household chores. This chapter highlights the point that everyday practices and routines can reinforce established cultural ideas about masculinity and femininity, but it is also revealed that such practices are changing in many households and the indications are that both women and men are becoming less rigid in their attitudes about who should do what in the domestic sphere.

The second half of this book shifts emphasis away from conventional heterosexual couple households to explore a range of household types including communes, gay and lesbian households, the domestic practices of migrant ethnic households, single people and older people. These chapters show that changes in the way that domestic life is organised are not wholly constrained by dominant social expectations even if, ironically, some experiments with domestic life can ultimately serve to reinforce the legitimacy of more conventional domestic practices. As Chapter 7 shows, most experiments with communal living tend not to fundamentally challenge conventional gender practices in the household. Indeed, in many cases, such experiments in communal life actually reinforce gendered roles rather than challenge them.

Chapter 8 recognises that the Western English-speaking nations with which this book is concerned are diverse multicultural societies. Within each nation there exist several cultural scripts on gendered domestic practices which operate in unison and sometimes in opposition. This chapter focuses specifically on adaptation or resistance to convention by first considering how recent migrant ethnic minority groups adapt conventional domestic practices from their home culture in a Western context. This is an issue of such complexity that it is impossible to do much more than scratch the surface of the diverse experiences of different ethnic groups, and consequently the chapter focuses only on the recent experiences of migrant black Caribbeans and South Asians in Britain. Second, Chapter 8 explains how gay and lesbian couples challenge the cultural conventions of heterosexual domestic practices. It is demonstrated here that gay and lesbian couples tend to emphasise the importance of 'equality' in domestic practices compared with the 'equal but different' model that is commonly adopted by heterosexual couples. While lesbian and gay couples do aspire to achieve a higher level of equality in relationships, the analysis indicates that the configuration of social class, education and personal factors also impact strongly on the experience of domestic life. In common with heterosexual couples, in sum, it is argued that the work that must be done to maintain a household is essentially similar and can produce arguments and resentments over disproportionate contributions to domestic work.

Over the last 25 years there has been a steady increase in the number of single person households. While the domestic situation of single women and men has not, as yet, been extensively researched by sociologists, it is clear that the position of single people in society is rising on the political agenda. Chapter 9 shows that being single can still be experienced as problematic in a society where heterosexual coupledom is still regarded as the cultural norm. The chapter explores the subjective experiences of women and men who live alone and, in so doing, the analysis demonstrates that being single is rarely a permanent status. Indeed, many people who live alone are currently in long-term relationships, have recently ended a relationship or have regular but short-term relationships. Nevertheless, perceptions of home and the way that domestic life is practised differs for single people because of their stronger reliance on friendship networks than may be the case among couples and the different way in which the boundaries of home are drawn as a consequence.

While this book concentrates upon the experiences of adults who are of working age, Chapter 10 takes a different point of view by addressing older people's expectations and experiences of domestic life. It is widely accepted in the sociological literature, as this chapter will show, that because older couples are more likely to subscribe to traditional views on gendered domestic practices than younger people, the process of transition to retirement can be problematic. Explanations of this are often justified on the grounds that women often find it difficult to accommodate to the idea of their husbands being at home. And in turn, because the routines of domestic life have been determined to a large extent by women over many decades, men often find it difficult to identify a role for themselves to play. This chapter reveals, in sum, that ideas about masculinity and femininity continue to affect the way that domestic practices are negotiated after retirement. In the concluding chapter of this volume, the prospects for further positive change in the way that gendered domestic practices are negotiated is contemplated. It will be argued that as women's and men's allegiance to strictly demarcated bread-winner and homemaker roles continue to be eroded, there are good prospects for greater equality in the domestic sphere.

2

Defining Domestic Practices

The term 'home' is often lodged in the imagination as a place to fulfil our dreams (Bachelard, 1958) and as a 'haven in a heartless world' (Lasch, 1977). It is an appealing idea and one to which many of us would like to subscribe but, in reality, domestic life can often be stressful and emotionally fraught. This is because running a home is so costly, because there never seems to be enough time to get everything done, and because members of the household cannot always agree on priorities. Investing in domestic life, in sum, is demanding in terms of time, money and emotion. And when the tension rises, people grumble, nag and often argue about the unfairness of it all. They say that it is not fair that they have to work so hard, that they have no time for leisure, that nobody will help to sort out problems, and that nobody appreciates what they have done for everybody else. Only too often, when women and men are caught in such a bind, they draw on stereotypical explanations to account for their feelings (Craib, 1995).

The purpose of this book is to take a step back from common-sense explanations for men's and women's conflicts in the domestic sphere and produce sociological explanations for the way that domestic practices have developed and are changing. As a first step in this analysis, it is essential to define in clear terms what domestic practices actually are. In the first section of this chapter, therefore, I invite the reader to set aside commonly held gendered assumptions about home life in order to think sociologically about domestic practices. Taking gender out of the formula even for a few moments is difficult, because cultural attitudes about what should be done, who should do what, and who does what best are so deeply ingrained. Thinking dispassionately about domestic practices requires a degree of honesty that is sometimes difficult for women and men to admit to in the coffee shop, bar or even, in my experience, in the seminar room. The difficulty arises from the fact that people find it hard, even temporarily, to set aside the crucial element of power from the equation. By power, I mean that one partner has a vested interest in influencing the ways that practices are defined or undertaken or, conversely, that one partner has the opportunity to avoid doing certain tasks while the other may feel unable to do so.

The second section of this chapter will explore the way in which domestic life is gendered in 'ideal typical' terms. The purpose of this exercise is to gain a clear understanding of the way that gendered ideological assumptions underpin conventional notions of what constitutes a 'breadwinner' and 'homemaker' and how these definitions are closely linked to perceptions of masculinity and femininity. This section of the chapter will also explore the way that power relationships in wider society impact on gender relationships. It will be argued that patriarchy and capitalism continue to impact on the way that domestic practices are defined in the home. But it will also be shown that domestic practices are subject to constant renegotiation by women and men as society changes. In so doing, the analysis reveals that while social institutions impact on domestic practices, the reverse is also the case as men and women make new demands on each other and society as a whole in order to mould domestic practices to suit their interests. This argument reflects a more general theoretical shift in sociology to identify the home as a key social institution which both responds to and produces social change: the home is a 'structuring structure' as Bourdieu (1984) would have it, or a 'form of structuration' according to Giddens (1984). As Donley-Reid has argued, home is in this sense 'a medium and the outcome – both enabling and constraining people and action' (1990: 208).

Defining domestic practices

As a starting point in this analysis, it is important to explore in some depth what is understood by the term 'domestic practices'. Table 2.1 provides a set of definitions that will be explored throughout this text. At face value, these definitions seem to be entirely straightforward and self explanatory, but in fact they rest on a set of implicit cultural and economic assumptions about the way that contemporary home life is practised. Beginning with underlying economic assumptions, it is clear that the contemporary household is primarily a unit of consumption rather than production: that is, income is gained from

Table 2.1 *Defining domestic practices*

Domestic Practices	Definition
Housework	Including tasks such as laundry work, cooking, cleaning, maintenance, gardening, home improvements, household shopping, etc.
Parenting	Including tasks such as intensive caring for babies and infants, helping older children with school work, ferrying children to and from sport, music, leisure classes, etc., liaison with schools.
Leisure	Can include many of the above tasks, including gardening, DIY, cookery, playing with children, family outings, home-based leisure (watching television, playing games, talking, reading, entertaining, etc.), home fitness training, preparing to go out, hobbies, household shopping, etc.
Providing income/wealth	Can include full-time life-long employment career, occasional, seasonal or part-time work; private income (savings, inheritance, trusts, etc.); state benefits; entrepreneurial activity, production of food, goods or services for the household, etc.
Strategic planning	Making decisions about careers, deciding about having a family/adopting/fostering, how to bring up children, choosing not to marry, choosing to remain single, setting goals, deciding how to apportion tasks in the household division of labour, etc.
Managing money	Including decision making on financial regimes (i.e., pooling incomes, setting spending targets, agreeing regimes of consumption, etc.), mismanaging money (i.e., constant overspending, failing to discuss money matters, keeping secrets, contrary spending priorities between partners), coping with financial crises, and strategic planning (see above).
Caring	Doing emotion work within households to maintain/nurture relationships with partner, children, extended family, colleagues, friends, neighbours; worrying about older children, providing support for nephews/nieces, grandchildren/great-grandchildren, etc.

economic activities that take place away from home, or at least the source of economic gain is monetary even if householders work at home. In Western consumer societies there is considerable pressure placed on households through retail psychology, advertising and marketing to invest in new products and services. Consequently, assumptions are made about the raised necessity for both men and women to take paid jobs to earn enough money to get the products and services they feel that they need. While such dual-earning households may be work-rich and perhaps also relatively affluent, there may be a tendency towards households becoming time-poor because they have to work harder to maintain their domestic life-style.

At a deeper level of analysis, it is clear that the definitions of domestic practices presented in Table 2.1 also implicitly assume a number of fundamental cultural principles. First, it is clear that the home is conceptualised with reference to secular rather than spiritual criteria. In the West, the home represents both a rational investment in voluntarily chosen interpersonal relationships and also a financial investment in the future. This in turn mirrors a tendency in the contemporary West to place the importance of individual happiness and self-fulfilment at the centre of people's lives rather than to subjugate self-interest to the spiritual world, kin networks and community. While these values may seem natural, especially to Western house-holders, they are not universal.

It is useful to provide just one example to demonstrate that many cultures organise domestic practices very differently in order to make the point that what seems 'natural' in the West is in fact a cultural construction. As Kent (1990) shows, for the Betsileo who live in the south central highlands of Madagascar in a highly domesticated subsistence rural economy, the use of domestic space signifies the existence and importance of gendered domestic practices, but this delineation of space is defined in relation to the spiritual world rather than the secular. The north of their large one-room houses is associated with nobility and seniority, while the south is associated with humbleness and lowliness; the east is associated with the sacred, and the west with profanity. Calendrical division of the year is important in defining, in spiritual terms, the use of space. Different months of the year are associated with benevolent or malevolent fates, and these, in turn, are associated with the north/ south, east/west axis. January in the north-east of the house 'bestows dignity and sovereignty', for example. In Betsileo households, gendered power relationships are symbolised by a patterned use of space. Senior males (and sometimes senior females) sit and sleep in the north-east of the house while other women and children sit in the south-west and younger males sit on the axis between them. As Kent points out, when she and her colleagues attempted to sit in the south-west of the house, presuming that this would be taken as a mark of deference to the householders, chaos ensued because it was expected, as guests, that they would be seated in the highest status corner of the house, in the north-east.

The 'strangeness' of other cultures works in both directions, of course, as Barley (1989) demonstrates in his study of homes as seen from the perspective of a party of Indonesians he was showing around Britain. From a traditional Indonesian perspective, many aspects of contemporary British domestic life seem bizarre: for example, the practice of investing great effort and money in front gardens that nobody ever sits in, or indeed working so hard to pay for a home when so little time is actually spent there. These observers found it especially hard to understand why the British invested their earnings in something as trivial as a home when they could invest this effort in building magnificent monuments for their ancestors. Because British culture is no longer profoundly shaped by religious belief, we forget that, in our early medieval society, we too invested in the spiritual world. From the eleventh to the thirteenth centuries, the wealthy invested much of their resources in the building of immense cathedrals and monasteries instead of opulent mansions for themselves. This changed as the centuries progressed when the richest landowners spent more and more money on the display of their own power and wealth in their mansions and estates. And so, while we may play around with spiritual ideas in the way we decorate and manage our homes by, for example, buying a coffee table book on feng shui, this does not signal an abandonment of the acquisitive and aspirational individualistic culture of capitalism.

The point of the above discussion, in sum, is to demonstrate that the categories listed in Table 2.1 provide a discrete 'snap shot' of contemporary domestic practices. Bearing these points in mind, it is now possible briefly to discuss some of the implicit cultural assumptions underpinning each of these categories. The first category in Table 2.1, *housework*, incorporates an unwritten set of cultural assumptions about what constitutes the right standard of comfort, order and cleanliness that should be achieved in homes. This is not to say that such standards are essential needs, in terms of health, security or other aspects of emotional or personal well being; but they represent what people expect. In early twenty-first century Western households, for example, it is generally assumed that an appropriate level of tidiness and cleanliness and fashionability should be maintained. It is tempting to argue that such standards are not universal across the world because the financial expense of achieving them is beyond the pockets of the majority of the world's population. While this may be true in purely economic terms, such an assertion would represent a gross underestimation of the importance of culture in defining what constitutes appropriate standards. Take, for example, the issue of the maintenance of appropriate levels of 'hygiene' in Western homes. As Douglas has argued, much of our tidying and cleaning is not just about dirt avoidance but represents compliance with cultural expectations.

> As we know it, dirt is essentially disorder. There is no such thing as absolute dirt: it exists in the eye of the beholder. If we shun dirt, it is not because of craven fear, still less dread or holy terror. Nor do our ideas about disease account for the range of our behaviour in cleaning or avoiding dirt. Dirt offends against order. Eliminating it is not a negative movement, but a positive effort to organise the environment... In chasing dirt, in papering, decorating, tidying we are not governed by anxiety to escape disease, but are positively re-ordering our environment, making it conform to an idea. There is nothing fearful or un-reasoning in our dirt-avoidance: it is a creative movement, an attempt to relate form to function, to make unity of experience. (Douglas, 1966: 2)

Douglas argues, therefore, that people in contemporary or pre-literate society ritualistically compartmentalise their domestic spaces to meet social expectations about respectability, privacy, authority and cleanliness. As a consequence, she writes:

> we must treat the spring millinery and spring cleaning in our towns as renewal rites which focus and control experience as much as Swazi first fruit rituals. When we honestly reflect on our busy scrubbings and cleanings in this light we know that we are not mainly trying to avoid disease. We are separating, placing boundaries, making visible statements about the home that we are intending to create out of the material house. If we keep the bathroom cleaning materials away from the kitchen cleaning materials and send the men to the downstairs lavatory and the women upstairs, we are essentially doing the same thing as the Bushman wife when she arrives at a new camp. She chooses where she will place her fire and then sticks a rod in the ground. This orientates the fire and gives it a right and left side. Thus the home is divided between male and female quarters. (Douglas, 1966: 68)

Domestic practices, especially in capitalist societies, are subject to constant incremental change. Indeed, the above quotation has a distinctly anachronistic quality about it, because less than four decades later the essentiality of spring cleaning (or being seen to be doing the spring cleaning) has been all but abandoned in most households. Change tends to come more quickly in capitalist societies than in traditional societies because companies must, if they are to survive, persuade us to modify our practices and, in so doing, buy new products and services (Lodziak, 2002). The need to increase household cleanliness is a particularly modern obsession that has been promoted by detergent manufacturers who encourage us through advertising to live in fear of germs lurking under the rim of our toilet, or persuade us to buy plastic products infused with anti-bacterial agents to prevent the risk of disease. We are encouraged to buy more and more powerful vacuum cleaners to suck up dust mites, or replace our carpets completely with laminated wooden floor coverings to protect ourselves and our children from allergies. And now that some members of the medical profession are suggesting that keeping things too clean can actually lower our resistance to disease, perhaps it will not be too long before a manufacturer starts selling the *right kind* of bugs in an aerosol to spray around the house to keep our children healthy!

The success of such companies cannot be guaranteed unless they can tap into and heighten consumers' desires and anxieties when it identifies new markets. As will be shown in Chapter 5, the public sometimes resists change at first, although over time such innovations are often accepted as indispensable. Statistically, Western homes are remarkably similar now in terms of their basic facilities. The vast majority of households have washing machines, refrigerators and microwave ovens. Indeed, items such as electric or gas cookers and vacuum cleaners and other such devices are almost universally owned. The fact that most houses own the same equipment is very significant sociologically, for it demonstrates that households are organised, and practices are undertaken in more or less the same way across the whole of society.

The second category in Table 2.1, *parenting* (and indeed the concept of childhood itself), is also loaded with contemporary cultural values. Until the nineteenth century, infancy and adulthood were not separated by a period of time known as childhood. Instead, minors were thought of as diminutive adults who were not so much in need of our care, but were providers of work to sustain the household (Ariès, 1988; Pollock, 1983; James and Prout, 1990). It was not until the nineteenth century that childhood became socially constructed as a significant life transition that required, in middle-class families at least, particular forms of nurturing, supervision, discipline and even different kinds of clothes, play and dedicated space in houses. Instead of children bringing economic advantage to households through gainful employment, they now represented a very significant cost to parents and for longer periods of time. These costs are not just related to factors such as the expense of children's school and university education; as Buckingham (2000) has shown, many aspects of domestic consumption are affected by children's 'pester power'. In the USA each year it is predicted that this amounts to $130 billion a year. Indeed, children's own spending is not insubstantial at $10 billion a year (see also Kline, 1993; Seiter, 1993; Gunter and Furnham, 2000; Kenway and Bullen, 2001).

Contemporary parenting practices are also characterised and shaped by cultural expectations that adults hold about what family life should be like. Such expectations have changed substantially over the last 30 years as more married women have taken paid jobs to help to meet the financial costs of raised expectations of domestic comfort and facility and to increase their personal independence. Consequently, most mothers cannot be available to care for their children full time as was the case in middle-class households in the 1950s and early 1960s. This shift in emphasis has required parenting values to change significantly from a position in the 1960s where working mothers were vilified for 'neglecting' their children, to the current perspective where parents argue that it is 'better' for children to be in childcare because they get more confidence and experience than could be provided by parents. The term 'quality time', when set in this context, speaks volumes about changed attitudes.

Leading from the above point, it is clear that the third category in Table 2.1, taking *leisure*, has also become an imperative for parents and children in contemporary households. The pattern of family leisure has changed dramatically since the 1960s, however, as the entertainment industry has built new expectations of what it is like to have fun. Ostensibly, the purpose of leisure is to achieve relaxation and pleasure but, as will be argued in Chapter 6, leisure activities can put additional pressure on time and resources and demand that householders work even harder to afford to use their free time as they choose. Furthermore, contemporary culture has established the principle that adults should enjoy leisure separately from children, and often individually within marriage. In fact, men have expected to take leisure as a reward for their efforts as a breadwinner for more than a century, as will be shown in Chapter 4. Married women's leisure, by contrast, was more commonly associated with housework such as craft work or cookery, the facilitation of children's leisure or 'tagging along' with husbands in their leisure pursuits (Deem, 1985; Green, Hebron and Woodward, 1990). But this pattern is changing as women have gained greater financial independence and higher expectations of personal fulfilment.

Providing income and wealth, strategic planning and *managing money*, as Chapter 6 reveals, are complex processes that are negotiated in the context of significant gender power differentials in wider society. It is clear from the above discussion that these domestic practices are shaped by capitalism in the sense that the capacity of a household to earn money is often defined by external factors. Similarly, decision-making and strategic planning are affected strongly by the way that capitalism raises expectations about the standards, status and facility of domestic life. In so doing, capital draws a close relationship between consumption and happiness which tends to increase pressure on households to make more and more money. In this sense, chasing desires for bigger and better houses and newer products to put in them can actually produce anxiety for those who cannot achieve their goals, and disappointment for those who can because they may not have the time to enjoy what they have earned (T. Chapman, 1999a).

Finally, the practice of *caring* is also a complex and culturally loaded issue (Morgan, 1996; Smart and Neale, 1999). In Western societies is it generally accepted, in cultural terms, that women invest more time in caring for family and the household than men. Social interpretations of what this caring represents varies over time. Current sociological thinking favours a distinction between the idea of 'caring for' home and family (that is, doing the actual work that is required) and 'caring about' the family. But this emphasis on caring about other family members and the idea of the family itself is often interpreted in a very negative way. This is because it is recognised that taking principal responsibility for caring necessarily results in lost opportunities. Furthermore, some writers now define caring about the family and its members as a type of 'emotional labour' (see Hochschild, 1983, 1989; Jagger and Wright, 1999; for a more general discussion of emotions, see Bendellow and Williams, 1998): that is, a kind of work rather than an expression of love. Such an idea would seem, as Chapter 5 demonstrates, to be most inappropriate in the 1950s where women's selfless approach to family life was, in cultural terms, revered. But this was a time when family life was framed within a particular model of romantic love that is less current now (Cancian, 1987; Giddens, 1992; Beck and Beck-Gernsheim, 1995). Looking further back in history, it is clear that the idea that a connection between caring and love has not always been thought to be a necessity, if indeed they were associated at all, for marriage used to be defined in more contractual or companionate terms (Trumbach, 1978; Stone, 1979; Houlbrooke, 1984; MacFarlane, 1986; Shoemaker, 1998).

This discussion of the underlying cultural meanings that are attached to the definitions of domestic practices in contemporary households has revealed that nothing should be interpreted at face value. And so, if some aspects of domestic life are commonly assumed to lack meaning, value or pleasure, it is important to ask ourselves *why* this is the case. The term 'housework', for example, has negative connotations: it is something that people claim that they would rather avoid (or leave for someone else to do) in order to do something more interesting, stimulating or socially valued, but it is possible to interpret housework in less negative terms. For example, it can offer opportunities to develop skills that cannot obviously be used in employment. It may be an outlet to use creative energy in decorating, cooking or entertaining, the outcome of which can elicit praise from significant others. Furthermore, even if some tasks are repetitive, it does not necessarily follow that they are intrinsically dissatisfying. Some people may enjoy the routine of chopping vegetables or mowing the lawn. Others might get a real sense of satisfaction from ironing clothes for no other reason than to gain pleasure from seeing a task completed (a situation which may always be denied them at work). Satisfaction could even be gained from the sensations surrounding a task such as the sight, feel and smell of freshly folded linen or a waxed table top. And finally, pleasure may be gained from caring for other people. While such experiences of pleasure may be more or less fleeting, I doubt that anybody experiences all aspects of housework as negative all of the time although they may, as I have already noted, be unwilling to admit to their enjoyment of particular tasks.

As has been demonstrated above, anthropologists argue that housework can be 'creative' and 'integrative'. But from a sociological viewpoint, it is equally apparent that such processes are also affected by power relationships. Indeed, because the task of managing dirt can be stigmatised, there is a tendency for the relatively powerful to delegate such tasks to social subordinates. As Hughes has argued, in the workplace the process of delegation of dirty work reflects underlying power relationships. As professions have become established, for example, professionals attempt to increase the 'social distance' between themselves and the dirt they deal with. Doctors delegate the duties of cleaning patients' wounds to nurses, while they in turn delegate other tasks to auxiliaries. And yet most occupations involve some aspects of dirty work, as Hughes (1958) has noted:

> [work] may be dirty in one of several ways. It may be simply physically disgusting. It may be a symbol of degradation, something that wounds one's dignity. Finally, it may be dirty work in that it in some way goes counter to the more heroic of our moral conceptions. Dirty work of some kind is found in all occupations. It is hard to imagine an occupation in which one does not appear, in certain repeated contingencies, to be practically compelled to play a role, of which he thinks he ought to be a little ashamed. (cited in Woollacott, 1980: 194)

The delegation of tasks to social subordinates is not always a desirable outcome. Doctors, for example, still generally keep control over the process of examining patients' bodies in order to retain command over the prestigious and powerful practice of making diagnoses even if they have to do this dirty work as a consequence.

In short, even powerful people are prepared to do dirty work if it is likely to provide them with more power and resources. In medieval patriarchal societies, for example, men tended to gravitate towards domestic service because the great baronial households of Europe were the political and economic powerhouses of the time. Men with aspirations for power and influence offered their own or their sons' service and performed all the principal domestic duties including cooking, waiting at table and providing personal services. Some of these services were degrading by any standards, including the ignominious practices of the 'groom of the stoole' who attended in the most intimate detail to the King's toilet (Girouard, 1978). It is not surprising, given these circumstances, that medieval households were populated mainly by men. The fifteenth-century Northumberland household, for example, included 166 men but only nine women (Girouard, 1978: 27). The near absence of women in the great households (see, for example, Shahar, 1983; Herlihy, 1985; Kirshner and Wemple, 1985; Labarge, 1986; Mertes, 1988) therefore signifies the political and economic importance of service at that time.

Long before the industrial revolution began, gendered practices in British and American households had been transformed because men recognised that little was to be gained in terms of their status, resources and power from giving service to their social superordinates. Consequently, the responsibility for the organisation and service of the household fell to women, as Chapters 3–5 reveal, although it remains the case that the reality of women's household work depends to a large extent on their class position (Gregson and Lowe, 1994; B. Anderson, 2000).

Analysing gendered domestic practices

In early twenty-first century society, as has already been demonstrated in Chapter 1, there is a tremendous variety of family and household formations. This makes the analysis of domestic practices complicated. In order to move forward, it is useful to construct an 'ideal typical' representation of gendered practices in households in order to provide a benchmark against which different life-styles, such as communal households (discussed in Chapter 7), gay and lesbian households (discussed in discussed in Chapter 8), single person households (discussed in Chapter 9), or retired persons' households (discussed in Chapter 10) can be compared. The concept of the 'ideal type' does not refer in any sense to an ideal world, or assert that these are the types of practices men and women should or do have. Instead I am using Weber's ([1922]1978) concept of the ideal type which, as Coser notes, 'never corresponds to concrete reality but always moves at least one step away from it. It is constructed out of certain elements of reality and forms a logically precise and coherent whole, which can never be found as such in that reality' (1978: 223). The purpose of Table 2.2, then, is to act as a 'benchmark' against which contemporary family forms can be compared. Analytical work of this kind helps to highlight the conflicts that occur when the values that men and women have internalised can clash with changed circumstances. For example, in dual-earning households, if a husband earns less than his wife he has to reconcile this with the role model of the breadwinner which insists that his 'masculinity' is signified by his capacity to be the primary earner. Similarly, the woman must reconcile her own position with the role of the homemaker which suggests that 'femininity' requires a degree of submission to men in exchange for security and status. In such dual career households, as Chapter 6 concludes, there is a higher degree of tension between husbands and wives who attempt to adhere too closely to rigid breadwinner and homemaker practices than for couples whose values are more flexible (McRae, 1986; Gill, 1999).

It is clear from the ideal-typical model of gendered domestic practises presented in Table 2.2 that men and women do not enter into relationships on equal terms. Indeed, a definitional characteristic of the breadwinner is that person's 'head of household' status in cultural, legal, political and economic terms. The effort bargain in this model of the breadwinner/homemaker household is that the husband provides the principal income through paid work while the wife runs the household, cares for children and perhaps also earns a secondary wage. In exchange for this wives should expect economic security and social status derived from their husband's employment status. The representation of domestic life presented in Table 2.2 seems now to be to be outdated but, as will be shown in Chapter 6, men and women continue to buy into this model of family life through the way they select marriage partners. That is not to say, of course, that they are necessarily satisfied with the outcome of that marriage when it becomes apparent that many contradictions and stresses can be created by such domestic practices, but of course not everyone who marries or cohabits fall neatly into this model of the nuclear family for a number of reasons. First, while it remains the case that men are more likely to be the principal earners at the point of marriage, it is not necessarily the case that they will remain so because their wife might outperform them in career terms. Second, it cannot be assumed that men will be satisfied with a secondary role in parenting or that women are happy to settle for a conventional motherhood role, or indeed that either or both partners will want children at all. Third, it cannot be assumed that all men who become breadwinners are happy and successful career men; many men have little or no ambition at work, and do not particularly enjoy work or the responsibilities that breadwinning entails. Finally, while many people do establish themselves in conventional nuclear families, many do not survive and end in divorce or separation. One does not have to be a sociologist to recognise that the portrayal of domestic life presented in Table 2.2 provides some ammunition to cynics who may suggest that conventional breadwinner and homemaker households may represent something of a tinder box.

Analysis of gendered power relationships in the domestic sphere requires theoretical analysis at two levels. First, it is necessary to draw upon broader social-structural analysis to demonstrate that society and its institutions help to shape the way that men and women behave. Several chapters of this book reveal that social institutions can stop women and men from participating in certain types of activity. For example, in Chapter 3, it will be shown that women were barred from certain forms of paid employment by the state in the nineteenth century. While it is important to recognise that legislation can be

Table 2.2 *Ideal-typical representation of polarised gendered domestic practices in the functionalist and feminist sociological analysis of the 'traditional' nuclear family*

Domestic practices	Men's expectations about principal practices	Women's expectations about principal practices
Housework	Secondary (helping)	Primary ('homemaker' role)
Parenting	Secondary (expectation of social distance)	Primary (parenting and motherhood as synonymous)
Leisure	Primary (expect right to leisure)	Secondary (to partner's, children's leisure)
Provide income/ wealth	Primary (breadwinner role)	Secondary (supplementary income)
Strategic planning	Primary (career decisions, geographical mobility)	Primary (family size, children's upbringing, household order and priorities, house style, location)
Managing money	Primary (major expenditure, houses, cars, own interests/ hobbies)	Primary (household goods, children's needs, holidays)
Caring	Secondary (supporting partner)	Primary (care for partner's, children's emotional needs)

used to force men and women to behave in certain ways, it is relatively rare in Western industrial societies to depend wholly upon such constraints. A much more powerful tool at society's disposal is to harness or generate a set of beliefs that legitimate social expectations. As was noted in Chapter 1, men and women bring to their domestic relationships a range of resources, including 'economic power', 'socialised skills', 'physical capabilities' and 'sets of ideas' that give them power over each other. The most important of these resources, arguably, are the sets of ideas that define what it is 'possible' or 'desirable' for women and men to do in their adult lives.

While there are competing explanations for the way that sets of ideas shape social practices, it is generally accepted within sociology that 'ideology' is a valuable conceptual tool to explain power relationships. Sociologists use the term ideology to argue that commonly held ideas or values help to justify and regulate patterns of social behaviour. The concept of ideology is not generally used to argue that social values necessarily serve the best interests of people in general, however. On the contrary, the principal purpose of ideology in a society is to persuade people to accept that it is legitimate for some people to have more power and resources than others. Most famously, Marx explored the importance of ideology for the maintenance of the power of propertied classes in society when he stated that: 'The class which has the means of *material* production at its disposal, has control at the same time over the means of *intellectual* production, so that thereby, generally speaking, the ideas of those who lack the means of intellectual production are subject to it' (cited in Giddens, 1971: 41). One does not have to be a Marxist to recognise that capitalism embraces many ideas that do not necessarily serve the interests of the majority, but these ideas have become so deeply embedded culturally that many people do not even notice that they hold such beliefs. Arguments that draw upon the concept of ideology are not necessarily fatalistic, however, in the sense that it is assumed that nothing can ever be done about fundamental conflicts of interests. On the contrary, the use of ideology in political writing is often a call to arms, as in the case of both Marxist and radical feminist writing on revolutionary change.

In the context of this book, ideology is a useful analytical device because it helps to demonstrate how capitalism seeks to persuade women and men to work hard in order to promote its fundamental interest in increasing the profitability of business enterprises. It also reveals why the state and its institutions help to facilitate the success of business enterprise by indoctrinating people into a disciplined approach to work through, for example, the education system. In its attempt to legitimate gendered patterns of social inequality in society, capitalism also draws upon patriarchal ideology. In simple terms, patriarchy means the 'rule of the father': that is, male governance of the behaviour of women, subordinate adult males and children in families or households. While there is much evidence, across history, of this pattern of governance being dependent upon male violence in interpersonal relationships, it is more generally argued that men's power over women is legitimated through patriarchal ideology.

Some feminist writers have asserted that there exists a 'system' of patriarchy, which operationalises the institutions of marriage, family, education, work, religion and so on to serve men's interests. In such writing, there is a tendency to assume a systematic male conspiracy to oppress women (see, for example, Millett, [1970] 1977; Firestone, [1970] 1974). There has been much critical debate on the salience of this kind of theorisation especially amongst those writers who have attempted to explore the relationship between the sometimes competing interests of capital and patriarchy (Delphy, 1977; Eisenstein, 1979; Hartmann, 1979; Barratt and McIntosh, 1980) or, most ambitiously of all, to fuse together the contributions of capitalism, patriarchy and racism to women's oppression into a unified theory (see, for example, Walby, 1986). Instead of being diverted from the issue at hand by the complexity of these debates, I shall follow Bradley (1989), who argues that patriarchy is a useful descriptive term which is best applied where it fits, rather than adopting it as an all-embracing explanatory device. I take this position, first, because patriarchy (together with capitalism and racism) is but one of a number of sometimes competing and sometimes integrated ideological forces in society, and second, because such theories tend to exaggerate the importance of ideology in shaping women's and men's everyday social practices.

The analysis in this book proceeds from the view that ideology is fundamentally important in embedding justifications for gendered inequalities in economic, political, cultural and social practices; and furthermore, that taking into account individuals' potential to challenge and change such practices is also crucially important. In this sense, I follow Giddens' lead by adopting a notion of power that embraces both the notion that social structural forces shape patterned social relationships *and* the idea that human agency always makes a difference in the way that social relationships are played out. As Giddens notes:

> Anyone who participates in a social relationship, forming part of a social system produced and reproduced by its constituent actors over time, necessarily sustains some control over the character of that relationship or system. Power relations in social systems can be regarded as relations of autonomy and dependence; but no matter how imbalanced they may be in terms of power, actors in subordinate positions are never wholly dependent, and are often very adept at converting whatever resources they possess into some degree of control over the conditions of reproduction of the system. In all social systems there is a dialectic of control, such that there are normally continually shifting balances of resources, altering the overall distribution of power. (1982: 199)

Giddens' emphasis on human 'agency' is important because it demonstrates that in all social relationships an element of negotiation is necessary between the relatively powerful and the relatively powerless. Negotiation between the powerful and the relatively powerless does not necessarily, or even generally, lead to 'equality', but it can narrow the gap as is the case in negotiated relationships between capital and labour, in the West at least; and, as this book demonstrates, between men and women in the domestic sphere.

It is also now becoming more common for sociologists of the family and domestic life to accept that there is often a mis-match between society's expectations of what domestic practices should be like and the way that domestic life is actually practised by individual women and men. Following Morgan, this book adopts the principle that 'family life is often characterised in terms of flux and fluidity' (1999: 13) and that, as a consequence, it is better to conceptualise domestic living in terms of 'practices' rather than definite and fixed roles. By adopting this position, it is possible to engage in a more subtle analysis of the shifting and varied gendered expectations and experiences and domestic life than can be achieved by adhering to, for example, more rigid functionalist analysis which tended to focus on the conventional nuclear family as the benchmark against which all other household forms must be measured. As Morgan argues, the use of the term 'family practices' implies:

> a recognition that family life can be considered through a variety of different lenses and from different perspectives. Thus, family practices may also be gender practices, class practices, age practices and so on. This point is made in order to stress that family life is never simply family life and that it is always continuous with other areas of existence. The points of overlap and connection are often more important than the separate entities, understood as work, family, politics and so on. (1999: 13)

Morgan's conceptualisation of family practices is useful because he stresses the interplay between a number of factors that shape the pattern and experiences of family life. Importantly, he puts considerable emphasis on the agency of individual members of the family in framing domestic practices. By definition, this approach emphasises the point that domestic life is a process and not a fixed system.

This is, of course, a very modern way of considering power relationships in the domestic sphere. The idea that women and men both have a significant say in the way that domestic practices were established would have seemed preposterous to men and most women a hundred or so years ago. The next three chapters explain how this shift in attitudes has come about.

3

Separate Spheres

This chapter explores how the forces of patriarchy and capitalism combined in the nineteenth century to produce an ideology of separate spheres for men as breadwinners and women as homemakers. Patriarchy, as the first section of the chapter reveals, is deeply rooted in Western ideology and has far reaching consequences on power relationships between men and women in society. More specifically, patriarchal ideology has had a very significant impact on power in marriage and, furthermore, it continues to impact upon cultural understandings of 'masculinity' and 'femininity'. This section will also show how patriarchal ideology, in tandem with the emergence of the capitalist system, consolidated the principle that women and men should occupy separate spheres. Concentrating on middle-class households, it will be shown that this separation was never complete and that the 'cult of domesticity' that emerged as the century progressed was riddled with contradictions. The second section of the chapter considers the development of separate spheres for working-class men and women in the nineteenth century. This section reveals that while the patriarchal ideology of the breadwinner household became deeply entrenched in working-class culture, its practice was often undermined. While breadwinners did attempt to emulate their middle-class male counterparts by keeping a wife at home, they often were not successful in achieving this end. In some cases, as this chapter will show, this is because women chose to continue working, while other women (probably the majority) had no choice but to work.

Patriarchal ideology and power in marriage

In medieval Europe, patriarchal ideology sustained the legitimacy of men's authority over women in marriage. Medieval theologians believed that men were superior to women in terms of physical strength, moral character and intellectual ability. Their authority over women was justified further by a medieval interpretation of the story of the fall of Adam which asserted that women were inherently weak and sinful. The Christian church, following St Peter, taught that husbands should honour their wives and treat them with some consideration and restraint, but there was no question that men were regarded as the master of their household. This was clearly stated by St Paul who established the principle that 'Wives, submit yourselves unto your own husbands, as unto the Lord. For the husband is the head of the wife, even as Christ is the head of the Church' (Ephesians, 5:25; cited in Shahar, 1983: 66).

Medieval marriage, in the upper echelons of society at least, was not entered into merely to control women. Instead, marriage as a social institution was used to bring powerful families together to combine their power and influence, increase their property and to forge political allegiances. Consequently, women from influential households were considered as prizes to be won for they could provide both lineage and property, and therefore power and social status. As Heer notes, young women were pawns in the power games of the great households.

> These noble ladies knew well enough that they were not mistresses of their situation, that men regarded them as loot or merchandise, as objects they openly and secretly traded among themselves, as prizes sometimes taken by stealth. Lands, men and crowns might flow from such golden booty. In feudal society, marriage was an important political and commercial transaction. ([1962] 1990: 137)

The rituals of Christian marriage symbolised this transfer of authority from a woman's father to their husband by the 'giving of hands'. In eleventh-century France, for example:

> The bride was given to the groom by her father or another close relative acting as a guardian. The joining of the right hands concluded the transfer of a gift – with all the artifice and ambiguity implicit in the act...The man then slipped onto three of his wife's fingers, one after another, the blessed ring that signified marriage – and was supposed to protect her from assault by demons. According to ecclesiastical theory, it was given for love and as a token of fidelity; [but] the reciprocal gesture, the giving of a ring to the groom by the bride, did not appear before the sixteenth century. (Barthélemy, 1988: 130)

Culture runs deep. In the contemporary Christian marriage ceremony, a bride is still presented to the groom as her father's gift, and men continue to choose whether or not to wear a ring, while for women no such ceremonial option exists.

It would be a mistake to assume that the wives of powerful men in the early medieval period had no influence upon their husbands, the running of a household and upon wider social and political issues. Indeed, it is likely that women lent their support to their husbands since the alternative, returning to her kindred home, would mean the loss of her privileged social position as mistress of the household. And while marriage had a strong contractual element, it would also seem unlikely that all late medieval and early modern marriages lacked intimacy and love (Stone, 1979; MacFarlane, 1986; for additional reading on pre-modern family life, see Duby, 1985, 1988; Herlihy, 1985; Brooke, 1989; Abbott, 1993). But even if companionship or love was achieved, it was established against the backdrop of women's subordination to men. As Crawford and Gowing note: 'marriage necessarily involved both partnership and hierarchy, love and mastery' (2000: 164; for texts on women's lives in medieval and early modern Europe, see Kirshner and Wemple, 1985; Labarge, 1986; Erler and Kowaleski, 1988).

Until relatively recently, there were few alternatives to marriage if women sought to gain security, status and a measure of autonomy in society. It is not surprising, therefore, that for many centuries women have been encouraged to develop their marriage marketability. From the seventeenth century social recognition of the importance of marriage marketability led to the production of a large number of 'conduct' books. More than 500 editions of conduct books were published in England between 1693 and 1760 (Fletcher, 1995). The most successful books in this genre were Richard Allestree's *The Whole Duty of Men* (which ran to 64 editions from 1659 to 1842) and its companion, *The Ladies Calling*, first published in 1673. Echoing the principles of medieval Christian teaching on the differences between the sexes, such books defined the 'natural' attributes of men and women as separate and distinct, as Table 3.1 shows.

Medieval writing on women tended to describe negative traits such as their sinfulness and potentially uncontrollable sexual passion but, as the eighteenth century progressed, conduct books began to place more emphasis on women's superior moralistic and virtuous characteristics. Such distinctions between masculine and feminine traits were not informed by sociological insights about cultural socialisation of course, but instead character traits were thought to

Table 3.1 *The attributes of women and men in English conduct books*

Women's natural attributes	Men's natural attributes
Virtues	*Virtues*
Chastity	Intellect
Purity	Boldness
Modesty	Discretion
Meekness	Honesty
Patience	Sobriety
Tenderness	Ambition
Charity	Determination
Piety	Courage
Devotion	Restraint
Vices	*Vices*
Vanity	False pride
Affectation	Aggrandisement
Ambition	Haughtiness
Artifice	Tyranny
Confidence	
Stubbornness	

Source: adapted from Shoemaker (1998: 23–5); see also Kimmel (1987b), Hitchcock and Cohen (1999), Foyster (1999).

be natural, so it was commonly believed that women were ruled by their emotions: they were led *by their heart*, whereas men were ruled by reason, *by their head* (see also Hadley, 1999; Hitchcock and Cohen, 1999).

While men were regarded as the stronger sex, it was commonly believed that they should exercise their power with magnanimity. As one pamphlet, *The art of governing a wife, with rules for bachelors*, written in 1747, suggested, the good husband must:

> be sober in speaking, easy in discourse, faithful where he is entrusted, discreet in giving counsel, careful of providing his house, diligent in looking after his estate, prudent in bearing the importunities of his wife, zealous of the education of his children, vigilant in what relates to his honour, and very stayed in all his behaviour. (Shoemaker, 1998: 26)

For a great many upper and middle-class men of the seventeenth and eighteenth centuries, such good advice fell on deaf ears. Instead, many men subscribed to the 'double standard' whereby men insisted upon the fidelity of wives, while allowing themselves illicit sexual relationships (Stone, 1992: 9–11; see also Meldrum, 2000). Consequently, men faced a far lower risk of public reprobation for their sexual infidelity.

By the turn of the nineteenth century, as evangelicalism swept through the new middle classes in England, such flagrant abuse of patriarchal privileges could be more costly (Davidoff and Hall, 1987; Tosh, 1999; for a history of evangelicalism in Britain, see Hilton, 1988; Bebbington, 1989). It is often assumed in popular histories of nineteenth-century domestic life that the middle classes wished to emulate the old aristocratic upper classes. In reality, the new middle class that emerged in the nineteenth century reacted against the hedonism of the older aristocratic order and sought to reflect in the design, furnishing and organisation of their households their belief in 'moderation'. It was not just the tendency of the old order to flash their wealth and influence that appalled the new middle class, it was their moral disregard. The inclination of men of influence to openly flaunt their mistresses and amass colossal gambling debts, together with their heavy drinking, gluttony and duelling, was anathema to the moderate men of the middle classes. Indeed, as Davidoff and Hall (1987) show, nineteenth-century middle-class life centred on 'religious belief', 'political practice', 'commercial activity' and 'family life' (1987: 14).

Domestic life also came to be regarded as a retreat from the public world and, by the latter part of the century, a cult of domesticity had developed which was celebrated in poetry, novels and in conduct books. As one contemporary writer notes:

> Home! it is a little world, it has its own interests, its own laws, its own difficulties and sorrows, its own blessings and jobs. It is the sanctuary of the heart, where the affections are cherished in the tenderest relations – where heart is joined to heart, and love triumphs over all selfish calculations. (Ferris, 1864: 179; see also Cobbett, [1830] 1980)

Even though many men continued to work at home throughout the nineteenth century (Davidoff and Hall, 1987; Hinchcliffe, 1992), an increasingly large majority worked away from home as the century progressed. This was partly because the workplace was more likely to be physically separated from the home, but also because the middle classes began to retreat to the suburbs in response to the deteriorating environmental and social conditions in the industrial cities (see Engels, [1844] 1969; Briggs, 1968; Gauldie, 1974). As the evangelical William Cowper's verse suggests: 'The statesman, lawyer, merchant, man of trade/Pants for the refuge of some rural shade/Where all his long anxieties forgot,/Amid the charms of a sequester'd spot' (in Davidoff and Hall, 1987: 164).

The scale of urban growth was very substantial. In England, the population grew from only 10.6 million to 25 million between 1800 and 1900, while the population of London increased from one million to 6.5 million during this period. At the turn of the nineteenth century there were only 15 towns with a population over 20,000, but this had risen to 63 by 1891 (Power, 1993: 166). In just one century, the proportion of the population that lived in towns grew from 20 per cent to 77 per cent. As Briggs puts it, overcrowding in cities had a tendency to 'convert elegance into squalor' (1968: 28).

The physical separation of suburban domestic life from enterprise, commerce and the industrial work of the cities impacted on gendered domestic practices. One account of life at Alderley Edge, near Manchester, in the latter half of the nineteenth century, illustrates this point:

> After the 9.18 train had pulled out of the station the Edge became exclusively female. You never saw a man on the hill roads, unless it were the doctor or the plumber, and you never saw a man in anyone's house except the gardener or the coachman. The quiet day was given over to correspondence, overseeing the servants and gardeners, and paying morning calls, until the evening came in and the male procession took place again in reverse. (cited in Girouard, 1990: 288)

House design also came to reflect contemporary expectations that women's and men's attributes and roles were distinct and should be kept separate. This was especially pronounced among the newly established entrepreneurial upper middle classes whose mansions provided separate spaces for men and women. In addition to their private library or study, exclusive space was allocated for men's leisure, often comprising a smoking room and a billiard room. This allocation of dedicated space was justified in terms of the different personal attributes and interests women and men were supposed to have. For example, in *The Gentleman's House* (1871), Robert Kerr explained that men needed private space because he assumed that women would not tolerate their disreputable habits:

> The pitiable resources to which some gentlemen are driven, even in their own houses, in order to be able to enjoy the pestiferous luxury of a cigar, have given rise to the occasional introduction of an apartment specially dedicated to the use of Tobacco. The Billiard-room is sometimes allowed to be more or less under the dominion of the smoker, if contrived accordingly; but this would in other cases be

impossible; and there are even instances where, out of sheer encouragement of the practice, a retreat is provided altogether apart, where the *dolce far niente* in this particular shape may solely and undisturbedly reign. (Kerr, 1871: 129)

Such was the Victorian preoccupation with sexual propriety that the separation of younger members of the household was also judged to be an issue of paramount importance (Girouard, 1978; M. Mason, 1995). In larger houses, bachelors' quarters were often physically isolated by a separate staircase. Kerr justified the avoidance of the 'bedroom thoroughfare', so that bachelors could gain 'unceremonious' access to their private quarters. He recommended a private lobby for the 'young ladies' and that 'The Governess' room…ought to be not too far off; because the young ladies must in some cases be under her charge' (1871: 141).

Social expectations about men's and women's interests and traits tended also to govern social manners. In England, women and men separated after dinner, for example, so that men could smoke and drink and engage in 'men's talk' which, it was presumed, would hold little interest to women. As one contemporary writer recorded in 1845, even watching women eat was regarded as 'an unpoetical thing: Lord Byron disliked to see women eat' (in Davidoff, 1976: 137). Indeed, women could not eat much because they were strapped tightly into corsets, so it is hardly surprising that they gained a reputation for being weak and feeble when they fainted. Women's 'dizziness', it was presumed, also accounted for their tendency (or prerogative) to change their minds, unlike men, who bore the burden of sticking to their guns in debate, even if they were self-evidently wrong.

In the Victorian middle classes, it was expected that men's authority over the household should not be challenged. Many were unabashed in exerting this right; as Thomas Carlyle told his future wife, 'I must not and I cannot live in a house of which I am not head' (in Tosh, 1991: 51; see also Clarke, 1991). While it was accepted that 'the Englishman's home is his castle', husbands were expected to exercise that power with magnanimity and restraint. As Davidoff and Hall argue, most did:

There is scattered evidence that some men exercised their power in a direct and domineering manner. But the local sources more often point to an intense involvement of men with their families, and a loving interest in their children's lives. In any case, the religious community would have checked an openly harsh display of naked power and many of these households were still open to the coming and going of numerous visitors and kin. (Davidoff and Hall, 1987: 329)

The 'natural' authority of men was strongly reinforced in conduct books which extolled the virtues of wifely deference. Mrs Sarah Stickney Ellis, for example, urged women to recognise 'the inalienable right of all men, whether ill or well, rich or poor, wise or foolish, to be treated with deference and made much of in their own homes' (in Hammerton, 1992: 78). That said, her awareness of the fact that many men fell short of the ideal led her to advise women that husbands needed to be managed to some extent, although she claimed to deplore the 'utterly revolting' habit of manipulating husbands. She cautioned against the use of a 'single rash or hasty word, especially if it implied an assumption of the *right to choose* [which] would have effectually defeated their ends' (cited by Hammerton, 1992: 78: my emphasis).

There existed, therefore, a peculiar tension between the idea that masculinity was dependent upon men being master of their own house, while the running of the home was ultimately the responsibility of women. This conflict was particularly acute for some men; as Tosh comments, 'for those young men who were touched by Evangelical influence, the contradiction was intensified by the novel idea that domesticity was a *defining* attribute of manliness – and this was a time when home was associated ever more closely with women, and femininity was counterposed ever more sharply to masculinity' (1999: 113). As Pugh (1983) has observed of American households at that time:

> American men unwittingly placed themselves in the dual and contradictory role of patriarch and eternal child, one the breadwinner, the other the grateful recipient of motherly attention. In both roles he was safe from the threats he saw in women: for the stern provider, they were helpless children; for the adult turned child, they were providers of another kind who would attend to his comforts without distracting him with unmotherly demands. (Tosh, 1991: 56; see also, Peterson, 1989)

Similarly, notions of the emotionally 'distant' father may have been overexaggerated (Davidoff and Hall, 1987; Tosh, 1999), although many men may have withdrawn from open displays of emotion to their children, and especially their sons, fearing that they must be prepared for the hard realities of the outside world. Contemporary commentators certainly expressed the importance of a father's authority in blunt terms: 'A mother has a most important place, and her hand must be felt always; but she should not be left alone. The burden is not primarily or justly hers. Invaluable, blessed, thrice blessed auxiliary, she leads and moulds, while the authority which has chief control is one step beyond' (Ferris, 1864: 183). The exercise of patriarchal authority did not necessarily run smoothly and often the father and son relationship could be particularly strained, especially in relation to a son's career. Often sons were expected to join the father in business and resistance could produce animosity. Anxieties about sons were nearer the surface because young men were exposed to more choices than daughters whose options were limited and activities confined. As a Birmingham clergyman wrote in a letter of 1838:

> I can truly say, that the older my children grow, the more difficulty do I find in the discharge of parental duties. The best mode of attempting the formation of character occupies much of my thoughts. With respect to the girls, the path appears to me comparatively clear; but the boys, who must eventually mix with a variety of characters, occasion me much anxiety. They must be exposed to vice; how, in dependence on the divine blessing, they may be most effectually prepared to encounter it, is a deeply important question. (cited in Davidoff and Hall, 1987: 332–3)

Women clearly held considerable authority over children and servants because they were charged with the responsibility of effecting the smooth operation of the household and of providing an appropriate level of 'comfort' for its members. As Grier (1988) points out, the term 'comfort' was less to do with facility than with 'the presence of the more family-centred, even religious values associated with "home", values emphasising perfect sincerity and moderation in all things. Social commentators claimed comfort to be a distinctively middle-class state of mind' (Hepworth, 1999b: 24–25). In smaller houses, as Halttunen (1982) has argued, the parlour was women's '"cultural podium" from which [a woman could] exert her moral influence' (Hepworth, 1999b: 23).

> The right furniture was thought to ease social intercourse by helping visitors to look their best, and, when correctly arranged, by encouraging circulation. Similarly, the hostess who tastefully arranged potted shrubs, plants, and flowers throughout the room helped 'brighten' and 'enliven' the company by placing them in 'almost a fairy-like scene.' In addition she selected and displayed the 'curiosities, handsome books, photographs, engravings, stereoscopes, medallions, any works of art you may own,' which were the stage properties of polite social intercourse. Such conversation pieces, according to one etiquette manual, were the good hostess's 'armour against stupidity'. The polite Victorian hostess was not simply an actress in the genteel performance; she was also the stage manager, who exercised great responsibility for the performances of everyone who entered her parlour. (Hepworth, 1999b: 24)

The cult of domesticity, for most middle-class women, was achieved on the back of cheap domestic labour provided by working-class women and girls. As the century progressed the demand for servants intensified: in Britain, there were just over 1,135,000 servants in 1851 rising to 2,127,000 in 1911 (John, 1986: 37). The life of servants has been romanticised in the popular imagination in historical novels and television series such as *Upstairs, Downstairs*. Such evocations of life 'below stairs' suggest opportunities for gossip, sexual intrigue and hearty meals shared in the servants' hall under the watchful eye of a benevolent, though strict, butler and housekeeper. Barstow's account of life in the English country house epitomises this romantic view:

> Domestic service was not then considered demeaning work for the free-born Englishman or woman: on the contrary, there was a good deal of prestige, even glamour, attached to being part of a noble household where the standard of living for the humblest scullery maid was higher than she could expect in her own home. (Barstow, 1998: 169)

Servants in mansion houses could often expect more reasonable conditions of work and some prospect of social mobility through the servant hierarchy, but such appointments were rare and certainly not all wealthy householders treated their servants fairly (for American studies, see Katzman, 1978; Dudden, 1983; Dill, 1994; J. Jones, 1985; Palmer, 1989;).

In England, the majority of servants worked alone in harsh conditions. In a study of the nineteenth-century servant population of Rochdale, Lancashire, Higgs shows that more than 60 per cent of domestic servants worked alone as a 'maid-of-all-work'. In Rochdale, in 1871, 53 per cent of servants were aged between 15 and 24, and 71 per cent were aged under 30 (1986: 137). Conditions of work were unenviable. Working hours were long, lonely and hard, for which servants received low pay and few perks. Isolated and unprotected by trade unions, servants were susceptible to all manner of abuse by their employers (Gillis, 1983). As F. Thompson points out, 'Their work was regarded as servile and degrading, they were trained to be subordinate, deferential, and obsequious, their manners and morals were by definition derivative and imitative' (1988: 248). The threat to 'let them go' without good 'character' references weakened their resistance to the demands of employers, and yet, because servants witnessed much of middle-class private life, employers perceived them as a threat (Davidoff *et al.*, 1999: 170–8). Wealthy women were often, and sometimes justifiably, preoccupied by fears of their servants stealing their possessions or telling their secrets. Certainly, servants had the power to make their employers feel uncomfortable by getting 'revenge against unfair treatment, using familiar weapons such as sulking, mishearing orders, semi-deliberate spoiling of materials, wasting time, "the sullen dumb insolence and petty irritations" bemoaned by employers' (Davidoff *et al.*, 1999: 171).

In sum, the middle-class cult of domesticity was built upon the labour of working-class servants. Sustaining such high standards of domestic life would soon become impossible, as will be shown in Chapter 5, when young working-class girls gained other employment opportunities after the First World War in factories and shops. From that point onwards, most middle-class women faced the task of doing the bulk of the housework themselves.

Separate spheres in working-class domestic life

Popularly held images of working-class life in nineteenth-century Britain are strongly influenced by the contemporary writing of novelists, social reformists or radicals (Steedman, 1999). Certainly, for a substantial proportion of the working classes in the early to mid-nineteenth century, conditions were appalling, as is evidenced in the writing of, for example, Dickens ([1854] 1969); Gaskell ([1848] 1970); Mayhew (1851); and Engels ([1844] 1969). But the working class was not a homogeneous mass of people who suffered from the effects of industrialisation in equal measure and were wholly dependent upon the philanthropic interventions of those who campaigned to improve their lot. Poorer working-class people may have been susceptible to the regular invasions of intrusive middle-class visitors including Ellen Ranyard's 'Bible-women' who, she asserted in 1859, could 'penetrate every home' (Hewitt, 1999: 125). A principal source of pride, status and respectability amongst working-class men and women was gained through their ability to fend for themselves rather than depend on the charity and advice of others. Working-class men gained social respectability mainly from their breadwinner role, but they bolstered their social status further through nonconformism, self-improving study at local technical institutes, the trade union movement, radical politics, and co-operative ventures in retailing and in the building society movement (see E. P. Thompson, 1968; J. Benson, 1989; K. Burgess, 1990). Such projects helped develop a culture of fierce working-class independence.

By the mid-nineteenth century, many skilled workers and artisans were relatively well housed with the average family inhabiting a dwelling of four rooms. Owning a home, in particular, signalled financial prudence and independence. In 1850 around 5 per cent of working-class families owned their own homes, rising to about 10 per cent in 1918 and 19 per cent by 1939 (J. Benson, 1989: 73). In some areas the proportion of men who bought their own homes was much higher, including mining areas of South Wales, the Lancashire cotton towns, some shipbuilding towns (including Jarrow on the River Tyne) and, to a lesser extent, the West Yorkshire woollen towns. Houses were purchased through building societies which were set up by working men in northern towns to avoid the higher cost of renting. Unlike their forerunners, the 'terminating societies' – the large permanent building societies founded in the middle of the century, including the Leeds Permanent in 1848, the Woolwich Equitable in 1847, the Abbey National in 1849 and the Halifax in 1853 – provided for savers as well as investment in housing (Gauldie, 1974: 202). Working-class men also established co-operative retailing societies where customers could expect to gain a dividend of three shillings in the pound for cash transactions. As Thomas Cooper wrote in 1872:

> In our old Chartist time, it is true, Lancashire working men were in rags by the thousands; and many of them often lacked food. But their intelligence was demonstrated wherever you went. You would see them in groups discussing the great doctrine of political justice...*Now* you will see no such groups in Lancashire. But you will hear well-dressed working men talking, as they walk with their hands in their pockets, of 'Co-ops' and their shares in them, or in building societies. (cited in Hobsbawm, 1969: 126)

But, as Cooper ruefully observed, not all men were the same for 'you will see others, like idiots leading small greyhound dogs'. By 1880, the co-operative movement had half a million members, mainly in the northern industrial towns, and by 1914 it was nearer to three million (Hobsbawm, 1969: 163; see also Pearson, 1988).

Nonconformism became hugely influential in social, political and community life. In the absence, initially, of churches or chapels in the urban industrial areas, nonconformists engaged in street preaching. Their influence was enormous. While the population of England doubled from 1791 to 1851, the number of Methodists increased by nine times, Congregationalists by six times and Baptists by seven times (McLeod, 1984: 21; see also Gilbert, 1976; K. Brown, 1988;

Bebbington, 1989). Nonconformism provided a focus for the development of radical political agendas and extolled the virtues of self-determination and self-improvement (Hobsbaum, 1969). Embracing nonconformism gave people the self-confidence to challenge the paternalistic power relationships that had operated for centuries in the countryside. Opposition such as this required both spiritual and economic resources and, as a consequence, nonconformity appealed most to the class of artisans. But even in poorer sections of the working class, the role of religion cannot be discounted. For example, Primitive Methodists (or 'Ranters' as they were often known) may not have developed formal political agendas, but they were powerful leaders in poor communities. Believing in divine justice, their moral authority was firmly established by the notion that God was on their side: that is, on the side of injustice.

Men's emphasis on self-improvement and social respectability through nonconformism, education, hard work and self-restraint was often dependent upon the support and hard work of their wives, as will be shown below. This is not to say that women were entirely compliant. James Turner of Halifax, for example, who kept a diary of his day to day life in the 1880s, was exasperated by his wife's lack of support:

> I left word with my wife to have breakfast ready in an hour; I was back a little before the time, so I said, 'Get breakfast ready, Martha', when she immediately flew into a rage, and said words which caused me to retaliate; well we got to such a pitch that I felt I could slay her without the least compunction; but I restrained my temper and began to dress for chapel; my boots were uncleaned and my wife usually cleaning them, I went on dressing expecting she would clean them; they were not cleaned, and so I had to clean them myself; of course this caused another scene; through this I was late at chapel. (J. Turner, 1981: 29–30)

Reflecting on these altercations, Turner considered the prospect of behaving like other men.

> I have not spoke to her since, nor shall I yet a while; instead of giving me encouragement and urging me onto Christianity, she has been quite the reverse ... if I were to get drunk and abuse her, she would think more about me ... I don't wonder at married men seeking comfort in a public house. I myself have been tempted to throw all on one side, and go on as I did before, or perhaps to become even worse than I was then. (J. Turner, 1981: 29–30)

The separation of spheres along the lines established in middle-class homes was never fully achieved in working-class households because women continued to work. Even in households where skilled men commanded higher wages many women, as will be shown later in this section, continued to work through choice or necessity. That said, in the nineteenth century men commanded the highest wages and monopolised the most highly skilled industrial work (Cockburn, 1983; J. Lewis, 1986a; Bradley, 1989; Lown, 1990). The working-class population in general had insufficient financial resources to emulate the middle-class model of domestic life, but better-off men strove to 'keep' a wife at home. As Thomas Wright, the engineer, stated:

> Among the working class the *wife* makes the home . . . the working man's wife is also his housekeeper, cook and several other single domestics rolled into one; and on her being a managing or mismanaging woman depends whether a dwelling will be a home proper, or house which is not a home. (cited in Cockburn, 1983: 34)

Skilled workers and artisans achieved this by gaining a 'family wage' through trade union action and political pressure. From the 1840s, trade unions exerted control over access to employment in specific trades so that wages and working conditions could be improved (Coyle, 1980; Humphries, 1981; Breitenbach, 1982). At the 1877 Trade Union Congress, Henry Broadhurst justified the family wage in order to 'bring about a condition of things, where their wives should be in their proper sphere at home, instead of being dragged into competition for livelihood against the great and strong men of the world' (in J. Lewis, 1986b: 103). In some industries men were successful in achieving these aims. In the printing industry, for example, men gained a near monopoly over the task of compositing through the relentless efforts of the National Graphical Association(NGA). Even during the First World War, when many women were brought into the labour force to undertake jobs which had traditionally been undertaken by men, the print unions kept women out by bringing retired men back to work. The NGA encouraged prospective members to retain restrictive practices in the following terms: 'Do you know that non Society employers are engaging and training girls and women to work as compositors – case and machine? Are they doing this for "your" benefit? When the boys come home, will "your" position be better or worse? . . . Play the man and join now' (in Cockburn, 1983: 36).

For the more affluent members of the working class, 'independence' was the watchword of success. Thomas Wright caricatured the ideal 'working man' as someone who:

> can command good work and good pay all the year round, has a comfortable home, saves money, provides through his benefit and trade clubs for the proverbial

rainy day, is in his degree respected because self-respecting, and on the whole is a person rather to be envied than pitied. (cited in McClelland, 1991: 74)

Achieving the 'ideal' of keeping a wife at home was not always easy because the nineteenth-century economy was subject to serious fluctuations in prosperity. Booms and slumps sometimes occurred on a national scale, such as the great depression of the 1880s; in other cases, economic crises were precipitated by the collapse of particular industries.

A serious problem for working women, as the nineteenth century progressed, was that the range of occupations available to them was reduced. This was due to restrictive practices established by male trade unions and by the introduction of state legislation that limited children's and women's employment. Much of this legislation was fuelled by moral arguments about women working alongside men. Unease was officially recorded about women's factory employment as early as 1815 in the Peel Committee's report. As one contemporary writer noted: 'I must admit that ... some women prefer the crowded factory to the quiet home because they have a hatred of solitary housework' (in Oakley, 1974: 41) Contemporary accounts of the appalling pay, hours and working conditions of women and children who undertook such piece-work in the home show why factory work was a preferred option (see Hope, Kennedy and De Winter, 1976; Allen and Wolkowitz, 1986; Morris, 1986; Pennington and Westover, 1989).

Pressure for increased regulation of women's and children's employment was not universally welcomed because they provided a pool of cheap labour to entrepreneurs. As Marx commented, 'The nearer the deadline approached for the full implementation of the Factory Act, the fatal year of 1836, the wilder became the rage of the mob of manufacturers' (in Coyle, 1980: 4). Nevertheless, the campaign to limit women's employment opportunities intensified. The 1842 Mines Regulations Act, for example, arose in response to a Royal Commission which argued that the reliability of men as employees, and the health and morals of mining families, would be improved if men could afford to keep a wife at home. This was underscored by moral arguments about women working alongside men. As one of the Commission's investigators commented:

The system of having females to work in coal pits...I consider to be the most awfully demoralizing practice. The youths of both sexes work often in a half-naked state and their persons are excited before they arrive at puberty...Sexual intercourse decidedly frequently occurs in consequence. Women brought up in this way lay aside all modesty, and scarcely know what it is but by name. (cited in Humphries, 1981: 23)

Lord Shaftesbury's Act banned all women from underground work and all children under ten, but it was only partially successful as just one government inspector was appointed to oversee 2,000 mines, and he was reputed never to have gone underground. Nevertheless, the principle was established that men and women had different capabilities and temperaments and that they should be allocated to different forms of work (G. Burke, 1986; John, 1986). The range of opportunities for women, in comparison with men, were considerably limited by the 1850s as Table 3.2 demonstrates.

Some commentators assume that the family wage pattern was devised specifically to benefit the male breadwinner at the expense of the independence of his non-employed wife (see, for example, accounts by Barrett and McIntosh, 1980; Hartmann, 1979; Walby, 1986). But, as Creighton (1997) points out, while men may have gained greater authority and service from this arrangement, men's

Table 3.2 *Ratio of women in the labour force in Britain, 1851*

Industrial group	% all women	% of women in each occupation
Primary industries		
Agriculture, etc.	8.1	11.4
Metal manufacture	1.3	6.3
Mining, etc.	0.4	2.8
Manufacturing		
Textiles	22.4	49.0
Clothing	17.3	54.0
Food, etc.	1.9	13.2
Paper	0.6	20.5
Bricks, etc.	0.5	16.7
Wood, etc.	0.3	5.0
Chemicals	0.1	8.7
Services		
Domestic offices, etc.	40.1	85.5
Professional, etc.	3.6	38.9
Transport and communication	0.5	2.9
Public administration	0.1	4.5

Source: adapted from John (1986: 38), Appendix C.

employment was often dangerous and physically burdensome. The life expectancy of miners, for example, was short even if they were lucky enough to escape injury or death from accidents. Hours of work were long. In 1850, engineers worked on average a 60-hour week compared with a 72-hour week for coal miners and textile workers. Through trade union pressure and parliamentary reform, men in these trades had reduced their hours to 54 hours a week by the 1880s. In 1908 miners won an eight-hour day, whilst most factory workers did not achieve this until 1937 (J. Benson, 1989: 15).

Many women did not want to stop working for fear of the loss of their independence. As one woman who had worked in factories for 60 years told Cadbury, the philanthropic social researcher: 'A shilling you can earn yourself is worth two given you by a man' (Cadbury, Matheson and Shann, 1906: 6). More commonly, married women simply had to work because not all husbands were, in Cadbury's terms, 'sober, steady or industrious'; some were in 'bad health'. Cadbury's research demonstrated that non-working women cared better for their homes and for their children providing that the husband earned sufficient wages but, for poorer families, the choices were stark: 'it becomes a question of choosing the lesser of two evils, i.e. whether the children are to be almost starved or more or less neglected' (1906: 220).

Highly skilled artisans also often fell on hard times and as a consequence had to draw in their wives and daughters to work with them, or rely on their economic activity if the man was out of work. As one journeyman tailor told Mayhew in the early 1860s, 'I cannot afford now to let her remain idle...If I had a daughter I should be obliged to make her work as well' (in McClelland, 1991: 78). As was often the case, his wife did not work alongside him, because of the fear that women working in his trade would further depress their income. Instead, she joined the growing number of women working in sweated trades, in her case dressmaking, earning only eight shillings a week compared with his 24 (see also Morris, 1986). Income fluctuation was endemic in casual, seasonal or cyclical work. Bricklayers, joiners and plasterers, for example, often relied on their wives' earnings as ironers or in factory labour (McClelland, 1991). And so, while census statistics show that most women married to respectable working-class men were full-time housewives, these data can be misleading because much of women's paid work went unrecorded for one of several reasons: for example, a wife often worked to directly support her husband's work, and many married women took casual or temporary work or they were involved in 'penny capitalism', such as taking in washing, putting up boarders, childminding, selling home-made food or drink or opening small parlour shops (J. Benson, 1989: 30).

In some areas, married women worked as a matter of course. In the Leicester hosiery industry in 1851, for example, 40 per cent of married women in their twenties worked, although this had been reduced to 30 per cent by 1871. Indeed, 20 per cent of married women in their sixties worked. As Osterud notes:

> The relationship between women's employment and the family cycle was quite different from twentieth-century patterns. Instead of leaving the labour force during their childbearing years and returning when their children were older, as many women do now, wives in nineteenth-century Leicester remained in the labour force when their children were young and stopped working for pay when their children were old enough to replace them as contributors to the family income. (1986: 59)

Women were not driven out from all skilled trades in the nine-teenth century. In the Staffordshire pottery industry, for example, there was a very high concentration of skilled women and men work-ers. Skills were strictly segregated by sex, even though men and women often worked together on the same task: male pot throwers, for example, would often have two women assistants. Mostly, how-ever, women and men worked on separate activities in different parts of the factory. Men tended to dominate in the heavy 'mucky' work of clay preparation, moulding and pot making, kiln work and packaging. Women outnumbered men in the finishing room, including painting, gilding, burnishing and decorating, although men were more likely to do the more 'artistic' work. Even though painters had similar skills, women were paid less: in 1851, men earned between 20 and 50 shillings compared with between 9 and 12 shillings for women (Bradley, 1989: 121). Unlike many other industries, women were not driven from the pottery industry by their male co-workers, philanthropists or employers; the contrary is the case, as mechan-isation of the labour process led to the loss of men's jobs. In 1851 nearly 70 per cent of workers in the china and earthenware trades were men, but this had been reduced to just less than a half by 1929 (Bradley, 1989: 123; see also Sarsby, 1985, 1988).

The pottery trade was not amongst the highest paying industries in the nineteenth century, which would seem to explain why women continued to work in such large numbers. But in Preston, the largest percentage of working wives were married to the most highly paid cotton and metal workers (Savage, 1987), showing that there may not have been a strong impetus to become a dependent housewife. In sum, the local employment conditions had a significant impact on the pattern of work within households.

The nineteenth century, in conclusion, was a period of social upheaval that transformed gendered domestic practices in three principal ways. First, changes in the way that the labour market was structured strengthened existing values about separate spheres of work for men and women. Second, changed work patterns led to a clear separation of the workplace from the home in the majority of households which resulted in the home becoming a site of consumption of products rather than their production, as had been the case in the eighteenth century. Finally, the idea of what constituted a respectable home changed substantially first in the middle classes but later in the working classes too. A keystone of respectability was the ability of the male breadwinner to earn sufficient money to keep his wife at home. It is generally agreed now that relatively few working-class men fully achieved this aim because women continued to work by choice or economic necessity; but the principle had been established that women's key role in adult life was to be a homemaker.

4

Breadwinniners

The advantages and disadvantages of breadwinning

In much of the sociological literature on gender and domestic life, as has already been shown in Chapter 1, there is a tendency to assume that there are few benefits to be gained by women from devoting time and energy to the task of homemaking. And further, the advantages to be gained from undertaking the male breadwinner role are assumed to be such that men, as husbands, are ultimately responsible for the lost opportunities of their wives. As was shown in Chapter 3, there is compelling evidence to show that men, as trade unionists, did mobilise their powers to keep women out of certain occupations and industries in the nineteenth century, just as male politicians produced laws to drive women out from certain forms of work. The consequence of this, in working-class households at least, was that by the beginning of the twentieth century, women's employment opportunities were severely limited and their economic independence stifled. Many commentators have drawn on evidence such as this to argue that women's oppression in the family is sustained through men's economic domination which is achieved through their paid employment (for a review, see Crompton, 1997). As the aim of this book is to consider paid work as a vital element in the analysis of gendered domestic practices, it is important not to dismiss the problems paid work can bring to men, and it should also be recognised that men's defence of their position as breadwinners at this time entailed social, physical and emotional costs. This point is illustrated in Table 4.1.

New (2001) has argued that while men have participated in the oppression of women, they too are subject to the repressive forces of capitalism which have 'systematically mistreated' them in the workplace. As she points out, men are mistreated by capital in both physical and emotional terms:

capitalist economies accumulate value at the expense of the living bodies of men, through the requirement to overwork in paid employment...The acceptance of overwork has traditionally been supported by the 'man as provider' ideology, now less widespread, but also by the fear of unemployment. Overwork falls also on middle-class and upper-class men, although working-class men are assigned the dirtiest, most dangerous and exhausting jobs. Their bodies are treated as disposable. (2001: 740–1)

New's argument is strengthened by her recognition that the concept of masculinity itself is imbued with an expectation of cheerfully accepting the sometimes intolerable burdens of work. As she notes, 'The masculine ideology of strength and endurance encourages

Table 4.1   *The advantages and disadvantages of breadwinning in the mid-twentieth century*

Advantages	Disadvantages
Escape primary responsibility from domestic work	Inescapability of work due to responsibility for gaining income to maintain family
Escape from day to day responsibility for childcare role	Loss of opportunity to play a full role in parenting
Escape primary responsibility for maintaining kin and family friendship networks	Become marginalised from decision-making and lose of influence over pattern of kin relationships
Gain status in community and family for being a successful breadwinner	Obliged to undertake dangerous/ stressful/exhausting work that may require compliance with personally unacceptable organisational goals and practices
Gain a 'right to leisure'	Leisure pattern constrained by employment-based culture of masculinity
Gain control over wife and children through economic power and reserve income for personal spending priorities	Fear of unemployment or downward social mobility through career failure
Gain self-fulfilment from work and unrestrained career opportunities	Work may be an alienating experience and signify lost opportunities

men to accept and even take pride in these destructive effects, with serious implications for men's health' (2001: 742). Support for this kind of argument can be found in unexpected places. In *Women's Oppression Today*, for example, Barratt recognised that the cultural association between masculinity and paid work could disadvantage men because they would have little time with their children:

> If we take the assumed dependence of women upon a male breadwinner, it is not self-evident that the role of 'breadwinner' is intrinsically a desirable one...For one thing, the assumption of the male breadwinner locks men effectively into wage labour, with considerable pressure to remain politically docile in order to safeguard their jobs and hence provision for their households. Second, although many men evade domestic labour and responsibility for childcare by assigning this work to women, there is now a growing expression of dissatisfaction with the degree to which this has deprived men of significant access to their children. (1980: 217)

At the time of writing, in the late 1970s, Barrett was right to state that there were few jobs that men could take which would allow them the flexibility to care for children. There is still a tremendously long way to go in this respect, but many employers do now formally recognise in their personnel policies the importance of men's participation in family life, and those who do not are obliged in many countries at least to provide time for paternity leave (Lewis and Lewis, 1996) The problem is that many men feel that they cannot take advantage of such opportunities because they perceive a risk of a detrimental impact upon their career development and the ability to meet their responsibility as the principal economic provider.

New's analysis is also important because she recognises that women and men as social agents can justify and reproduce their own disadvantaged situation by behaving in conventional masculine or feminine ways, but they do so in the context of manipulative institutional settings that seek to exploit gendered subjectivities. Even men's sense of social superiority and advantage that they traditionally assume over women does not, of itself, mean that they too are not exploited. As New comments:

> The fact that men are also told that they are superior and deserving of privilege does not cancel out the effect of this mistreatment, which can realistically be called oppression. Part of our [i.e., feminist sociologists'] reluctance to call it so stems from the fact that men act as agents of their own oppression – yet we are not confused when women are the agents of *women's* oppression. Our reluctance also comes from the view that if men benefit from the gender order, they cannot also be mistreated within it. (2001: 744)

In the next two chapters of this book, I will be not just be exploring the way that men and women came to accept their roles as home-makers or breadwinners under the influence of institutions such as the education system, employment organisations, employment law, the trade union movement and so on; in addition, it will be shown how they actively defended their position in undertaking these roles even if, ultimately, they could be seriously disadvantaged and endan-gered by them. Because the same principles of analysis are applied to men and women, in the spirit of New's argument as outlined above, this does not of course mean that I am assuming equality or equivalence of experience between women and men. But by leaving aside the politically and emotionally charged issue of who suffers the most or is advantaged the most, and all the heated arguments that invariably surround that issue, it is anticipated that a clearer understanding can be gained of the way that gendered practices are socially produced, reproduced and transformed over time. The evaluation of who is likely to benefit or be disadvantaged by such situations will be delayed until Chapter 11.

It is clearly beyond the scope of a single chapter to explore every type of work men undertook in Western industrial societies in the twentieth century. Instead, the chapter will focus on two areas only. The next section will concentrate on the experience of British working-class men in those heavy industries such as mining, shipbuilding and fishing which tended to produce particularly polarised gendered relationships in the home and community in the first half of the twentieth century. The main reason for this clear separation of roles, it will be shown, was the assimilation of a particular form of masculinity that helped men to withstand the rigours of physically demanding, dirty and dangerous work. The masculine culture that prevailed required the maintenance of a collective class consciousness and cohesiveness that denied the possibility of personal achievement or advancement that clashed with the interests of the whole community of men. While such communities ceased to exist in Britain after the collapse of traditional heavy industries towards the end of the last century, the cultural association between hard manual labour and masculinity continues to inform, albeit in a diluted way, working-class men's attitudes about, and expectations of, domestic life.

The section after that, by contrast, will focus on the link between masculinity, employment and the imperative to succeed in the USA from the early to mid-twentieth century. Unlike the British example, this second example will explore how the demands of career success could disadvantage socially upwardly mobile men. This section will also demonstrate the potentially catastrophic impact of career failure on perceptions of masculinity. In the concluding section, the chapter will assess the extent to which married men today benefit in financial and career terms from adopting the role of the breadwinner in comparison with unmarried men. And further, the section will ask whether these men are successful because they are married, or whether or not they attract marriage partners because of their potential to succeed.

Masculinity and the avoidance of domestic life

As has already been shown in Chapter 3, in the nineteenth century many skilled workers in Britain consolidated their position in society as self-reliant, proud and respectable working-class men through trade union action, self-help and hard work. A keystone to their status was their ability to keep a wife at home while they attended to the masculine role of breadwinning. Well into the twentieth century this model of working-class family life was sustained in those communities where heavy industries, such as steelmaking, shipbuilding or mining, dominated the local economy. British industrial sociologists and class theorists from the 1950s through to the early 1970s were preoccupied with the effects of men's work experience on patterns of class formation, class consciousness and political action. Sociologists' concern with men's employment did not signal a complete disinterest in family life; however, the strong association drawn between a man's job and social class attitudes led many researchers to conclude that a man's job shaped not only his attitudes, but the attitudes and behaviour of his wife too (see, for example, Goldthorpe *et al.*, 1969).

The masculinist research agenda of British sociologists at that time shows how deeply ingrained the notion had become that the term *work* was synonymous with men. And further, it helps to explain why, as a consequence, the role of women's work in the home or in the labour market (or their absence from it) was generally ignored (R. Brown, 1976). In a groundbreaking critique of class theory, Acker asked this question: 'In a society in which women, as well as men, have resources of education, occupation and income...why do we assume that they are inoperative if the woman is married?' (1973: 938). Since the 1970s these gaps in sociological knowledge have been filled with a wide range of contemporary and historical studies of women's and men's participation in most industries and occupations (see for example, John, 1986; Bradley, 1989; Crompton, 1997). In so doing, these studies demonstrated that women's working lives were affected by capital, male trade unions, the state and by cultural notions about women's and men's family and work roles. Additionally, these studies demonstrated that women could, and were, breaking into new forms of work from which they had been previously excluded if they challenged conventional notions of the housewife role. These issues will be discussed in some depth in the next chapter but, for the moment, it is useful to take a step back and consider what forces separated gendered roles so strictly in the mid-twentieth century in traditional working-class communities and gauge what impact this had on women's and men's domestic practices.

Studies of work, class and stratification in Britain in the 1950s and 1960s drew a strong association between work and masculine self-identity. As Lockwood noted in his highly influential article, 'Sources of variation in working-class images of society', skilled male manual workers concentrated in large industrial communities took 'Pride in doing 'men's work' and [had] a strong sense of shared occupational experience [which] make for feelings of fraternity and comradeship' ([1966], 1975: 17). Men not only shared 'class loyalties', but were also 'leisure time companions, often neighbours and not infrequently kinsmen. The existence of such closely knit cliques of friends, work mates, neighbours and relatives is the hallmark of traditional working-class communities' (Lockwood, 1975: 17). While there were many studies of closely-knit industrial communities in this period, only two will be discussed here: first, Dennis, Henriques and Slaughter's (1956) study of a mining town, and second, Tunstall's (1962) study of fishermen.

Dennis, Henriques and Slaughter's study of the mining town, 'Ashton', in the north of England in the 1950s, provides clear evidence of the existence of strictly polarised gendered expectations about roles in the community, at work and in domestic life. The study shows that a particular form of masculinity had developed which embraced a strong sense of fellowship, pride in their work, and strong class and political solidarity. These bonds were forged by common experiences of dangerous team work. In the early 1950s as many as 400 miners were killed each year in British pits and about 250,000 injured (Dennis, Henriques and Slaughter, 1956: 132–3). Under these circumstances it is not surprising that miners tended to adopt a 'live for today and not tomorrow' approach to leisure and a 'hand-to-mouth' attitude to money which was reflected in high levels of strategic absenteeism (colloquially known as 'miner's Mondays').

The prevalence of this attitude to money also suggests the miners' lack of interest in social mobility either for themselves or their children; but it actually led to a stronger emphasis on class solidarity in a community of men. Often men's personal interests were put in front of their family's. It was common for miners to deceive their wives, or refuse to tell them how much money they earned in order to reserve a sizeable proportion of their income for their male-only leisure activity. Of the eight working men's clubs in Ashton, all but one refused membership to women. Women were only allowed in for Saturday night concerts and on Sundays. Officially, the clubs aimed to provide 'for working men the means of social intercourse, mutual helpfulness, mental and moral improvement, and rational recreation' (1956: 142). In reality, men spent most of their time drinking socially, telling jokes, talking sport or about work incidents whilst avoiding intellectual matters which were dismissed as 'talk'. Only in the 'best room', which was the preserve of local councillors, union officials and other working-class men with positions of responsibility, were wider issues discussed.

Women's lives were circumscribed in much the same way as men's by the existence of the colliery. The opportunities for paid employment amongst women were limited, so forcing upon men and women a division of labour which demanded that men became the breadwinners and the women homemakers. Expectations about women's roles were clearly understood and accepted by men and women. As Dennis, Henriques and Slaughter show:

> The miner feels that he does an extremely difficult day's work; he makes it plain that he thinks it 'a poor do' if his wife cannot carry out her side of the contract. The wife is invariably found to support this view strongly. Housewives boast of their attention to the needs of their husbands, and of how they have never been late with a meal, never confronted a returning worker with a cold meal, never had to ask his help in household duties. If a miner returns from work on a wet day and finds the washing crowded round the fire-place to dry, he will show a greater or less degree of anger, according perhaps to his state of fatigue and the kind of day he has spent, but every woman knows that to present her returning husband with such a scene is not encouraging good marital relations. (1956: 181)

Marriage itself was viewed in contractual terms, following a brief romantic courtship, after which men and women expected to live largely separate lives. This pattern of domestic life survived longer in the relatively isolated pit communities than in other industrial areas where the idea of joint home-based leisure was becoming established (Zweig, 1952; Goldthorpe *et al.*, 1969; Young and Willmott, 1975).

In mining communities, rigidly defined gendered divisions of labour started to break down when more women took paid work. As Hebron and Wykes (1991) show from their study of three English mining communities in the 1980s, this was a slow process: only about 29 per cent of married women worked, usually part time in the village, compared with about 50 per cent nationally. While many women continued to accept the role of the full-time housewife, men were becoming aware that attitudes were changing. As one politically active miner stated:

> You see the mining communities have always been male oriented environments, but it's like steel, any heavy industry, it always tends to be like that. Woman plays her domestic function not by desire, but by necessity. You know, shift work, heavy industrial work, men don't have enough energy really to carry out any other function than just working. And of course new technology taking the real hard work out and shorter hours and more leisure time obviously forced women to start to reconsider their position: 'Am I continually working seven days a week and he's getting more and more leisure time?' And there's a challenge come from the women, which of course has already taken place away from the heavy industrial areas. (1991: 166)

The national miners' strike in the late 1980s changed women's perceptions further as they too became heavily involved in political action. This raised women's political awareness in the domestic arena too. As a village teacher told the researchers:

> In families, some things have changed quite drastically in terms of relationships and roles. I think there's been an increasing awareness amongst women, and rejection of their role...I also think there's a lot of tension amongst men who can't cope with the sort of shifting role that some women are expecting, and are deeply distressed and concerned by it. Not, I believe, in a sense of wanting to restore the power base, but of just coping with it and adjusting to it. (1991: 169)

It should not be assumed that all traditional male-dominated manual occupations produced uniform patterns of domestic life in the mid-twentieth century. Tunstall's study, *The Fishermen* (published in 1962), makes this clear by showing how men who worked on trawlers for three weeks at a time had varied experiences of domestic life. Many fishermen, like miners, adopted an attitude of 'live for today, not for tomorrow' to spending and leisure. But others had home-centred lives when on shore. Nevertheless, fishermen generally shared strong views on their sole responsibility for breadwinning. Their reluctance to 'allow' their wives to work was shaped to some extent by their worries about marital infidelity when they were away at sea if their wives had social contact with men outside the home. As Tunstall put it:

> Fishermen often think it is an insult to their capacity, or perhaps to their status as men, if their wives go out to work. What is the point in his, his willingness to go fishing and to accept its hardships in order to get money, if his wife then decided to go out to work as well? (1962: 161)

While the number of divorces amongst fishermen were twice the average in Hull, and most men stated frankly their worries about their wives' behaviour when they were at sea, it is probably more likely that it was the unsocial nature of their work which disrupted marital harmony. Indeed, some wives seemed equally unenthusiastic about their husbands spending time on shore:

> I don't like it when he comes home for long. He had a big trip recently – settled with £100. He drank it all himself . . . in two weeks. He drinks only whisky, and he can sup it, I'm telling you. He gets very restless, and I'm glad when he goes back to sea. (Tunstall, 1962: 163)

Or, as another fisherman's wife commented:

> Well, I'm not ashamed of it – I don't get on with my husband. He always talks fishing and how miserable it is. He's always complaining and feeling sorry for himself. What I say is: 'Why did you go into it then?' He takes me out once each trip, and most of the time he sits at home watching television. I just don't like having him here. When he's out of a ship and home all the time, I hate it. (Tunstall, 1962: 163)

To claim so openly that she did not like her husband being at home seems incongruent with contemporary expectations about marriage. Indeed, by the 1960s, sociologists were demonstrating that there was a movement towards more egalitarian and companionate marriage in the working class even if it was yet some way off achieving the kind of symmetry that some sociologists predicted (Young and Willmott, 1957, 1975).

The importance of wider cultural changes in gendered expectations about marriage and domestic life should not, therefore, be underestimated. Indeed, later studies of men who worked away from home over long periods of time demonstrate different frustrations from those expressed by Tunstall's fishermen *because* of their domestic and family orientation. For example, in one study of offshore oil workers' families in Newfoundland in the mid-1980s, one woman commented: 'I don't think you ever really adjust to it – you accept it' (Lewis, Shrimpton and Storey, 1988: 163). Adjustment was difficult because women and men lived double lives. On the rigs, men talked of a deep sense of loneliness because they missed their families, and often spoke of life on the rig as a prison-like existence. This is partly explained by its 'blokey' environment, where masculine 'virtues' of making the best of things are fiercely reinforced. The men expected each other to leave their problems behind them and converse always at a superficial level. As one man stated: 'I love to grumble when I get home at first 'cause I don't have anyone at the rig to grumble at' (Lewis, Shrimpton and Storey, 1988: 172). Such attitudes could produce real disappointment for family members who looked forward to the man's return. As one woman said, 'Here I am preparing for the great day, when he gets home, psyching myself up for a good time and everything else, and then he comes home and all he can do is sleep for the first week. It's like a slap in the face' (Lewis, Shrimpton and Storey, 1988: 176).

Some characteristics of traditional working-class masculine attitudes to domestic life still emerged from this study, however, especially the notion that men had done their work by spending 30 days on the rig. As a consequence, some men resented pressure to get involved in household chores. One man pointed out: 'after coming off – I just want to rest for a day or so, I don't need to be hit with something that's *her* job' (Lewis, Shrimpton and Storey, 1988: 174). By contrast, other men were concerned by their wives' tendency to retain aspects of independence which was crucial in their absence. Even though these men knew that their wives could deal with problems, they often wanted to take up the reins as head of the family immediately on return. This caused stress to women and children who found their own lives disrupted as men demanded attention and expected them to put on hold their normal activities. A mis-match often developed between men's *imagined* view of home while they were on the rig, and its *realities* when they arrived back. As Solheim has shown, amongst offshore workers, home became 'a fixed and immutable reality... frozen in his imagination as it was when he left' (1988: 149).

These studies of miners, fishermen and offshore workers show that paid employment, especially in closely knit industrial communities, can impact on gendered domestic practices. But it has also been shown that other factors affect attitudes about the relationships between work and family life. As the twentieth century progressed in Britain, there was a gradual blurring of class boundaries and class attitudes as the occupational structure became more complex. Old traditional working-class communities collapsed and attitudes to marriage changed from a relatively polarised model of the private domestic roles of women and public work roles of men to a more companionate model as more married women entered the labour market. Two other key factors should also be taken into account: first, the adoption of a more aspirational culture within the working class that led to expectations of social mobility, if not for themselves then for their children as educational and occupational opportunities were opened up; and second, the progressive development of a property owning, consumer society in Britain from the 1950s onwards which lessened the impact of work on the way that men, in particular, constructed their images of masculinity.

Masculinity and the imperative to succeed

Industrial relations in Britain, up to the 1980s, were characterised to a great extent by an oppositional, or 'us versus them', culture that divided capital and labour. Working-class life, although often romanticised by labour historians, was characterised to some extent by social, economic and political solidarity and a consequent suspicion of those who openly aimed to 'better themselves' rather than improve the position of the majority through collective action. In the USA, the labour movement was never as strong as in Britain for a number of complex reasons. But at root, the most important cultural explanation for this is that the ideology of self-improvement through competition and hard work was much more important in America than in Britain. The emphasis on individual freedom, independence and self-fulfilment that underpins the ideology of the American Dream is not just reflected in labour history in the USA: it is also reflected in different attitudes to patterns of consumption which in turn affected notions of achievement and social status amongst the working classes in Britain and America. These differences may be explained partly by the fact that America is a much more wealthy country than Britain and that standards of living in general have been higher for a longer period of time. But there remained, for much of the earlier part of twentieth century, a significant difference in the way that class identity was perceived and, as a consequence, in the way that masculine identities were constructed around the relationship between work, social mobility and the success imperative.

Since the turn of the last century the ideology of the successful breadwinner in the USA has demanded high levels of achievement from married men. In a society that puts its faith in the principles of meritocracy and upward social mobility, failure is not an option. The 'getting ahead' imperative in America that became established in the nineteenth century was reinforced by social Darwinist philosophy which asserted that only the fittest, brightest and most competitive men would achieve their goals. Henderson's study of businessmen, published in the first volume of the *American Journal of Sociology* in 1896, illustrates this point:

> Men of splendid abilities find in the career of a manufacturer or merchant an opportunity for the most intense energy. The very perils of the situation have a fascination for adventurous and inventive spirits. In this fierce, though voiceless, contest, a peculiar type of manhood is developed, characterised by vitality, energy, concentration, skill in combining numerous forces for an end, and great foresight into the consequences of social events. (cited in Bendix, 1956: 256)

In sociological terms it was clearly unfair to compare the life chances of the average middle-class or working-class American man with the very few who had made great strides forward through their insightful opportunism. But even if, in statistical terms, it was impossible for more than the very few to achieve greatness because there were too few places for them to occupy at the top, it did not dampen writers' enthusiasm for encouraging men to achieve their aspirations.

A flourishing trade in self-help books emerged in the USA to teach men how to make a success of their lives. The 'New Thought' movement, which reached its height of popularity between 1885 and 1915, claimed that men could overcome any hurdle if they had the right attitude. Atkinson's 1901 edition of *Thought Force in Business*, for example, stated that, 'Anything is yours if you only want it hard enough. Just think of that. *Anything*! Try it. Try it in earnest and you will succeed. It is the operation of a mighty law' (in Bendix, 1956: 260). Orison Swett Mardon was so successful as a writer of self-help books that parents named their children after him. Between 1907 and 1923 Mardon sold three million copies of his books, including *Pushing to the Front, or Success Under Difficulties*, *Architects of Fate*, *The Secret of Achievement* and *Prosperity: How to Attract it* (Bendix, 1956: 261).

Persuading optimistic men to reach high was sometimes underscored by thinly veiled threats about the risk of failure. In some cases, men were deemed to fail unless they reached the very pinnacle of success in American society. Even to become a salaried man, according to some writers, was tantamount to failure. Fowler makes this clear in his guide book for fathers *The Boy, How to Help Him Succeed*, published in 1902:

> Many a man is entirely incapable of assuming responsibility. He is a success as the led, but not as the leader. He lacks the courage or willingness to assume responsibility and the ability of handling others. He was born for a salaried man, and a salaried man he had better remain. If he goes into business for himself, the chances are that he will fail, or live close to impending disaster. (cited in Bendix, 1956: 259)

In a society that put so much of a premium on success, there was little sympathy for men who failed to achieve. In many cases, this lack of success was explained by a fundamental lack of character, meaning that liberals who defended the less successful in society opened themselves to criticism. Hubbard's stinging rebuke shows this:

> We have recently been hearing much maudlin sympathy expressed for the 'down-trodden denizen of the sweatshop' and the 'homeless wanderer searching for honest employment', and with it all often go many hard words, for the men in power. Nothing is said about the employer who grows old before his time in a vain attempt to get frowzy ne'er-do-wells to do intelligent work; and his long, patient striving with 'help' that does nothing but loaf when his back is turned. In every store and factory there is a constant weeding out process going on. No matter how good times are, this sorting continues, only if times are hard and work is scarce, the sorting is done finer – but out, and forever out, the incompetent and unworthy go. It is the survival of the fittest. (cited in Bendix, 1956: 265)

Suspicion that less successful men were lazy, incompetent or intent on sabotage were seized upon by early organisational theorists. Taylor's (1917) *The Principles of Scientific Management*, for example, had a powerful impact on patterns of industrial management. Taylor believed, in line with contemporary Social Darwinist thinking, that there was a best fit between every job and every man's capabilities. But he was also extremely suspicious about the poor effort most men put into their work, unless they were supervised very closely and incentivised through piece rates: 'Underworking, that is, deliberately working slowly so as to avoid doing a full day's work...is almost universal in industrial establishments...and the writer asserts without fear of contradiction that this constitutes the greatest evil with which the working-people of both England and America are now afflicted' (1917: 14).

Taylor's writing influenced new patterns of industrial management and the division of labour in factories which helped to inspire the assembly-line factory system that came to dominate American manufacturing systems in the early twentieth century. The Ford Motor Company's pioneering use of assembly lines, for example, systematically controlled the pace and pattern of work in automobile manufacture to avoid underworking. While the experience of work on the assembly line was exhausting and the management regime often brutalising (Beynon, 1973; Rose, 1988), this did not produce a strongly unionised work force as was the case in Britain. Breaking down worker resistance was partly alleviated by the incentive of relatively high pay – the 'five-dollar-day' package – but also by the high levels of unemployment at that time and intense management opposition to labour unions. But above and beyond that, it is apparent that factory workers themselves did not necessarily think of their position in collective terms. Instead, by internalising the ideology of the American Dream, they dreamed of escape by saving enough money to buy their own land or business (Chinoy, [1955] 1992).

In this example, there is a close association between the notion of escape from industrial work and the possibility of achieving an independent 'masculine' identity away from paid employment as head of their family and in charge of their own business or farm. Within paid employment, however, there was much scope for men to bolster their sense of masculinity by reproducing cultural notions that the public world of work was a male preserve while women's place was in the private sphere of home. Indeed, some management theorists asserted that men had a monopoly over successful attributes. For example, McGregor's (1966) management theories, which were developed in the 1950s, strongly emphasised the link between success and masculinity. In defining his 'model of the successful manager', he asserted that such a man must be 'aggressive, firm and just. He is not feminine in the womanly sense. The very expression of emotion is widely viewed as a feminine weakness that would interfere with effective business procedure' (cited in Spencer and Podmore, 1983a: 7).

The general tendency in the mid-twentieth century to celebrate the single-minded, competitive and hard-working role model of the successful corporate manager, executive or professional did not pass entirely without criticism. In one contemporary study, *The Organisation Man*, Whyte was highly critical of the notion that family life must be sacrificed for corporate success. In his chapter entitled 'The Neuroses of Organization Man', Whyte assessed the impact of excessive careerism on the 'non-well rounded man'. He began by painting a stark picture of the effort required of the organisation man in terms of his weekly workload.

> Typically, it would break down something like this: each weekday the executive will put in about 91/2 hours in the office. Four out of five weekdays he will work nights. One night he will be booked for business entertaining, another night he will probably spend at the office or in a protracted conference somewhere else. (Whyte, 1957: 136)

Whyte's impressionistic insights have proven to be well founded. Even in the 1950s he noted that while 'corporations warn against such a work load as debilitating, in practice most of them seem to do everything they can to encourage the load' (1957: 136). As one man told him, 'what it boils down to is this, you promote the guy who takes his problem home with him' (Whyte, 1957: 137). Male professionals and managers also expected to neglect their families in order to pursue work-related leisure. Submitting to the expectation of complete devotion to work is reproduced by the tendency of senior managers to promote men (and more recently women) who are moulded in their own image; people, that is, who put work first and family last. It was easier for men to make such a 'sacrifice' because they readily adopted the 'man as provider' model of marital and parental responsibility, rather than demanding a fully participant parenting role. In the 1950s and 1960s in the USA, sociologists recognised that the gendered division of labour in the middle classes consigned men to full-time breadwinning and women to full-time homemaking, but this was not conceptualised as problematic. As Parsons stated:

> To be the main 'breadwinner' of his family is a primary role of the *normal* adult man in our society... Consequently, 'housekeeping' and the care of children is still the primary functional content of the adult feminine role in the 'utilitarian' division of labor. Even if the married woman has a job, it is, at least in the middle classes, in the great majority of cases not one which in status or remuneration competes closely with those held by men of her own class. Hence there is a typically asymmetrical relation of the marriage pair to the occupational structure. (Parsons, 1964: 191 my emphasis)

Parsons supported the view, therefore, that occupational success demanded total devotion from the husband at the expense of his wife in career terms. As many feminist writers later pointed out, it was often wives and children who were consigned to a life-style with fewer opportunities in the suburbs while he was away at work. But as was noted in the introduction to this chapter, sustaining a career also had costs for men in terms of lost opportunities. As one man from Whyte's study pointed out:

> Executives try to be dutiful husbands and parents, and they are well aware that their absorption in work means less time with their family even when they are physically with them. Younger executives in particular accuse themselves. They are not, they say, the fathers they should be and they often mention some long-term project they plan to do with their boy, like building a boat with him in the garage. But, they add ruefully, they probably never will. 'I sort of look forward to the day my kids are grown up,' one sales manager said, 'Then I won't have to have such a guilty conscience about neglecting them'. (Whyte, 1957: 140)

In the 1950s and 1960s the advantages that were bestowed upon successful career men over their wives in terms of leisure, self-fulfilment, career advancement, status and disposable income may then have been tainted by some degree of guilt for not fully participating in parenting and domestic life.

Given the strong cultural pressure on middle-class American men to be successful careerists and the continuing association between primary breadwinning and masculinity, it is not surprising that many men find it difficult to face up to the consequences of career failure. In fact, the experience of downward social mobility is not particularly uncommon: about one in five American and British men are downwardly mobile in their working lives (Payne, 1987; Newman, 1988). It is not surprising that this situation is rarely remarked upon either in the media or academic literature, given the very strong emphasis on personal success, especially in the USA. As Newman notes: 'America's Puritan heritage, as embodied in the work ethic, sustains a steadfast belief in the ability of individuals to control the circumstances of their lives. When life does not proceed according to plan, Americans tend to assume that the fault lies within' (Newman, 1988: 8).

Newman's study of downward mobility in America set the experiences of redundant managers against the backdrop of the American culture of meritocracy where, even if men experience temporary setbacks in their careers, they will recover if they have the determination. Newman analyses an issue of *Fortune* magazine where the front cover photograph shows:

> a confident, elegant, powerful-looking man striding out the door of an unnamed corporate headquarters. His impeccable blue suit, conservative tie, and beautiful leather briefcase nicely complement his youthful, energetic face. This man is every inch the image of the modern executive, ready to take on the world. The

accompanying headline reads: 'Pushed Out at 45 – Now what?' *Fortune*'s readers might be taken aback by this, but their nerves will be calmed by the cover's fine print: 'Like many of the managers, Silicon Valley's Joseph Rockom lost his $85,000 job but has bounced back.' It seems that *Fortune* has discovered the phenomenon of managerial unemployment, but... concludes that the casualties of corporate restructuring 'have not lost [their] spirit,' and that 'most are winding up in new – and often better paying – jobs.' (1988: 42)

In reality, at the time of study, 27 per cent of unemployed executives were still out of work after six months, and nearly half of redundant managers had to take work in non-managerial or professional work (1988: 44). Newman's study of *The Forty Plus Club of New York* shows the practical difficulties outcast managers and executives faced in gaining a new job with the same status they had held previously. This study demonstrates the psychological impacts of job loss on men in their forties and fifties with the responsibility of supporting college-age children, and a wife who had not previously needed to take paid work. For some men, the humiliation of admitting their unemployment was so severe that they concealed their plight from their families for some time:

Joe Rigley, a refugee from the world of big oil, was so worried about the disappointment and upset the news would cause his family that he hid the fact that he had been terminated for nearly six months. He continued to dress in a suit and tie every morning, leave the house, and stay out all day, returning home at the normal hour as if nothing had gone awry. Jack actually spent the days in coffee shops reading want ads or trying to make contact with old friends in the oil industry. Since Jack handled the family bank accounts, giving his wife an 'allowance' to cover household expense and doling out 'mad money' to the kids on Saturdays, it was possible for him to conceal their declining bank balance, draw on his severance pay, raid the savings account, and keep the truth to himself for quite a while. (1988: 51)

By admitting his job loss, this man took what Newman describes as a 'first step in the symbolic stripping of his identity... he redefined himself in his family's eyes as someone unable to exert control over his own life and, by extension, the circumstances of theirs' (1988: 51). Men who have been made redundant from executive jobs do not necessarily internalise blame immediately, but feelings of failure can surface if an appropriate position is not gained quickly because financial problems make it impossible to sustain an outward expression of success to significant others. The inability to reciprocate the kindness of friends, abandon vacation plans, the need to sell cars or trade down in the housing market all increased former executives' sense of failure and isolation. As one man told Newman: 'All of

a sudden everybody stops talking to you. It's like a disease...
friends, associates, best friends...they start calling you less or stop
calling you altogether. People don't know what to say. They think
they're going to upset you, they don't know how to talk to you'
(1988: 59). Men's loss of self-esteem could also be reinforced by
their spouse. Initially, women accepted that their husband's unemployment was unfair and did not reveal personal failings or lack of
commitment to his career. But, as Newman points out, suspicions of
failure emerged over time because women were unable to reconcile
the 'real' cause of their husband's unemployment with their belief
that reward flows to the deserving.

The experiences of redundant family men cannot necessarily be
transposed directly on to men in general. Indeed, Newman shows
that gay men executives who lost their jobs fared considerably
better. They were generally less depressed, were more optimistic
about the future and did not feel that their friends had either
rejected them or regarded them as failures. Unlike the family men,
gays could draw on financial and social support from friends without
as many strings attached and, while they were concerned about loss
of income, the pressure to maintain status in their circle of friends
was less acute. For the family men, downward social mobility signalled
emasculation by contrast. To offset these feelings a number of men
employed what Newman calls a strategy of 'categorical fate': that is,
they claimed that they were carried along by independent social forces
rather than accept the possibility of personal failure. Paradoxically,
however, some men argued that it was their exercise of masculine
traits that led to their downfall. As Newman notes:

> They believe they were too aggressive, too rational, too smart, too experienced, or
> too committed to principle... [these are] praiseworthy attributes in American
> business. Executives are supposed to be tough and forthright... Hence to be fired
> for being too forthright is, according to the theory of manly flaws, a backhanded
> compliment. (1988: 72)

The fact that some men accused former colleagues of emasculation
because they had yielded to the organisation, while others felt
responsible for their own fate, provides useful insights into the variety
and complexity of responses to downward mobility. The common
factor, however, is that all of these men were caught, temporarily or
permanently, in an in-between or liminal world (V. Turner, 1987)
because of the loss of their privileges gained from their former
primary breadwinner status.

Are married breadwinners more successful than other men?

In the introductory section of this chapter, it was asserted that breadwinning may be advantageous for men in career terms. As the analysis has proceeded, it has become clear that the presumed advantages of breadwinning, such as having more time for leisure and disposable income, more interesting work, career opportunities and so on are not achieved by all men. Indeed, it has become apparent that many of the once taken-for-granted meanings attached to breadwinning, shown in Table 4.1, have been undermined by social, economic and cultural change (these changes are summarised in Chapter 11).

While much has changed, there remains a good deal of evidence to suggest that men, as married breadwinners, do benefit in career terms compared with unmarried men. In relation to income, research shows that married men earn between 10 and 40 per cent higher salaries than never-married men. For married and single women by contrast, income differentials are insignificant (Nakosteen and Zimmer, 1997; Gorman, 1999; Leslie, 2000). These researchers provide a range of explanations for such wage differentials between married and single men which can be summarised in five key points. First, employers may discriminate against non-married men, or positively discriminate towards married men. Second, married men may work harder than single men because of their family responsi-bilities. Third, married men may have more time to devote to work because they gain practical and emotional support from their wives in career building. Fourth, men in emotionally stable relationships may devote less energy to leisure, dating and so on, and may be more healthy and more likely to avoid high risk activities. Finally, married men may take fewer risks with their careers for fear of losing their job, and may be more alert to opportunities for career advancement. All of these factors remain under-researched at present and those sociologists who are exploring such issues are hampered by the complexity of modelling data which takes into account the very many other factors that need to be incorporated in explanatory equations such as age, education, race, class background, occupational type, career potential and so forth. Furthermore, a similar range of variables would need to be included for married men's wives. Given the difficulties of resolving these analytical problems, researchers in the field recognise a conundrum which can be illustrated by posing two different but related questions: *are married men more successful because they are married*, or *are successful men more likely to marry*?

It may well be the case that men with good prospects are likely to be more attractive to women for they can offer economic stability and security. Having a prestigious job, social status and power, similarly, may make such men seem more interesting and therefore more attractive to women. Research on partner selection implies that women may have a vested interest in marrying successful men and, indeed, expect to see further progress in men's careers as a part of the marriage bargain. Presenting marriage in this light may seem to be offensive to both women and men but, as will be shown in Chapter 5, several studies show discernible statistical patterns to demonstrate that women's patterns of partner selection is associated with economic and status prospects.

Once married, it seems that couples may choose different strategies to achieve economic security and social status through investing in men's careers. Nakosteen and Zimmer (1997) suggest that there are three competing explanations to account for such differences. The first is a 'rational choice model' which assumes that husbands and wives take a cool rational overview of their situation and, given the prevailing labour market conditions that generally suit men best, decide that it makes economic sense to put most resources into *his* career building. The second is to adopt an ideological explanation which asserts that couples draw heavily, but possibly unconsciously, on traditional attitudes and beliefs and establish conventional gendered domestic practices that support men's careers. The third explanation is a 'power perspective' which asserts that men, because of their economic dominance, can make decisions without paying much attention to the arguments or interest of their wives because they know that their income is essential to maintain the household. Each of these arguments could be of importance for the analysis of any particular couple, of course, but it is probably not possible to generalise on which is the most salient. What is clear, however, is that the situation is becoming more and not less complex, as the next chapter will show through an analysis of the changing role of the homemaker in the twentieth century.

5

Homemakers

Juggling work, domestic and caring roles

In Chapter 4 it was shown that for much of the last century the breadwinner role produced a degree of certainty in men's lives. They knew that society expected them to marry, to work full-time in life-long careers so that they could financially support a wife and children. In return for their part in the marriage effort bargain, they expected to have sufficient money to enjoy their leisure, and to have most of the work of the home and caring for children done for them by their wife.

At the start of the twentieth century it was expected that women's principal role in life was to be a homemaker. As was shown in Chapter 3, there were few alternatives available to women other than marriage if they were to gain security and status in society. Much has changed since the start of the last century, however, as this chapter will show. Most importantly, women now have many more options in occupational and educational terms than was the case a hundred years ago and, furthermore, there has been a sea change in attitudes about women working which has led, for example, to the establishment of equal opportunities legislation in most Western nations. Increased opportunities for women to gain economic independence was also accompanied by a challenge to the principle that women should stay in unsatisfactory marriages.

The shift from the relative certainties of the breadwinner/ homemaker household of 1900 to the more diverse structures of family life in 2000 which has already been discussed in Chapter 1 has meant that the homemaker role has changed significantly. In order to illustrate this point, Table 5.1 presents a set of work, relationship and family circumstances that women may find themselves in and outlines the potential impact such situations may have on their

Table 5.1 Impact of homemaker, career, marriage and parenting situation on autonomy, affluence, time resource and status

	Personal autonomy	Financial autonomy	Time resources	Occupational status	Parenting/family status
The 'traditional' housewife with no paid employment and full-time parenting and homemaker	Flexibility and control over organisation of household but wider options constrained by caring responsibilities	Dependent on husband's income and domestic financial regime	Time constrained by availability of support from family, age of children and attitudes to standards of housework	None	May be subject to praise or criticism depending on cultural attitudes and work status of family, neighbours and friends
Single woman in a professional career with low homemaker commitment and no dependent children	Likely to be higher as there is nobody to share decisions	Medium to high depending on stage of career	Likely to have more free time after fulfilling work commitments	Likely to have more potentiality due to lack of family/ relationship constraints	May be subject to envy, praise or pity from friends family members for not marrying/parenting
Married to a man in a successful career, with no dependent children in a professional career of their own with low homemaker commitment	Medium autonomy (may be mediated by husband's career, attitudes and behaviour)	Medium to high depending on husband's level of support or constraints	Likely to be higher depending on own and husband's career and relationships demands	Likely to have more potentiality due to lack of parenting, homemaking constraints if husband is supportive	May be subject to pressure from husband, friends and family members to have children

Situation	Autonomy	Affluence	Time	Occupational status	Esteem
Married to a man in a successful career with dependent children, a part-time job and high homemaker commitment	Likely to have lower autonomy to facilitate husband's career and care for children and home	May be lower due to heavier dependence on husband's wage	Low to medium time resource depending on childcare support, nature of work and husband's domestic support	Likely to be low unless professional career was established prior to having children	May gain esteem for spending more time with children and supporting husband's career from family, friends and neighbours
Married to a man in a successful career, with own professional career, dependent children and low homemaker commitment	May enjoy a higher degree of personal autonomy due to career position	May be a higher level of affluence due to dual career income, but moderated by childcare costs, domestic help, etc.	Likely to be heavily time pressured to meet needs of career and parenting and maintain basic homemaking commitment	May achieve medium to high occupational status depending on husband's support and willingness to divert attention from home and children	May gain esteem from some for achieving career and maintaining family, but criticism from others for neglecting children and home

levels of personal autonomy, affluence, time, occupation and family status. It is not the purpose of this exercise to produce a typology of the whole range of experiences of homemaking, but simply to demonstrate that changed domestic relationships can affect women in both positive and negative ways. When examining the first row of this table which presents the situation of the conventional home-maker with a range of alternative situations, it becomes evident that escaping from the 'pure' homemaking role does not necessarily make for an easy life. Hochschild's (1989) work, for example, emphasises the point that many women face an intolerable work burden as they attempt to manage a household, sustain a job and, on top of that, remain responsible for the emotional well-being of family members.

It is clear that the number of columns and rows in Table 5.1 could be extended almost indefinitely to include a range of situations covering single parents, women living with unemployed husbands, higher paid women living with men with lower wages, women living with unco-operative and obstinate partners, and so on. It is up to the reader to explore these possibilities if they choose to do so. As it stands, however, the table sets the scene for the discussion that follows in this chapter on the social, economic and cultural circum-stances that has led to change in women's opportunities for (and expectations about) their role in the public and private worlds of work and home.

The text of this chapter is divided into three parts. The first part of the chapter explains how middle-class households were trans-formed in response to the loss of servant labour in the first half of the twentieth century. In so doing, the chapter shows how house design, new technology and scientific management techniques were introduced, ostensibly to ease women's workloads. The second part of the chapter discusses the circumstances under which women came to challenge the conventional breadwinner/homemaker household during and after the Second World War. The section shows how society attempted to pressure women into accepting an often isolated and unrewarding homemaking role. The final section of the chapter shows that there were fundamental challenges to the homemaker role from the 1960s onwards which were encouraged by feminist thinking and action; but it goes on to show that, while attitudes to homemaking and breadwinning have changed, women still often find themselves supporting their husband's career. This situation is explained by discussing culturally resilient patterns of marriage that reinforce conventional homemaking and bread-winning practices.

The ideal housewife

By the beginning of the twentieth century, middle-class householders in English-speaking Western societies generally accepted the principle that men should take most responsibility for earning money while women should take most responsibility for running the home. These roles were legitimated by the establishment of a set of cultural values that highlighted the differences between men and women in terms of their personal attributes, interests and capabilities. The idealised image of the homemaker and breadwinner household encouraged most families to manage their lives, or at least manage the public appearance of their lives, to match such social expectations. While the gender script had become established in cultural terms, however, the economic and political conditions that underpinned it had already started to change. The most important of these changes, arguably, was increased occupational opportunities for working-class women which led to a significant shortage of domestic servants for middle-class households as the century progressed. In Britain, for example, many working-class women had experienced better paid work, better working conditions and shorter hours during the First World War than they had in domestic service. Consequently, after the war working-class women sought factory or shop work instead of becoming maids.

The 'servant problem', as it became known, caused considerable annoyance to the middle classes and is reflected by this outburst from one contemporary British writer, Walter Shaw Sparrow: 'Among the poor we find the first action of compulsory Board Schools on impulsive young minds, generating odd and wayward ideas about personal freedom, as if girls in a tea-shop for example were either freer or more comfortable than maid-servants in a home' (Shaw Sparrow, 1908: 42–3). Many middle-class commentators proposed that young working-class girls should be banned from alternative forms of work, but such attitudes were not universal. As Mabel Atkinson made abundantly clear, 'no improvement would be attained by shutting other avenues of employment to women and forcing them back into this. Such a line of action is, of course, quite imprac-tical, whatever be the difficulties of mothers of families and mistresses of households' (1910: 193). Given the currency of feminism in the middle classes at that time (see Dyhouse, 1989), some writers thought it unfair to treat working-class women differently. Mrs F. S. Carey's *A Profession for Gentlewomen* offered this advice:

> In all classes of society fresh careers have been found and are still opening up for energetic girls; and at a time when educated women clamour loudly for freedom and equality, we must not be surprised if their humbler sisters take up the cry, and demand some form of employment that will give them liberty in their leisure hours. (1916: 97–8)

Instead of complaining about servants, Carey recommended treating servants with greater respect: 'we have no right to impose dullness on any young lives, or to assume that complete control of action, speech, and even thought which some mistresses apparently consider their right' (1916: 93). There was a proliferation of writing on the better management of servants in Britain in the first quarter of the century, but the project was a hopeless one because the supply of servants was declining.

Few Victorian households had contemplated the idea that middle-class women might do the housework *themselves*, but by the second decade of the twentieth century, a more pragmatic approach began to emerge (Phillips, 1923). As Carey advised, 'What I do urge is, first, that the work of every house should be of such a kind that no mistress need shrink from undertaking it; and, secondly, that only in this way can the housewife achieve that perfect independence which must form the basis of happiness' (1916: 13). Carey advocated a number of changes to the way that households were run to meet the changing circumstances of the homemaker. These included a new 'scientific' approach to housekeeping; second, the introduction of 'labour saving' devices; and finally, substantive changes to the way that houses were designed to make them more easy to run. Each of these will now be discussed in turn.

The interest in the 'scientific management' of the household reflected changing patterns of industrial organisation at this time. Inspired by the ideas of Frederick Taylor, many industries were undertaking 'time and motion' studies of work roles in order to find the most efficient way of getting a particular task done. Taylor advocated that 'one best way' of doing any task must be scientifically determined. In the USA, Christine Frederick was a principal exponent of scientific management of the home (1920). As a contributing editor for *Women's Home Journal* between 1912 and 1919, Frederick worked tirelessly to persuade American housewives to abandon their old inefficient ways and apply Taylor's 'one best way' principle. As the magazine's editor, Bok, recalled:

> We are beginning to understand that, as men are revolutionizing business methods with greater efficiency, so the housewife by introducing more system in her work, is finding the simplifying results of efficiency entering the home. No; housekeeping is no longer drudgery. Women are beginning to see in it a science: a vital factor in life; an act that calls for the highest intelligence, a business as big as the affairs of men. It is the women who hang on to the old methods of housekeeping that find it drudgery. (Cited in Scanlon, 1995: 64)

Arguably, Frederick's zealous adaptation of business practice into the home made more work than was necessary. For example, she argued that women should also keep records of practically every aspect of their work. In her own case, she 'decided that if my husband and other men used modern filing systems and cards in their offices I could do the same to keep my house in order' (in Scanlon, 1995: 66).

In Britain too, 'expert' writers recommended the re-education of middle-class women for their future role. Schiff argued that women must embrace science so that 'the drudgery of housekeeping will diminish' and so that the housewife 'will cease to be a slave to household duties'. In so doing, she would free sufficient time for 'the cultivation of her own mind, and thus, while becoming a more real companion to man, she will be free to take a more enlightened interest in the education and development of her children' (Schiff, 1910: 25). While Schiff's project of reducing the effort women spent on housework was laudable, it is clear that she had no interest in challenging assumptions about gendered domestic practices, or the primacy of the husband in decision-making. Gauging how many middle-class women actually adopted a 'scientific' approach to housekeeping in Britain and America is difficult to establish, although Frederick claimed that she received 1,600 letters in one month in response to one of her articles in the *Women's Home Journal* on scientific house-keeping (Scanlon, 1995).

In Britain, the transition from being the 'mistress' of the middle-class home to the 'lone housewife' was relatively slow because many households continued to employ day servants up to the Second World War (Higgs, 1986). Progressively, however, the 'servant prob-lem' opened up a huge market for 'labour saving' devices once initial worries about the use of electricity in the home had been overcome by the campaigns of Electrical Development Association (EDA). As one EDA pamphlet stated: 'Electricity comes as a timely solution to the servant and other problems, which threatened to disturb that most potent factor in civilisation – THE HOME' (cited in Forty, 1986: 207). Such campaigns were supported by middle-class women's pressure groups such as the Women's Engineering Society founded in 1919 and the Electrical Association for Women which followed in 1924 and gained 10,000 members in 90 branches by the 1950s (Worden, 1989: 130).

Not all domestic appliances were accepted by consumers. One early example is that of the domestic sewing machine introduced first in the USA by companies that produced industrial machines. The main opposition to the idea of a domestic sewing machine was an association with industrial labour, which was something that middle-class American women most emphatically wished to avoid. Singer's advertising copy-writers tried to break down resistance by claiming that 'The great importance of the sewing machine is in its influence upon the home; in the countless hours it has added to women's leisure for rest and refinement' (in Forty, 1986: 98). Design was important, too: the classic Singer sewing machine looked more like a piece of furniture than a machine. Other appliances were easier to sell to middle-class women. Washing machines, which dispensed with the hard labour of boiling water, using a dolly tub and posser and mangles to wring clothes dry, were a great success in Britain and America (although, in the USA, middle-class women had generally used professional laundries prior to their introduction). Ironically, as Schwartz-Cowan (1989) notes, in America, 'the decline of the commercial laundry is, in fact, one of the few instances we have of a household function appearing to be well on its way to departing from the home – only to return' (in Scanlon, 1995: 55).

Writers had been extolling the virtues of good house design since the turn of the century in order to cut down the labour required to run a home. In Britain, architects also began to focus on the ergonomics of kitchen design in the inter-war years. Lillian Gilbreth's *The Kitchen Practical*, published in 1930, stressed the importance of uniform fitted work surfaces and ergonomic planning (see also Gilbreth, 1930; Faulkner and Arnold, 1985). This fashion for efficient kitchen design was not short lived: indeed, by the 1950s ergonomic route plans had become a regular feature in house and home magazines and at shows such as the Ideal Home Exhibition. The *Daily Mail Ideal Home Book 1949–50* tested the efficiency of two kitchen layouts with the following results:

In the first kitchen, which was quite a good one by ordinary standards, it took eighteen minutes for the housewife to cook the breakfast, and she walked no less than 199 feet while doing it... With the improved layout it took only eleven minutes to cook the meal, and the cook walked only 55 feet. (Kernahan, 1949: 43)

Experiments with domestic space in Britain led to the widespread use of open-plan designs that had been popular in America for some time. The advantages of the open-plan design with an integrated kitchen-diner were clarified by Bryan Westwood, who asked, 'Why banish the housewife for great part of her day to an uninspiring corner, cut off from all social life, except that of the back door?' (in Sherman, 1949: 23). This approach led some architects to invert floor plans by putting the kitchen at the front of the house facing the street. One architectural adviser to local authorities, Elizabeth Denby, supported such innovations on the grounds that 'workers and children have a surfeit of communal life during the day. Not so the women... the kitchen, the workshop, should look onto the street, so that the woman can join, however indirectly, in the life of the neighbourhood' (in Attfield, 1989: 177). This design option was used in Harlow New Town in the 1950s, but many women disliked it because they felt that the more public positioning of the kitchen meant that it had to be kept spotlessly clean at all times.

For British council house tenants, especially in the period of post-war reconstruction, modernist strictures on how the working classes *should* live could not be ignored and so, in both high-rise and estate housing, open-plan design became increasingly common (M. Roberts, 1991; Brindley, 1999; Jeremiah, 2000). This is not to say that open-plan design was wholly unpopular. Many welcomed the idea of moving to a new council house or flat, for this was seen as a great improvement on the old terraced house 'slums'. By the 1960s, open-plan design had also become a popular style in speculatively built private houses, and people who owned older houses followed the fashion by knocking-through rooms and stripping away the original features such as delft racks, picture and dado rails, panelled doors and walls, fireplaces and staircase balustrades (M. Thompson, 1979). This minimalistic aesthetic may have cut down the dusting, but it opened the whole house to scrutiny and may have made more work for women.

What this analysis demonstrates is that much of the design criteria used was underscored by a set of gendered assumptions about whose responsibility it was to care for house, home and family. This was reinforced by retailing, marketing and advertising strategies at the time. It would be a mistake to assume that women did not welcome many of the new products and designs that eased their work in the home. That said, capital does not just create demand: it responds to it, too. And as households became more affluent, at first in America but later in Britain, middle-class women as consumers began to shape the market itself in response to a change in the way that household work was perceived. By shaping and responding to changed middle-class consumer behaviour, advertisers perhaps unwittingly produced an image of affluent, white middle-class women's life as 'universal'. This, in turn, affected the way that the model of a successful home was constructed by other women even if they were excluded economically from experiencing it by not being white, affluent or married. In the USA, as Scanlon suggests:

> This 'average' woman had certain characteristics: she was, for the most part, married, living what might be called a 'his and hers' marriage divided by strict gender definitions of work, nurturing, and communication. She was white and native born. A middle-class woman, she resigned her job or career at marriage and preferred spending money to producing goods. Truly modern, she purchased the latest appliances, served her family canned foods, participated in leisure activities. Finally, although she occasionally griped about her husband's lack of attention or her children's selfishness, the 'average' woman felt enormous satisfaction with her life. (1995: 7)

How well this socially constructed 'average' matched reality is difficult to judge. But certainly, by the end of the Second World War, there is evidence of the façade cracking.

The decline of the cereal box family

It is not possible to define a clear point in history where the traditional breadwinner/homemaker model of the middle-class nuclear family began to decline. It is more useful to conceptualise change in the way that households were organised as a process which occurred over time as women took advantage of new opportunities in the labour market. That said, one key historical event that many sociologists have focused upon as a watershed in women's changed attitudes to the homemaker role is the Second World War where women were drawn into many occupations from which they had previously been excluded by trade union action, protective legislation and discriminatory practices by employers (such as the 'marriage bar').

During the Second World War, cultural expectations about women's 'traditional' roles were strongly challenged by governments that faced up to serious labour shortages because men were drawn into the armed forces (R. Brown, 1992). In many countries, commonly accepted assumptions that women did not have the temperament, interest, strength or requisite skill to undertake men's jobs were temporarily abandoned. In Britain more than six million women took jobs during the war, many of whom were effectively conscripted into the labour market. Under the Registration for Employment Order of 1941 and the Control of Engagement Order of 1942, women were directed into strategically vital areas of employment as defined by the Ministry of Labour (Riley, 1983: 64). While mothers with children aged under fourteen were exempt, many of them volunteered for war work or undertook voluntary work for organisations such as the Women's Royal Voluntary Service. Employers were encouraged to recruit married women on the strength of their reliability and adaptability as this extract from a Ministry of Labour report, *Women in Shipbuilding*, shows:

> It is no exaggeration to say that the average woman takes to welding as readily as she takes to knitting, once she has overcome any initial nervousness due to the sparks. Indeed, the two occupations have much in common, since they both require a small, fairly complex manipulative movement which is repeated many times, combined with a kind of subconscious concentration at which women excel...A healthy, and not too heavy, sensible woman who has to run a home is marvellously adaptable, and will turn her hand to anything with good will, once she has made up her mind to do it...She has more balance than the young ones. (cited in Riley, 1983: 68)

In America too, six million women took paid jobs for the first time, increasing the number of working women to 57 per cent, the majority of whom were married (Woloch, 1996: 302). Federal government propaganda made huge demands on 'womanpower', with hoardings carrying messages such as: 'If you've used an electric mixer in your kitchen, you can learn to run a drill press' (Woloch, 1996: 308; see also Hepler, 2000). As there were few jobs that women could not do once they were 'released' from the domestic sphere, it is tempting to argue that the war produced a new sense of independence and self-confidence. Certainly, war-time conditions changed social attitudes and engendered a *live-for-today, not-for-tomorrow* culture, especially in Britain where the immediacy of the war was everywhere to be seen. People became more promiscuous because they were constantly on the move and social life was collectively lived out in the public arena instead of being anchored in the private domestic sphere. And yet marriage became more popular in the early years of the war and the age of marriage fell, suggesting that conventional notions of morality remained high (Haste, 1994). However, when men returned from the forces, couples often could not adapt to women's changed expectations of freedom and independence (Turner and Rennell, 1996).

After the war, women left work in droves. By 1946, some 2 million women in the USA left the labour force and another million were laid off. Part of the explanation for this is that the government withdrew many of the childcare services it had provided for married women. In the early post-war years, women were exposed to a barrage of government propaganda to encourage them to take up their new patriotic duties as mothers and homemakers. In America, as Woloch points out, 'Once the war was over, the woman worker was no longer a symbol of patriotic ardor but rather a threat to social and economic security' (1996: 310). In Britain, this was reinforced by the closure of almost half of the war-time nurseries by 1947 and pressure on women to leave their jobs to make way for demobilised soldiers (Riley, 1983).

Tremendously adaptable though women proved themselves to be during the war, it is a mistake to assume that such work was necessarily welcomed or enjoyed. In Britain, tens of thousands of women worked in munitions factories for between 65 and 80 hours a week, and for many there was still the shopping, housework and children to take care of. Rationing worsened the situation, making shopping, cooking and housekeeping frustrating and time consuming and often leading to high rates of absenteeism. One Mass Observation survey reported that some factories cut down absenteeism by issuing 'a weekly ration of cigarettes and cosmetics to every female member of the staff, and did it on a Saturday, their worst absentee day normally' (in Riley, 1983: 70). In America too, it was recognised that fatigue from running a home and working produced high levels of absenteeism. In many factories, women counsellors were employed to give advice on diet and health and to help sort out childcare and housing problems (Hepler, 2000: 79–81). New workplace opportunities were, however, a mixed blessing, and as defence work was run down towards the end of the war, many women sought escape from the double burden of paid work and homemaking.

Government policy in post-war Britain and America re-established a gendered categorisation of 'breadwinner man' and 'homemaker woman'. While there may not have been an *orchestrated* campaign to push women out of the labour market by government, employers and trade unions, the ideology of separate spheres for women and men re-emerged. A number of factors contributed to the return to domesticity, ranging from government policies on the family, patterns of post-war town planning and housing reconstruction, education and employment, together with the effects of the mass media and expert advice on good parenting and homemaking.

One of the most serious consequences of this was the increased social isolation of housewives, especially for women who were rehoused in new towns or moved out to the suburbs (see, for Britain, Miller, 1983; Little, Peake and Richardson, 1988; Booth, Darke and Yeandle, 1996; and for North America, Fava, 1980; Saegert, 1980; Wekerle, Peterson and Morley, 1980; P. Wagner, 1984). Attfield's study of Harlow New Town near London, for example, shows that the new women residents missed the day to day contact with their extended family, friends and neighbours that were customary in traditional working-class communities. As one woman in Harlow commented: 'When I used to look out of the window, I couldn't see a thing...I thought I was the only person on earth...It took me years before I classed this as a home' (Attfield, 1989: 218). This was a condition known locally as *Harlowitis*, and led a doctor to give this ill-judged advice to women in the *Harlow Citizen*: 'Buy yourself net curtaining for every window in the house, shut yourself in for a week and forget the place ever existed. It will do you the power of good' (in Attfield, 1989: 219).

Planners did not *intend* to make women feel isolated, but they failed to recognise that the role of a 'housewife' may be insufficiently stimulating. It may not even have occurred to them that women could be anything less than happy if they had a modern house, garden and a local parade of shops. Influenced by current ideology on men's breadwinner and women's homemaker roles, British town planners were actively discouraged from providing employment opportunities for women. The Hopkins Committee set up in 1943, for example, was established to explore ways of persuading skilled men to move away from local unemployment blackspots to other areas of Britain. Inducements to move included secure and well-paid work, with good prospects, and good quality affordable family housing. As Roberts (1991) shows, print works or engineering works were the most likely industries to attract 'chief householders' and their families. As the influential planner, Abercrombie, warned in 1945, it was necessary for new towns not to depend too much on trading estates of unstable firms because:

frequently, these concerns are large employers of young persons and low-paid female labour. Their conditions can create very difficult social problems, which

are not conducive to a sense of citizenship, unless the number of such firms in any
one area is limited. A balance should be built up with stable concerns employing
skilled male labour. (in M. Roberts, 1991: 72)

There remained considerable pressure on women to retain their
principal role as homemakers through to the 1960s even if it was
tacitly recognised that it could produce frustrations. Women's
magazines and manuals on household management, in particular,
devoted space to give advice to women on how to perform their
roles appropriately. In such texts, men were judged to have exercised
their principal duties at 'work' and so they expected to be greeted at
home by a smiling wife, who had taken off her apron, put on some
make-up and had dinner in the oven. As Knox instructed her readers
in the *Daily Mail Ideal Home Book*:

> The wise man is he who confines his office troubles strictly to office hours. He
> leaves them behind when he grabs his coat and hat and legs it for the station. The
> wise woman is she who deals with her chores of home, housekeeping, and children
> in her own time, and does not meet her returning mate on the doorstep giving an
> impersonation of Cassandra, who, it will readily be recalled, spent her waking
> hours prophesying disaster. (1952: 244–5)

This 'pipe and slippers' scenario was endlessly reinforced in advertising, film, popular music, television and magazines. Contemporary
writers tacitly accepted that women were not fully realising their
potential intellectually, but seemed to be at a loss when it came to
giving advice on what to do about it, as Eirlys Roberts put it:

> We put everything we have into our homes to make them ideal – love, care, intel-
> ligence, hard work, tremendous interest ... [but] a woman can rarely talk to her
> husband about insurance or medicine or law suits, and he probably doesn't want
> her to. He is not in the least interested in the difficulties of making breakfast
> without bacon or in the problem of whether the bookcase should be by the wall
> opposite the window or the one next to it. They can't talk about their jobs very
> much ... And when the children and the neighbours have been exhausted, the
> split is seen. He is interested in the world outside, in what goes on in Parliament
> in local government, in foreign affairs. He is fairly well informed on these
> subjects and likes to talk about them. She isn't, and doesn't. And, sooner or later,
> he will stop trying to interest her, and keep his talk for other men. Why is it? Do
> we lack intelligence? We certainly do not ... But our minds don't get much
> stimulation. We may pass the whole day without talking to anyone except the
> char and milkman and they, although often entertaining, are rarely intellectual.
> If we do sit down with a book, there's always an unmended sheet in the linen
> cupboard which nags at us through the print, and wins in the end like most
> naggers. (1949: 224)

As educational and employment opportunities improved, expectations of women's cheerful resilience declined and women began to reject the role model of the designer housewife (Partington, 1989).

The re-emergence of feminism in the 1960s reflected the progressive challenge to conventional attitudes about women's domestic roles, especially by better educated women who recognised the possibility of gaining greater independence by developing a career of their own. Women were largely excluded from the public world of political life, leisure and employment, it was argued, first by Friedan in *The Feminist Mystique* (1963). And so from the 1960s, as more married women took paid work, homemaking lost social status. As Oakley argued, women must: 'reject uncompromisingly any attempt to stereotype them as housewives: "Housewife" is a political label after all, a shorthand symbol for the convenience to a male-oriented society of women's continued captivity in a world of domestic affairs' (1974: 241). In the face of men's opposition to housework and the unremitting pressure of mothers on daughters to fulfil traditional domestic roles, Oakley considered that radical action was necessary: the abolition of the family itself. 'The family's gift to woman,' she wrote,

> is a direct apprenticeship in the housewife role. For this reason, the abolition of the housewife role requires the abolition of the family, and the substitution of more open and variable relationships: not man-provider, woman-housewife and dependent children, but people living together in a chosen and freely perpetuated intimacy, in a space that allows each to breathe and find her or his own separate destiny. (Oakley, 1974: 236)

Some radical feminists proposed complete separation from men, arguing that heterosexual love was a patriarchal social construct that institutionalised women's oppression and justified men's sexual violence (for a recent critical discussion, see Kemp and Squires, 1997), while others, as will be shown in Chapter 7, attempted to redefine the structure and functions of the family by experimenting with communes.

Recognising that women themselves participated in the reproduction of domestic ideology, Oakley argued that women needed to be made conscious of the way that roles were learned and standards set through socialisation:

> Women must fight the standards set up by their conditioning; standards which insist that anything less than domestic perfection is a crime against their own

natures. Since they have no inherent natures, that crime is of their own imagining. It is on their conditioning that destruction needs to be inflicted, for those standards and ways of doing housework go back into the sub-conscious. They must be made conscious before the battle can be won. (Oakley, 1974: 241)

The cultural resilience of homemaking

As will be shown in Chapter 6, both women's and men's attitudes towards domestic work have shifted to some extent since Oakley published *Housewife* in 1974. Nevertheless, gendered domestic practices in the majority of conventional heterosexual households have proved themselves to be culturally resilient even though many women have successfully established careers in formerly male dominated occupations. As more women have developed careers in their own right, it may be assumed that it is less likely that men can expect or desire that their wives should adapt to or be incorporated into their own working lives.

It would be a mistake, however, to assert that all women want to become career women. Hakim (1995) has argued that women's work orientations have been misunderstood by many feminist sociologists because of their eagerness to show that women can, or even must, be independent from men. In relation to part-time work, for example, it has become commonly accepted that high levels of turnover of women workers are *caused* by the poor level of remuneration, low levels of training, poor promotion prospects and a lack of employment rights (Freeman, 1982; Robinson and Wallace, 1984). But Hakim interprets this differently and argues that women who *choose* part-time work do so because their principal commitment is to homemaking.

We conclude that by the early 1990s about half of adult women were committed to paid employment, compared to two-thirds of adult men. In effect, the adult female population divides into two fairly equal sectors. The first group of women are committed to careers in the labour market and therefore invest in training and qualifications, and generally achieve higher grade occupations and higher paid jobs which they pursue full-time for the most part. The second group of women give priority to the marriage career, do not invest in what economists term 'human capital', transfer quickly and permanently to part-time work as soon as a bread-winner husband permits it, choose undemanding jobs 'with no worries or responsibilities' when they do work, and are hence found concentrated in lower grade and lower paid jobs which offer convenient working hours with which they are perfectly happy. (Hakim, 1995: 435)

In Germany, Britain and the USA, Hakim demonstrates that part-time workers are twice as 'conservative' in their attitudes as full-time women workers, *'even when there are no children of any age at home*, that is, before there are children or when they have left home' (Hakim, 1995: emphasis in original). It is particularly important to emphasise the fact that many women without responsibilities for dependent children adopt the 'marriage as a career' perspective since this highlights the fact that being a homemaker with, perhaps, some part-time work is a choice many women want to make. Many women with dependent children, similarly, do not want to make a major commitment to work but choose to stay at home with their children. If Hakim is right to argue that about 50 per cent of women choose the 'marriage career' instead of an 'employment career' it is important to explore what advantages such women perceive they gain from being married. The possible advantages may include gaining social status through a husband's work, freedom from full-time employment, economic security and a chance to invest fully in the upbringing of children. In return, women may expect to do the bulk of the housework and childcare, and provide career support to their husbands.

It is important now to explore the importance of those factors connected to male career success that directly impact upon women's experience of domestic life. These factors include, for example, the necessity of geographical mobility to build a career, absence from home due to long working hours, the involvement of wives in supporting careers of men who work at home, and so on. Taking the issue of geographical mobility first, it is clear that many men must relocate their family several times if they are to climb the ladder of success. In some cases, mobility is an essential requirement, as is the case, for example, of the military, the church and the diplomatic service. Other careers, such as professional football, academic life, or work for large multinational companies also require career-minded men to move. Men on the move might, with some justification, claim that it increases a family's affluence, but it cannot be assumed that everyone benefits equally as moving area can sever kinship and friendship ties, childcare networks, and may arrest or curtail women's careers (Haour-Knipe, 2001). The extent to which women's lives are affected by a husband's mobility depends to some extent on their own occupational aspirations. In one study of in-migrants to Aberdeen in Scotland, for example, it was demonstrated that wives readily adapted to new situations and quickly established themselves in new jobs (Bonney and Love, 1991). Women married to careerist men often choose occupations which can be picked up elsewhere relatively easily, such as clerical and secretarial work, or teaching and nursing. As the numbers of dual-career families increase, however, it is likely that fewer career women will be prepared to abandon or damage their own career in order to facilitate their husband's social mobility, especially if their economic contribution to the household could not be offset by their husband's promotion.

Men's occupational mobility can produce chronic disorder in women's lives in other ways. The military wife, for example, is not just vulnerable to regular demands for mobility but is also expected to be fully incorporated into her husband's career in the sense that she, too, is subjected to the intense institutional control of daily life (Chandler, 1981). For example, military wives are expected to co-operate and respect the decorum of rank, meaning that women are discouraged from fraternising with women married to men of higher or lower rank, and such fraternising is particularly frowned on between the wives of officers and enlisted men. Similarly, men can also disrupt family life by working at home, This is a common pattern of work in many professions including, for example, the clergy, writers, farmers and people with small businesses. Men who work at home often have a high degree of autonomy over the way their work is done, but this can have the opposite effect on their wives and children. Often the home environment is adapted to meet the husband's work routine. Writers, for example, demand quiet and a lack of mental disturbance; they expect other members of the household to defer to their work by demanding silence so that they can achieve their goals (Sciama, 1984; Hartill, 1989). Also, men working at home tend to demand exclusive domestic space for their work. In a study of 84 predominantly self-employed teleworkers in London, Fothergill shows that men's work could have a negative impact on women's control over the domestic sphere. As one woman respondent stated: 'I think I was quite aware of having a large male presence in the house all day long. He was talking to me an awful lot, I was feeling quite pulled in different ways ... I felt actually having [him] setting up a business round the house was demanding all round' (Fothergill, 1995: 23). Not all women responded in the same way, however. One respondent told Fothergill that she was 'jubilant' when her husband got a teleworker's job at home:

I was pregnant when he applied for the job and he wanted something which was more useful than batting up and down the motorway, selling software to people ... and it would be less stressful because he did suffer from stress and high blood pressure at one point ... I thought he would enjoy it and because he wasn't going to be the absentee father, so I was delighted. (Fothergill, 1995: 23)

When both partners worked mainly at home, Fothergill shows, women generally retained most responsibility for housework and childcare. This was reflected in the spatial arrangements that joint teleworking couples adopted. Men colonised space that was dedicated to their work while women fitted theirs around other family spaces and activities. Other studies of women homeworkers have also shown that flexible patterns of work do not so much lead to a free use of time as the loss of free time (Allen and Wolkowitz, 1989; Pennington and Westover, 1989). Men in small businesses often work mainly from home, claiming that they have escaped the 'rat race' by getting out of regular salaried employment. Self-employment is rarely an easy option, however, and the precarious economic situation of many small businesses can lead to very long hours of work and a low prioritisation of family life. Ironically, many men who go into small business do so to gain the freedom to do what *they* want to do, but find it doubly hard to stop working because they fear business failure (see Scase and Goffee, 1980; Corden and Eardley, 1999).

Husbands can also disrupt domestic life by taking the 'culture of work' home with them, with soldiers using army-like discipline (Macmillan, 1984), policemen interrogating their wives (Young, 1984), or doctors suffering from being unable to overcome professional emotional disengagement (Fowlkes, 1980; Gerber, 1983). In Salaman's (1971) British study of railway workers and their families, one woman expressed the frustration of being married to a man who thought of nothing else but his work: 'It's railways, railways, railways with him. All railwaymen are like it, they just want to get together and talk railways. As though they didn't have enough. If you want to find out about railways, ask the wives. We're the ones who've had railways all these years' (cited in Finch, 1983: 34).

Finally, some professionals (including priests and politicians) are required to display high standards of respectability in both their public and private lives. Family members are also expected to live up to these standards. Consequently, vicars' wives find that their homes become semi-public places, which are subject to unannounced visits and surreptitious scrutiny for signs of slovenliness or unrespectability by parishioners (see Finch, 1983; Callan and Ardener, 1984). In sum, it is clear that many women are expected to do more than *facilitate* their husband's work by doing the housework and looking after children, but are also often *incorporated* into their working lives in the sense that they must present an appropriate image of themselves, their house and family to meet the expectations of clients or the general public.

Since these studies were published women's career opportunities have improved. That said, many women continue to recognise that marriage can provide opportunities for greater affluence than they can easily achieve themselves, together with the security to establish a family. To state this seems offensive in a culture which has become accustomed to the adoption of gender-neutral language in relation to labour market aspirations. And further, because people are loath to concede that they marry for any other reason than love, it seems offensive to assert that that women weigh up potential partners' current or potential economic worth. Nevertheless, it is important to take such factors into account because the evidence to suggest that women marry beneficially in economic and status terms is compelling (see Coltrane, 1998).

There are several of reasons why women tend to marry men who have higher incomes than themselves. The first is simply a structural one: in countries where gendered orientations to work and sex discrimination in employment continue to exist there are more men with high status and paid jobs than women. The result is a marriage market where women are more likely to find a partner who has a higher paying job with better prospects than they do. And while there is a significant narrowing of the gap in marriage partners' educational achievement in favour of women, this trend will continue until parity of occupational achievement exists (Gorman, 1999; Leslie, 2000). Women marrying men of a higher status than themselves is not just an outcome of statistical probability, but is also a cultural phenomenon, known by anthropologists as *hypergamy*. Men and women understand this, get to know their market value and sometimes even advertise it in the baldest terms. Studies of personal advertisements in newspapers and dating agencies in the USA show that men, knowing their own value, emphasise what they want from a woman, using expressions such as *attractive*, *slender*, *petite* and *sexy*. Women put more emphasis on terms such as *secure*, *affluent*, *professional* and *successful* (Coltrane, 1998: 47).

In the eighteenth and nineteenth centuries, as has been shown in Chapter 3, the advantages of marriage for middle-class women far outweighed the disadvantages as there were few, if any, legitimate alternatives which could lead to a respectable independent social status in the community. Families marketed their daughters openly on the social circuit and discussion of market value was a source of considerable societal fascination. In reality, marriage patterns continue to be predictably *homogamous*, especially in terms of class background, religion, race, ethnicity and age (although women generally marry men who are older than themselves, thus giving men a head start on the career ladder). Coltrane sums up these market factors as follows:

> women's dependence on marriage has made it less likely they will impulsively fall in love and more likely that they will work on their own feelings to make them fit the practical aspects of relationship possibilities. In contrast, men have been able to follow their impulsive feelings and trade their wealth or earning power to get a desirable wife, often marrying more attractive women slightly below them in social class. Such marital bargains tend to reinforce power differences between men and women in the larger society. (1998: 51)

The dream of an egalitarian marriage can often be upset by the choice of marriage partner whose job may shape a woman's life-style and block her opportunities to develop a career in her own right. It is likely that women may not always know what kind of life-style they are buying into which can be the cause of marital friction. In the concluding section of her study, *Married to the Job*, Finch (1983: 133) helpfully formulates a set of rules for prospective wives who want to avoid being incorporated in their husband's work. While she admits that the exercise is quite a frivolous one, it remains useful and interesting. Her rules are listed below.

1 Avoid a husband whose job entails frequent geographical mobility.
2 Any potential husband whose job has very flexible hours should be regarded with great suspicion.
3 If you want to try to work out shared domestic tasks, avoid a man whose job takes him away for blocks of time.
4 Be very careful about going to live in a house which is any way connected with your husband's work.
5 Under no circumstances marry a man whose work is going to be based in your home, or even one who can work at home if he wants to.
6 Beware of the seductions of self-employment...the man who employs himself often needs his wife's labour to make the business viable.

7   Avoid men doing work which contaminates the whole of their
    lives, work which is highly socially valued, or which has strong
    moral overtones.
8   Regard with great suspicion any man whose work entails certain
    tasks which look like women's work...he will off-load them on
    the nearest available and reliable woman – yourself.

Finch wryly observes that most potential husbands will have been
excluded by this process, leaving only, perhaps, 'a nine-to-five factory
worker with a job for life in the same place', and even then 'there is
no actual guarantee that she will be totally unaffected by his work'
(1983: 133). On this matter, she is entirely right. As a former assembly-
line worker in Britain told Beynon in *Working for Ford*:

> in those days it was terrible. That was before I was a steward. I was working on the
> headlinings and I never thought I'd survive. I used to come home from work and
> fall straight asleep. My legs and arms used to be burning. And I knew hard work.
> I'd been on the buildings but this place was a bastard then. I didn't have any
> relations with my wife for months. Now that's not right is it? No work should be
> that hard! (in Beynon, 1973: 86)

Some women might see some real advantages in having a partner
who brings in a wage, then sleeps in front of the television on the
sofa and does not bother them for sex. But, like as not, the arrangement would produce other irritations, for what is the point in being
married at all if one's partner is completely inert? There are several
ironies and contradictions at work here. If the man has stimulating
and demanding work, which carries social status, is well remunerated
and allows him some flexibility in the way he does his job, it may
make him seem like an *interesting person* (perhaps even an attractive
social asset in a marriage), but also it can make him impossibly selfish
as his work can take over his life and, by definition, hers too. On the
other hand, if the man has a less stimulating job which does not tire
him too much, then he might start getting *too* closely involved in his
wife's domestic territory.

Until relatively recently, the idea of marrying a professional man
was an attractive option for many women because it provided them
with a fair chance of achieving a relatively secure and affluent
lifestyle, social status and social mobility. Many women took this
option very seriously (that is, becoming a career wife) because they
had little hope of achieving such status in their own right. As Finch
put it:

> Being married to the job makes perfect sense for most wives, not simply because external constraints force them into it, nor because their socialisation makes their compliance inevitable, but because it has its own inherent internal logic. This internal logic has three strands: it makes economic good sense; the organisation of social life makes compliance easy and developing alternatives very difficult; it provides a comprehensible way of being a wife. (1983: 168)

Only two decades later, for educated women with good career prospects of their own, attitudes may be changing. No longer do women have to be pioneers to get a foothold in a professional career. Women are more likely to expect to have a higher degree of economic independence. And marriage itself, because of the constraints it imposes on women, is being postponed until later by women if, as we shall see in Chapter 9, they marry at all.

Women's opportunities increased substantially in the twentieth century in political, cultural, economic, educational, employment and relationship terms, but expectations about women's homemaking roles have not yet been abandoned. Far from it; women still do about 70 per cent of housework, are much more closely involved in childcare and still provide much support for their husbands' careers. In the next chapter, it will be shown that gendered domestic practices remain deeply rooted, but it also shows that *both* women and men need to change attitudes if a higher degree of equality is to be achieved in the domestic sphere.

6

Negotiating Domestic Practices

This chapter illustrates how women and men negotiate domestic practices. Following Morgan's (1996) conceptual work on family practices, introduced in Chapter 1, this chapter stresses the importance of exploring the everyday routines of domestic life for gaining an understanding of the way domestic practices and family life change (see also Jagger and Wright, 1999; Silva and Smart, 1999; Smart and Neale, 1999). Emphasising the everyday, the routine or trivial aspects of family life, Morgan argues, helps to make sense of the way that taken for granted practices act as foundations for the solidarity of social relationships within the household. It is, of course, important to recognise that every family negotiates and establishes everyday practices differently but, at the same time, as Morgan puts it, sociologists must take account of the fact that 'practices have a societal and an historical dimension as well' (1999: 19). As I attempt to show throughout this book, the interplay between established patterns of cultural, economic and political life always impact on the private world of domestic life. This can occur formally through the activities and dictates of institutions that establish building regulations, patterns of employment, mortgage contracts, health, safety and environmental regulations and so on. But most importantly, social and cultural mores impact on the private sphere informally through the social pressure exerted by family, friends or neighbours which in turn tends to produce continuities in social behaviour both inside and outside the home (see also Chapman, Hockey and Wood, 1999).

This chapter concentrates on the mechanisms and principles upon which domestic practices are negotiated in heterosexual couple households. While the emphasis is on negotiation it should not be presumed that men and women enter into relationships on an equal footing, however. As was argued in Chapter 1, women and men also bring different resources into relationships including 'economic power', 'socialised skills', 'physical capabilities' and, most importantly, 'sets of ideas'. Consequently, most couples have arguments about the day to day practices of domestic life because they have a greater say on some issues compared with others, and do not always share understandings on competing time pressures and priorities. That said, the purpose of the chapter is not merely to demonstrate that men or women have more power over each other in some important respects, but instead it is to reveal how they attempt to negotiate their way around the conflicts that power imbalances produce.

The chapter is divided into three sections. The first section concentrates on time use in households. It is demonstrated that the introduction of new technology, change in the design of houses and the introduction of new ideas about how to do housework has affected domestic practices in unpredictable ways. Most significantly, it is argued that there can be an inverse relationship between technological innovation and time spent on housework. Gendered patterns of time spent on housework are also changing. As this section will demonstrate, recent research suggests that many men are spending more time undertaking household tasks than in the past. While it remains the case that women spend most time on housework, in some circumstances men do more of the work than women.

The second section discusses patterns of financial prioritisation in households. Through a historical investigation of changing approaches to managing money in households, it is revealed that gender is a crucially important factor in defining how money is valued, apportioned and spent. In the final section of the chapter, I will return to the issue of housework roles that was introduced in Chapter 2. Through an analysis of differing circumstances within which couples approach household chores, this section highlights the extent to which everyday practices and routines can reinforce established cultural ideas about masculinity and femininity. That said, this concluding section reveals that such practices are changing in many households and the indications are that both women and men are becoming less rigid in their attitudes about who should do what in the domestic sphere.

The changing patterns of domestic time use

Judging from the sales-pitches of companies that manufacture products such as washing machines, vacuum cleaners, microwave ovens and so on, it would seem to be self-evident that new technology saves time. Ironically, the reverse can sometimes be the case: new technology sometimes increases time spent on housework. Vanek's (1980) analysis of homemakers' time use from the 1920s to the late 1960s in America, for example, indicates that women consistently spent about 50 hours a week on housework, even though the nature of the tasks themselves had been transformed. It was also argued that the amount of time spent shopping increased substantially from about two hours a week in the 1920s to a whole day by the 1960s. While it might be expected that the introduction of one-stop shopping at supermarkets or malls which were accessed by car might reduce shopping time, Vanek argues that the reverse is the case because there are more products to choose from, more money to spend, and a more complex life-style to attend to. It may be the case, however, that the apparent consistency of time spent on housework identified by Vanek may have concealed substantial differences between the social classes. As Gershuny and Robinson (2001) have argued:

> in the UK at least, this apparent constancy reflected two counterbalancing processes: a decline for working-class women due to the diffusion of 'labour-saving' appliances, and an increase for middle-class women reflecting the decline in paid domestic service. From around the end of the 1950s housework time declined for all groups, so that by the 1980s women did substantially less routine domestic work (cooking and cleaning) than women in the 1960s. (2001: 335)

Table 6.1 provides, firstly, a comparison between early twentieth century and contemporary twenty-first century households in order to demonstrate how tasks have changed in response to improvements in household technology. Second, the extent to which labour-saving technologies actually save time is illustrated. It is apparent from this analysis that one of the most important time-saving technologies was the introduction of efficient plumbing, heating and lighting. Houses that relied on gas lighting, coal fires and perhaps only one cold water tap created a tremendous amount of work for working-class housewives – or servants in the case of middle-class homes – in the early twentieth century. Cleaning fireplaces, bringing in coal and lighting fires in every room of the house was a labour intensive activity in itself but, additionally, the dirt created by coal fires produced

Table 6.1 *Time saved and created by household technology*

Type of technology	Time saved	Time increased
Heating and lighting Central heating systems Gas fires, electric fires Hot water cistern/geysers	Saves time cleaning conventional fire grates, collecting and chopping wood, ordering fuel, carrying in fuel, making fires. Reduction in time required for heating water, especially for baths.	Negligible time spent switching on heating system, gas or electric fires. Fashion of wood burning stoves and open fires may redefine fire-lighting as leisure rather than work. The availability of hot water cuts down time required for general cleaning tasks. May increase the number of and use of bathrooms as expectation of body cleanliness increases.
Laundry work Automatic washing machines Tumble dryers Steam irons	Considerable time saving on manual washing, drying and ironing.	There may be a tendency to wash clothes more frequently due to demands of fashion, use of different clothes for a range of activities; may also be raised expectations of cleanliness/freshness of clothes.
Food storage Refrigerators Freezers	Keep food fresh for longer thereby cutting down regular shopping requirement.	The ready availability of a range of food encourages snacking, multiple meal orders from different family members, facilitates family eating at different times of the day thereby producing more washing up, cooking time.
Cleaning equipment Vacuum cleaners, carpet cleaners Floor polishers	Quicker and cleaner to use than carpet beaters, brushes, mops and manual floor polishing.	May have encouraged greater use of carpets that require time consuming maintenance; may have raised expectations of cleanliness.

Table 6.1 (Continued)

Type of technology	Time saved	Time increased
Cooking equipment Electric and gas cookers Microwaves Food processors, mixers, breadmaking machines, etc.	Kitchen ranges required constant attention to keep them in working order. Prepared meals can be defrosted and cooked in microwaves.	New cooking technology is quick and efficient but may encourage more regular preparation of meals for flexibility of members of household. Food processors, bread machines, etc., may increase expectations of home cooking.
Clearing up after meals Dishwashing machines	Saves time washing, rinsing and drying plates. Keeps dirty pots and pans off kitchen surfaces. Achieves better finish than manual washing, saving polishing of glasses and cutlery.	May encourage more flexible patterns of meal production.
DIY equipment Power tools Portable work benches System built furniture	Requires less time, energy and strength in undertaking tasks.	May create demand for jobs to be undertaken such as building furniture, shelving, home improvements, etc., which were once undertaken by skilled paid workers. May decrease the time between replacement of furniture due to fashion/durability of furniture.
Gardening equipment Lawn mowers, lawn edgers, leaf vacuums, etc.	Reduces time, strength and effort required to undertake tasks.	May encourage higher standards of gardening. May create work formerly undertaken by paid workers.

more cleaning work throughout the home. The introduction of gas, electric or oil-powered fires and water boilers or a central heating system had a dramatic impact on the pattern of housework, especially in the eradication of the slow process of boiling water for bathing and laundry work.

A second important technological innovation was the introduction of automatic washing machines. As was shown in Chapter 4, such appliances were sold on the back of a promise that they saved the time and hard physical labour involved in laundry work. But the introduction of such machines also had the effect of raising expectations of cleanliness. Clothes are now washed more regularly and garments are dedicated to particular activities, such as leisure wear, work wear, sports club wear and so on (Deem, 1985; Faulkner and Arnold, 1985; Schwartz-Cowan, 1989; Silva, 2000b). Similarly, the introduction of refrigerators and freezers reduced the need to take delivery of, or to shop for, fresh food on a daily basis. Encouraging householders to stock up with a growing proliferation of ready-made products had the effect of undermining the social institution of the daily family meal and replacing it with a television dinner or snacking culture that encouraged different members of the household with varied leisure and work patterns to expect meals on demand (Mennell, 1985; Charles and Kerr, 1988; Lupton, 1996; Grieshaber, 1997). This, in turn, helped to open up a market for dishwashers which could hide away a constant current of kitchen activity. The latest technological addition to most Western kitchens is the microwave, which has speeded up the process of cookery but also increased flexibility and demand for instant meals (for discussions of the impact of the microwave and other cooking technologies, see Cockburn and Ormrod, 1993; Cockburn and Fürst-Dilic, 1994; Silva, 2000a).

The introduction of new cleaning equipment, such as vacuum cleaners, floor polishers, carpet cleaners and so on, have not just made the process of cleaning more simple, but they have also, increased expectations of cleanliness. The proliferation of hygienic cleaning products such as anti-bacterial surface cleaners (which claim to avert health risks) also raise standards to such an extent that more work may be created. The fact that more people can now expect to have larger houses and apartments also increases the work of the household. Most newly built houses and flats have several bathrooms and toilets, for example, which require more cleaning; moreover, their provision means that people clean themselves more often than was the case a hundred years ago, thereby producing more mess. As was shown in Chapter 4, the design of homes, especially when open plan, increases the prospect of the surveillance of household cleanliness and respectability by significant others which in turn raises the necessity of keeping the home clean and tidy the whole time.

The work of the home is also increased by the availability of DIY equipment and products which has been bolstered by a fashion-led desire to redecorate more regularly. At the beginning of the last century furniture was constructed from solid wood with heavy-duty upholstery to make it extremely durable, and high quality carpets were expected to last for 20 years or more. Durability is a less important selling point in contemporary society because people want to change things regularly and often long before they wear out. This is reflected in Britain by a spate of hugely popular television programmes, such as *Changing Rooms*, *Fantasy Rooms* and *Perfect Homes*, which have raised awareness of interior design and decoration. Such television programmes have established the careers of a number of flamboyant celebrities. DIY has become sexy, and as a consequence leaving things as they are, for many, is no longer an option (Tomlinson, 1990; Chapman, 1999b). The content of Table 6.1, in sum, suggests that the introduction of household technology has been both a blessing and a curse in terms of its time-saving advantages.

There has been a wide range of sociological studies on the time spent on housework, but there remains little agreement on how long, on average, it takes to look after a home. There is one consistent finding, however, which is that in heterosexual couple households women do between one-third and one-half more housework than men (see Coltrane, 2002, for a review of 200 studies). This is illustrated in Table 6.2 which lists men's and women's time spent on housework in Britain. There is some evidence to suggest that this is changing, however, as Gershuny and Robinson conclude in their cross-national analysis of time use studies:

> With respect to routine or core domestic work time (i.e. cooking, cleaning and clothes care), there is, after controlling for the structural variables, a consistent *increase* in men's time, amounting to eighteen minutes per day. Contrasting with this, is a quite vertiginous *decline*, of an hour per day over the period, in the time spent in these activities for women (though of course, from a much higher initial level). (2001: 339)

Even if there has been an increase in the amount of free time for women and men, it may be the case that it is not experienced as

Table 6.2   *Hours spent on household tasks*

	Fathers	Mothers
Cooking, preparing meals	2.50	13.30
Cleaning	2.00	13.15
Washing and ironing	0.55	9.05
Spending exclusive time with children	5.05	8.45
Household shopping	2.50	5.50
Washing up	2.00	3.40
Driving children to school	1.45	2.55
Gardening	3.00	2.00
Sewing/mending	0.10	1.20
Other activities	2.55	1.40
Total hours of work per week	23.30	62.00

Source: *Social Trends* (1997), Table 13.4.

such. As Gershuny and Robinson note, 'It could therefore be that, even though leisure time as a category has increased slightly, the time that is spent in it has come to feel more intensive in character, and consequently more pressured' (2001: 345). The distinction between work and leisure is less clear cut for married women, especially if they are full-time housewives or part-time workers (Deem, 1986; Green, Hebron and Woodward, 1990). Research on married women in Britain, for example, shows that leisure time is often defined as a 'break' from family work and usually takes place in the home by watching television, talking to friends, reading or craft work (Wearing and Wearing, 1988; Hunter and Whitson, 1991; Green, 1996). Most research has focused on the experience of white Western women, but limited evidence suggests that, for Asian women living in the West, leisure is even more concentrated on home-based craft and entertainment or visiting friends and relatives (Green, 1996: 144). Married women in full-time employment, by contrast, tend to draw a more clear cut distinction between leisure time and paid work/ housework time. This suggests that it is not a question of non-working or part-time working women not *having the time* for leisure, so much as not having the right mind set to *take the time* (for a fuller discussion, see Le Feuvre, 1994; Adam, 1995; Kingdom, 1996).

Resentments over the use of leisure time can lead to relationship discord and can be exaggerated when both partners work full time but only one takes proper responsibility for housework. Many studies have shown how frustrating it is for women who effectively do a 'second shift' (see, for example, Hochschild, 1989; Layte, 1999; Baxter, 1993). There are clear indications that conventional gendered practices are breaking down in some categories of household. As Sullivan notes:

> there has been (i) a clear reduction in gender inequality in the performance of some of the normatively feminine-associated tasks, (ii) a larger proportional increase in the time contributed by men from lower socio-economic strata, to a position of near equality with those from higher socio-economic strata, and (iii) a substantial increase in more 'egalitarian' couples, especially among the full-time employed. (Sullivan, 2000: 453)

The extent of men's participation in housework is not consistent (Sullivan, 2000). As Table 6.3 shows, on average husbands do *more* housework if their wife works part-time or does not have any employment. Sullivan also questions the commonly held assumption that men from middle-class households get more involved with housework and childcare than their working-class counterparts. Table 6.3 also reveals that men from manual/clerical households make about the same contribution to domestic work as technical and professional men. Finally, and most importantly, Sullivan shows that in one-third of full-time working couples, men do *more* domestic work than their wives.

There is a paradox at work here. It appears that when men have more time available to do housework than their wives (either

Table 6.3 *Proportion of domestic work undertaken by women by employment status of partners and socio-economic status of the household*

	Manual/clerical		Professional/technical	
	1975	*1997*	*1975*	*1997*
All	0.78	0.63	0.74	0.66
Both full time	0.69	0.60	0.62	0.62
Husband full-time, wife part-time	0.80	0.68	0.74	0.71
Husband full-time, wife not employed	0.82	0.73	0.80	0.73

Source: Sullivan (2000: 443), Table 2.

because these men are unemployed, or because the wife has a more demanding or higher-status job than her husband), they do *less* housework. This may explained by the tendency of unemployed men to feel a loss of self-esteem and economic powerlessness which, in turn, threatens their sense of masculinity. One British study of unemployed men found that many men felt that it would be degrading to be 'kept' by their wife. As one man said:

> I'd have the feeling as if people would be staring behind my back, my missus keeping me, she's paying for all the food, the clothes, the roof over our heads, paying for me to go out and have a drink...If she just worked alone I'd probably go round the bend. (in McKee and Bell, 1986: 141)

Women often accepted their husband's point of view, as one woman said, 'I'm not going to slave myself to death while he sits at home all day on his backside doing nothing' (1986: 141).

Many studies of British unemployed men in the 1980s recession showed them to be in a state of chronic despair or inactivity (see, for example, Platt, 1986; Warr, 1987), but such reactions were not universal. R. Pahl's (1984) study of the unemployed men on the Isle of Sheppey, for example, discovered that men found alternative forms of work from which they gained a degree of status, remuneration or exchange of services (see also Wheelock, 1990). Drawing a contrast between those men and women who cannot adapt to new circumstances (such as unemployment or unconventional income differentials) and those who can is best explained by recognising the fact that some women and men are more wedded to the idea that masculinity and femininity are defined in relation to particular gendered roles in society. As will be shown in the last section of this chapter, however, the indications are that such rigid associations with traditional roles are beginning to break down, especially amongst younger people.

Setting priorities and spending money

Sociological research on the nuclear family up to the 1960s tended to conceptualise household income as a general resource that was unselfishly divided up in the interests of all members of the household. Most family studies at this time adopted a relatively uncritical assumption that the gendered division of labour between homemakers and breadwinners represented the 'natural' order of things. It is not surprising, therefore, that when married women actually sought to gain paid work it was regarded as a 'problem'. In early 1950s Britain, for example, the rising number of married women workers was often met with astonishment by social commentators because it was assumed that the welfare state would have eradicated the 'problem' of married women needing to work. Some writers did recognise that women's principal motivation to take paid work was to gain a degree of personal independence; however, as Willoughby suggested in 1951:

> Her husband gives her a housekeeping allowance but it is rare in this country for the woman's share in running the common enterprise of home and family to be recognized by a personal allotment from her husband's income. Her personal expenditure has to come out of the housekeeping or she has to ask her husband for the amount she requires for a new dress or hat. The higher the economic and social status of a woman before marriage the more she may resent this situation. She continues to work, in part, for the psychological satisfaction of remaining independent. (cited in E. Wilson, 1980: 32)

From the 1960s, studies began to show that if women were in long-term employment, they had considerably more influence on decision-making. While some commentators continued to argue that this put couples under 'strain' because it interfered with traditional gendered divisions of labour (Blood and Wolfe, 1960), other studies revealed that married women's increased economic independence through paid work actually benefited them in psychological terms because they did not have to depend wholly upon their husbands (Klein, 1965). It is a mistake, however, automatically to assume that the more money married women contributed to the household budget the more power they had. This is because married men's and women's income may be 'valued' in different ways. Classical economics states that the value of money is a constant: a dollar is a dollar, no matter who has it in their pocket or purse. While the 'exchange value' of money in the market may be equal, its value to members of the household is affected by many other factors. Pocket money, for example, is of minimal value to parents, but of huge importance to children.

Drawing upon anthropological research on traditional societies, Zelizer (1989) shows that money is valued differently depending upon its 'special purpose', such as a daughter's dowry, funeral or marriage gifts. In Western society, too, money is 'earmarked' for particular purposes. As Douglas (1967) argues: 'many of us try to primitivize our money…by placing restrictions at the source, by earmarking monetary instruments of certain kinds for certain purposes, by only allowing ourselves or our wives certain limited freedoms in the disposal of money' (in Zelizer, 1989: 349). Zelizer shows that money is valued differently according to its source. 'Gift money' can be used for only one purpose, buying a present, because the giver may want to know how it was used, or may even demand that it is used for a particular purpose. 'Stolen money' or 'borrowed money', similarly, has different value from 'earned money' (see Finch, 1989). 'Savings' can be allocated only to specific priorities, especially savings for children or holidays. Most importantly, the issue of who *earned* the money affects its value.

The money married women earned in the nineteenth century was often known as 'pin money'; that is, extra money, not the more important 'breadwinner's' money. In the USA, there were many court cases in the nineteenth and early twentieth centuries which dealt with the issue of whose money was whose in marriage. In 1914, Charles Montgomery sued his wife, Emma, for the $618.12 she had saved over the 25 years of their marriage from her 'allowance'. Brooklyn Supreme Court Justice Blackman ruled for the husband, arguing 'that no matter how careful and prudent has been the wife, if the money…belong to the husband it is still his property, unless the evidence shows that it was a gift to his wife' (Zelizer, 1989: 357). In Buffalo in 1905, Joseph Schultz was taken to court by his wife when he put a rat trap in his trouser pocket to stop her from taking his small change. The police court judge rejected her complaint.

The way money is managed in marriage has changed over time. It was commonplace in the USA for women to be given 'dole' money by their husbands in the nineteenth century: that is, money 'doled out' for particular purposes. This arrangement was abhorred by many women because they had to make requests for all spending, which led to a campaign for women to be given 'allowances'. Even as late as 1938, a national *Women's Home Journal* survey found that 88 per cent of women were in favour of allowances (Zelizer, 1989: 361). Popular advice books on how to manage home life tended also to adopt this perspective. Bruce-Milne's mammoth four-volume *The Book of the Home* (1956) devoted 50 pages of text to the 'business of the home'. Bruce-Milne did not question the legitimacy of a husband's control over the household income, but cast doubt on the wisdom of keeping financial secrets from their wife.

Some husbands believe that so long as a wife gets her regular housekeeping money and her personal allowances, that is all she need worry about. Some men genuinely take this view because they want to protect their wives from money and business worries; others because they fear that if their wives knew the full extent of their annual income, it would make them unduly extravagant... If she has a suspicion that her husband could afford to give her a larger housekeeping allowance, she will tend to be extravagant and overspend, in the hope of getting an increase. Again she is reduced to nagging and wheedling or, at worst, she may develop into a hard, grasping woman. (1956: 559)

This quotation reveals Bruce-Milne's recognition that there was a dimension of unequal power between husbands and wives in their domestic financial relationships, and also, that women could employ a number of strategies to increase their resources including overt pressure on their husband by 'nagging', or covert manipulation of his moods, interests and priorities by 'wheedling'. This text also seems to assume that husbands were generally magnanimous in their command over financial affairs, as shown by Bruce-Milne's warning to women that they may become 'hard and grasping' unless they subordinate themselves to his authority. Assuming that husbands discharged their financial power with magnanimity was often misplaced. As has already been shown in Chapter 4, in the British coal mining industry, for example, men collectively agreed to keep their incomes secret from their wives so that they had enough money to enjoy their leisure time. Indeed, in Britain, male-dominated trade unions resisted the introduction of direct salary payments into bank accounts because their wives would find out how much they earned. Instead, they favoured the weekly pay packet so that they could take their cut before they handed over what remained to their wife. In other cases, men generally regarded 'overtime' payments as separate from family money (Oakley, 1981).

The popularity of allowances in the USA and Britain gave way to a preference for a 'joint account' in the 1960s and 1970s. The use of money in joint accounts is now a common method of managing domestic income and would appear to offer evidence of a movement towards 'equality' in marital relationships. But, as Burgoyne's (1990) work on pooling money in sole breadwinner households shows, women are often reluctant to regard family money, even if it is in a joint account, as accessible to them for *personal* spending. Using pooled money for gifts or treats can produce feelings of unease in women, while men's treating or gift-giving is regarded as more authentic generosity because it is 'their' money (see also

Mauss, [1927] 1966; Goffman, 1967; Bell and Newby, 1976; Cheal, 1987, 1988; Berking, 1999).

The above analysis suggests that money is valued in different ways, but this is only half the story because the way that men and women account for spending is also gendered. For example, there can be a disjuncture between the ways that women and men 'say' they spend money and the way they 'actually' do. Giving the appearance of not spending money can be employed to suggest selflessness. As one woman in Burgoyne's study stated: 'I wouldn't go and buy a magazine – I mean I have a magazine if I'm ill or something so that – somebody buys it for me. I never would – I wouldn't dream of buying a magazine or something like that'. But, as Burgoyne points out, 'Yet she had no difficulty spending child benefit, which she had saved, on special items of furniture of her own choice' (1990: 659). Some of the men in Burgoyne's study were perplexed and irritated by women's reluctance to spend money on themselves; but men can use this martyrdom strategy too, denying themselves things in order to make themselves seem 'selfless' in comparison with their wives' extravagance, thereby making their wives feel guilty when they spent money.

Gendered attitudes about spending money has produced a catalogue of excuses to justify or conceal extra spending. Husbands' suspicions are raised when their wives claim that a new garment was 'from a charity shop', that they had 'had it for ages', or had 'bought it in the sales', just as men can conceal extra spending by not divulging the true level of their incomes, by claiming that nights out were 'on expenses', or that clothes, cars and computers were 'essential for work' or an 'investment in their careers'. Zelizer argues that a man's income is generally regarded as more important and that this therefore affords him more influence over its disposal. But this may also, presumably, rebound on married men because married women's extra income could be regarded as their own money, not family money, and therefore beyond men's influence; while, on the other hand, men's money is regarded wholly as family money. As the woman's oft-quoted comic line goes, 'What's yours is *mine*, and what's *mine* is mine.'

As money is valued in such a complex manner, this complicates the project of researching financial matters in households. Consequently, researchers have tended to side-step this issue and concentrate on measurable distinctions between patterns of 'everyday' spending from the 'strategic control' over money. J. Pahl's (1983) research on family spending distinguished between money *manage-ment*, *budgeting* and *control*. Money management (how priorities are set) and budgeting (how the money is saved or spent to achieve given aims) are vital functions in the household but, according to Pahl, it is the question of who controls the budget which is most important even if, ultimately, that control can be experienced negatively. In theoretical terms, it may be expected that the person who controls the finances has the most power because they choose what the priorities are. But this may not always be the case, especially in poorer households, because the person (usually the woman) who controls the budget takes responsibility for the restriction of other people's needs and wants. Indeed, in some cases, men blame their wife's shortcomings as a money manager, when in reality there just is not enough money to go around. This is illustrated by the following quotation:

> She spends too much. I don't know why she can't manage better. We always seem to be behind: she just can't save anything. As soon as she's got a couple of bucks in her hands she finds something to spend it on. It makes me mad as hell sometimes when I work so hard and there's not enough money for me to spend on something I want. (in Vogler, 1998: 693)

This man's complaint appears to rest on an assumption that his wife is spending all the money on herself or is spending wastefully when, in reality, she may be juggling an inadequate income to meet many competing demands.

Vogler and Pahl (1994) further developed research on money management in a large survey of 1,200 couples in six British towns. In this study they identified six ways in which couples managed their money. In so doing, a distinction was drawn between 'strategic control' over resources and 'managing money' which, as in commercial organisations, impacts on the difference between actual decision-making power and day to day control of resources. The categories Vogler and Pahl defined are as follows:

- in the *female whole wage* system wives managed all the money except the husband's personal spending money
- in the *male whole wage* system husbands managed all the money, which could leave non-earning wives with no personal spending money
- in the *housekeeping allowance* system husbands managed most of the money, except for the wife's housekeeping allowance

- in the *joint pooling* system couples pooled all or most of the money and managed it jointly. (Vogler, 1998: 692)

The fourth definition was, in turn, divided into three categories: the *male-managed pool*, the *female-managed pool* and the *jointly-managed pool*. As Table 6.4 indicates, in about 50 per cent of households the relatively egalitarian model of the managed pool is adopted. Significantly, these findings also suggest that in the poorest households women take most responsibility; but as households become more wealthy, men become more closely involved in the management of money. Vogler argues that poorer households are more likely to maintain conventional gendered practices because both men and women have a more concrete or rigid adherence to the traditional roles of breadwinner or homemaker (see also Hardill *et al.*, 1999). Consequently, poorer men show some unwillingness to be involved in the minutiae of domestic affairs. But, of course, the conventional male breadwinner's lack of concern with general levels of household spending may be contingent upon those priorities *not* impinging upon his own spending (see, for example, Edgell, 1980). Even when facing the hardship that unemployment brings, some men expect to have money for leisure and thereby make it difficult for their wives to manage financially. Such men often fail to appreciate that their wives are not spending the bulk of the household income on themselves. This exasperated exchange of views illustrates the point:

Husband (unemployed bricklayer): There's been lots of times we've had £150 come in ... and I've ended up with about £10 or £15 and you've had the rest.

Table 6.4 *Household financial income and resource allocation*

	%	Standardised (£) income per month
Female whole wage	27	624
Female managed pool	15	658
Joint pool	20	719
Male managed pool	15	728
Male whole wage	10	755
Housekeeping allowance	13	679

Source: Vogler (1998: 694), Table 1; first published in Vogler and Pahl (1994).

Wife (former secretary): But it's like I keep telling you it's not *me* who has it. He thinks when we got £150 he'd want a bit of it and I have the rest. And he seems to think it's me who's having it, but it's not me. I spend it on paying the bills, buying food, clothes, things like that. But he seems to get the idea that it's me who's having it. Whereas with him, when he has his cut, it's *him* who's having it, it's being spent on him! (in McKee and Bell, 1986: 142–3)

The majority of recent studies on money management in marriage have tended to emphasise the negative aspects of women gaining control over day to day spending and decision-making on the presumption that the husband ultimately makes the big decisions about household finances. While it may be true to state that homemakers spend more time and energy managing the household budget, it does not necessarily mean that they do so without identifying some clear strategy of their own. It is likely that homemakers make heavier personal investments in the idea of the family instead of their personal occupational careers, and consequently their spending patterns may reflect the achievement of their idea of what home should be like. Such practices can be very subtle but can have enduring impacts upon the way that household life-styles develop and thereby shape the direction of future possibilities for both women and men.

There are many circumstances in which women's family spending on everyday items such as food can help to produce and maintain the buyer's definition of what constitutes an appropriate home life. Choosing more expensive 'organic' food products, for example, may signal a homemaker's serious concern for the health and well-being of family members. Buying environmentally friendly products, similarly, indicates a wider concern with what is going on outside the household. When buying food products, consumers do not just draw upon rational appraisals of what is best for them in terms of cost, nutritional value or personal taste and enjoyment. On the contrary, food shoppers create an image of the kind of household they want to live in and signal this clearly to their family, friends and neighbours through conversation about their shopping behaviour or when they invite people around for dinner. Positioning a household as one which will only tolerate environmentally-friendly products is costly in economic terms and, by definition, means that choices are being made about not spending money on other things. This kind of analysis could be extended to all kinds of everyday family spending including smaller items such as clothes, children's toys and books, and cleaning products, and also larger products such as washing machines, refrigerators and vacuum cleaners, or services including private nursery care or schooling, family holidays or even the location of the family home. All spending decisions, therefore, have opportunity costs: that is, something else must not be bought or some other activity may not be attended to as a consequence. When the homemaker does most of the shopping, then, it cannot be assumed automatically that they are simply shopping for the family; instead, it should be recognised that they may also be stamping their own authority on what the family's priorities are. They are shopping for themselves, albeit in a subtle, and perhaps even unrecognised way, because they are deciding what kind of family they want to live in.

This analysis suggests that all couples make more or less explicit bargains about what their collective and individual priorities are. This bargain is struck after each partner has drawn upon their personal resources of emotional, financial or cultural power. Striking a bargain does not imply absolute *agreement*, especially if one person has less power than the other in some important respect which can lead to a build-up of resentment in relationships. Arguments over money are one of the main sources of conflict in marriage because the resource allocation bargain is constantly being renegotiated as circumstances change.

Housework as a thankless task

As was shown in Chapter 2, much of the recent feminist and sociological writing on housework assumes that it is an intrinsically dissatisfying task. The source of this sense of dissatisfaction derives largely from the fact that housework is socially and economically unrewarded; but this is not to say that the person (usually the woman) who takes primary responsibility for housework, managing money and caring is completely powerless. On the contrary, power can be gained in two ways: first, doing housework provides *knowledge* about the people who live in the house. As Martin argues:

> She knows the minute details of all our personal habits and has the right to comment, instruct and require. She knows when daughters menstruate and sons have nocturnal ejaculations: whether anyone has been smoking or drinking: when outsiders have been brought in; what provisions have been used and when. Even without recognising it she becomes adept at fitting together all the clues that tell her exactly how the territory and resources of home have been used, even in her absence. (Martin, 1984: 31)

Second, because women do most domestic work, especially cleaning, they have a good deal of control over the way that things are done, and they also set the *standards* on the quality of work. Setting standards provides the opportunity to supervise others when they undertake tasks and to complain if they fail to do things 'properly'. As Martin argues, women patrol 'the boundaries of order spying out subversion, imposing rules and exercising sanctions' (1984: 24).

However, housework is often experienced as a thankless task because other members of the household do not witness the labours that make a home clean and tidy. Resentments arise, Martin argues, because a woman 'can experience her husband and children as a species of insatiable vandals, for ever intent on undoing what she has just achieved and consuming *her* time' (1984: 27). Consequently, 'The alienating effect of her control of domestic order is normally experienced, not as evidence of her *power*... She can never do enough for her men folk' (Martin, 1984: 34: emphasis in original). Early second-wave feminist writing on housework tended to emphasise the experience of the task in the starkest terms (Oakley, 1974; Malos, 1980). As Barrett and McIntosh (1980) put it, 'The daily regime in the prison...is long hours of working banged up in a solitary cell while the guards attend to other, more important business' (in Bell and Ribbens, 1994: 231). More recent analyses by feminists and gender sociologists have tended to be less critical of some aspects of domestic practices. This has been achieved by desegregating tasks such as caring from routine tasks. Following Morgan's lead on the conceptualisation of family practices, Smart and Neale draw the following distinction between caring and housework:

> As the concept of care became more and more refined, it became possible to see how carers were engaged in a reflexive project requiring skills and agency. In a way, feminist and sociological work on caring transformed women into socio-logical agents for the first time. No longer were they merely the 'put upon' and symbolic housewives of the domestic labour debate, nor were they simply a natural resource for other family members as implied in functionalist sociology; instead, they entered, conceptually speaking, into a sociological citizenship for the first time. (1999: 20)

Smart and Neale draw a distinction between caring and house-work because it is assumed that caring 'is qualitatively different from housework because it involves negotiations with others and responsiveness to others' needs; it is both a form of labour and of love' (1999: 20). In sum, the boundary between the two is more difficult to draw than it seems on the surface. Similarly, as was shown in Table 2.2, leisure can be experienced as work or pleasure. The same can be applied to cooking, playing with children and even cleaning; it depends very much on the family circumstances and upon one's own values and mood.

The fact that the process of caring generally goes unrewarded may undermine any last vestiges of pleasure that might be had from housework for the person who nearly always ends up doing a particular task. Some men may not recognise this problem because they only undertake certain tasks occasionally. As I have argued elsewhere (1999c), for many women the relentless routine of household cookery makes it an unpleasant task, while for men cooking can bring them immediate rewards because the task has an intrinsic novelty value, because they may gain praise from their wife for 'helping out', or their children may be surprised or amazed or join in and make the exercise more fun (instead of nagging and repeatedly asking 'Is it nearly ready?'). Furthermore, occasional cooks are more likely to get away with serving treat foods, and may be more likely to cater for social occasions such as barbecues or dinner parties where they can play at being celebrity chefs (Beardsworth and Keil, 1990: 142). Similarly, much of traditionally masculine household work tends to be occasional or seasonal, such as car maintenance, decorating, repairs or heavy gardening. While these tasks can consume a great deal of time, *choices* can be made about when the tasks are done compared with more routine domestic work. Furthermore, DIY can be creative and, because the outcomes are socially visible, men can gain credit for doing the job (providing, of course, that they can do the job competently).

Men's care for children can also be a source of praise because the dominant discourse of parenting asserts that women are 'natural' parents, while men 'choose' to be good fathers (Heubeck, Watson and Russell, 1986; Lamb, 1986; Richards, 1987; Lupton and Barclay, 1997). That said, when fathers want to be fully involved in the care of their children, this can create tensions (Russell, 1983, 1986). Because it is expected that mothers have principal responsibility for parenting, a father's involvement in childcare can be mediated or controlled by his wife. This can produce contradictory outcomes if women and men are uncertain about the kind of role they want to play in parenting. The following example illustrates, for example, how one woman genuinely wanted her husband to get involved in childcare, and yet she discouraged him at the same time.

I think he needs to be involved for his own sake and the baby's sake ... The first time he bathed her I insisted that he did. I can do it very quickly having done it before but I'm very aware of her losing body heat and of course he isn't, he was messing about testing the water with his elbow and I found I really had to restrain myself not to say 'come on, hurry up, she's getting cold'. He bathed her which took about half an hour and put her nappy on which fitted where it touched, it was awful, running down her legs and generally a mess. (cited in McKee, 1982: 131)

It is clear, in this case, that the woman feels that she has the authority to set the rules on how things should be done and reserves the right to supervise the process and criticise his performance. As Lummis argues, 'The performance of fatherhood roles cannot be divorced from socially imposed divisions of labour which have excluded the male from the home as effectively as they have tied women to it' (1982: 56).

A number of sociological studies on caring and housework practices show that men's and women's relationships can be seriously affected by role conflicts or role constraints. Such conflicts often derive from a tension between a close personal identification with traditional masculine or feminine cultural values which clash with the need for co-operation in defining and undertaking tasks. McRae's British study of marriages where women had a higher status and more highly paid job than their husbands illustrates clearly how couples with strongly traditional views found it difficult to cope with their unconventional roles. As one woman stated:

It is too much. I get very tired. But a lot of it is my own fault. I'll be honest, I keep the work to myself. I've spoiled them. I find it quicker and easier, without a lot of arguments, to do it myself. And that's how it's gone. And it's wrong – I pay. I'm tired. But then, no one could do it the way I wanted it done. I'm very house proud. It's my own fault. And if they do do it, I have to sort of bite my tongue and leave it for a day or two and then do it all over again. (cited in McRae, 1986: 137)

A number of the women in McRae's sample who had more traditional values about feminine roles knew that they effectively stopped their husbands from participating in housework. As one woman, whose husband did very little in the house, remarked:

I think he'd do more if I weren't so bossy. The thing is, I don't think he would clean the house as conscientiously as I do. I think he'd think that he did, but I would know that he didn't. He sometimes suggests changes – suggests helping – but I guess I'm a bit old fashioned. (cited in McRae, 1986: 138)

Other studies have shown that women who work full time and do most of the housework express resentment about role conflicts.

As a woman teacher with 'conventional' views about gender roles observed in a study by Evetts:

> The thing I would most like in my life would be to have time to be a housewife and mother. The biggest present anyone could give to me would be for *someone* to say you needn't work any more. You see magazine articles, you hear on the media about women wanting to be this and do this. They're obviously women who have never had to work all their working lives, otherwise they wouldn't feel like that. I would love to be a housewife and mother. I've worked all my adult life out of necessity. I would love to be at home, to take time to enjoy my house, to take time to cook, to sit, to sew. It's something I've very much missed out on and something my children have missed out on. (original emphasis, 1988: 526)

In McRae's study, a number of women openly expressed their dissatisfaction with their husbands' lower occupational status and set themselves the task of attempting to improve their job prospects. This example illustrates the case of a woman computer programmer married to a milkman:

> I suggested that he should get himself trained in something that would set him up for life. Make him fulfil himself more. Get away from dead-end jobs. He'd have to take a drop in wages to do this, but I'm quite prepared to go without. It's more important to have fulfilling work – something more worth while, more skilled. Something to give him more self respect. He lacks self-respect. I don't know how much of this I have caused – with the difference in our jobs – but then, there is a social stigma about being a milkman which comes out. I'm sure he's fully aware of the gap between our occupations. (cited in McRae, 1986; 105)

This woman admitted that she would prefer it if she had a husband whom she could 'look up to', and who could 'teach me' things. A head librarian, married to a telephone engineer, was also uneasy about being the breadwinner:

> I feel I am the breadwinner, but I wouldn't let him know I feel that. I play the helpless female because I think that's how he wants it. I think I'd like to be more stereotyped. I'd like him to take more responsibility. Perhaps because I think that's the way it *ought* to be. But then, I'd worry about whether the bills were paid. In some ways, on the financial side, I'm more mature in my approach. I wish it were different. (cited in McRae, 1986; 105)

A significant minority of respondents in McRae's study did not subscribe to traditional homemaker and breadwinner roles, and they also tended to be less concerned with standards of housework. One example of a woman administrative officer who was married to a heating engineer shows that they had a well defined division of labour; she did the ironing and laundry, while he did most of the household repairs and gardening; the rest of the work they did together. As they commented:

> The housework isn't organised. We both tend to leave it until we can't stand it any more. We do so much else we don't have time to fuss about it. I always feel I ought to do more. My wife tends to do more cooking than I do.

> We do it as and when we can. It's shared out and it tends to be a blitz. We get fits of cleaning and luckily usually at the same time, although he tends to do more cleaning than I do. I don't feel it's my responsibility to keep the house clean, or to get food on the table. (cited in McRae, 1986: 129)

Many of the studies that have been discussed in this section were undertaken in the mid- to late 1980s and so it could be the case that such traditional attitudes may be less strong among a new generation of women and men. As will be argued in the concluding chapter of this book, attitudes are likely to change because men now gain social capital not just from being good fathers, but also for demonstrating that they are competent in a whole range of domestic practices. Indeed, some men may invest in developing their skills so that they can participate more equally in domestic work as a matter of principle. By the same token, many younger women may resist pressure to maintain such high standards of housework as it limits their opportunities in other fields; and, because they adopt such an attitude, they may not feel so threatened if their partner or husband steps in and takes charge of some tasks. Anecdotal evidence suggests that such practices are common enough among young people, but sociologists have as yet tended not to explore such issues in much depth.

As was stated in the introduction to this chapter, sociologists generally agree that negotiating who does the housework tends to cause friction between men and women in households, and no doubt this situation will continue, but it is important to be sensitive to the fact that the nature of these arguments will change over time. Indeed, it is not inconceivable that men and women may argue because women may not let men get on with household jobs and do things their own way, just as women argue with men if they feel excluded from other avenues of social and economic life. In making this case, I am clearly challenging the oft-repeated but under-researched sociological assumption that most routine aspects of domestic work are necessarily unpleasant and are fundamentally dissatisfying and disempowering. Indeed, I would argue that many tasks can be pleasurable because they allow people to develop the kinds of skills and engage in types of creativity that they cannot gain at work. If this is the case, then there is surely some scope to argue that domestic life and the work it entails does not always have to be fraught with conflict. I may be wrong to assert that domestic practices could become more equally shared, of course, but at least by raising questions about these fundamental issues, new research agendas can be framed to investigate changing attitudes and changing practices.

7

Communal Alternatives

Challenges to the nuclear family

The preceding chapters of this book have demonstrated that the majority of heterosexual couples in long-term cohabiting or marital relationships more or less follow conventional gendered expectations on household practices. Following convention, in some ways, is an easy option for it eradicates the social, economic and political risks associated with unconventional behaviour and the potential stigmatisation that is often imposed upon those who dare to be different from the majority (see Chapman, Hockey and Wood, 1999). As this book has also shown, however, patterns of domestic life are also subject to change over time. Change in households generally occurs in response to transformations in wider social, political and economic circumstances. But as this chapter will demonstrate, changes in the way that domestic life is organised are not wholly constrained by dominant social expectations; even if, ironically, experiments with domestic life can ultimately serve to reinforce the legitimacy of more conventional domestic practices. In gendered terms, as this chapter shows, most experiments with communal living tend not to fundamentally challenge conventional gendered practices in the household. Indeed, in many cases, such experiments in communal life actually reinforce gendered roles rather than challenging them. The first section of this chapter will consider the way that strictly governed religious and utopian socialist commune movements attempted either to resist convention or to transform society. Following this, I will consider a range of less radical, but nevertheless unconventional experiments with communal dwelling types that were pioneered in the late nineteenth and early twentieth centuries to accommodate women who had not married. The second section, by contrast, explores the experiences of highly individualistic people who lived in hippy communes in the 1960s and early 1970s.

Christian and utopian socialist communes

There have been many experiments in communal living over the last two centuries in Europe and America which represent significant challenges to the conventions of wider society. Such movements were motivated by a desire either to show how much better society in general could be if radical alternatives were widely accepted or, conversely, represented isolated attempts to escape from convention. This section considers religious and utopian socialist communes.

The most enduring form of Christian commune is the monastery. Some monastic orders have been established for so long, in some cases for more than a thousand years, that society tends not to regard them as radical alternatives to convention. Nevertheless, the monastery is a good starting point for this discussion of communal life because it demonstrates the kind of discipline and rigorous compliance with rules that is required for such communities to sustain themselves over time. Monastic life in medieval England was not an easy option. Indeed, the rigours of monastic life were such that they represented beacons of self-discipline in a world which was more often characterised by its excess. Monasteries were generally built in inhospitable places to achieve isolation from the temptations of town life. Serlo, one of a band of dissenting monks, was sent by Archbishop Thurston of York to establish a monastery at the site of Fountains Abbey in Yorkshire in 1132. He described it as 'a place remote and uninhabited, set with thorns, amongst the hollows of the mountains and rocks, more fit, it seemed, for the lair of wild beasts than fit for human use'. Matthew Paris wrote of the same place a few years later in *Historia Anglorum* as 'a place of horror and of vast solitude, in a deep and gloomy valley about three miles from Ripon, where they began in extreme poverty to build a church' (in Drabble, 1979: 18). In so doing, they were attempting to emulate the ascetic lives of saints.

The strict ascetic life-style of the monk originated as a reaction to the excesses of the Roman empire during its long period of collapse (Leclercq, 1961; Milis, 1992). While different monastic orders applied different rules about, for example, poverty, silence, social isolation, fasting, sleep deprivation and a strict routine of work, celibacy, prayer and scholarship, all monastic orders expected complete obedience (Levi, 1987; P. Brown, 1988). Monastic life was hard on the body. The case of Aelred, a Northumbrian monk of the twelfth century, may be exceptional, but shows what these devout men endured in order to keep their faith. Aelred's conversion led him to Rievaulx Abbey in Yorkshire where he lived a life of torment. He fasted, contained his bowel movements, took cold water baths in the freezing current of the River Rye and whipped his own body to overcome his sexual desire by meeting 'fire with fire'. He suffered terribly: 'My God, what crosses, what torments that wretched one suffered until at last there was imparted to him a delight in chastity, so that he could overcome all the desires of the flesh which could be felt or imagined' (in McGuire, 1988: 305). Aelred won his battle and became Abbot at Rievaulx in 1147. But at what cost? As he wrote to his sister, 'I want you never to be secure but always be afraid' (McGuire, 1988: 308).

The longevity of monastic life was dependent upon the establishment of strictly ordered regimes that reinforced the sublimation of self-interest to the goals of the whole community. Furthermore, it was essential that monastic orders were regarded as legitimate organisations by wider society, and the power elite in particular. European history is littered with examples of religious intolerance and so, for many religious societies, the only options were either to practise their beliefs in secret and risk discovery, or to emigrate to a more tolerant society. One example is the Hutterites who fled from Switzerland in 1528 because of religious persecution. Regarding the society of their time as 'carnal, corrupt, idolatrous and fun-seeking and therefore removed from God' (Rigby, 1974: 24), their aim was to establish a communal society that was based on the principle of hard agricultural work from which no members of the community were exempt, including the minister and colony steward.

Embracing alternative life-styles and belief systems does not necessarily eradicate traditional gendered domestic practices. Hutterite colonies were organised, for instance, on egalitarian principles but they were profoundly patriarchal, meaning that only men could participate in reaching majority decisions that affected communal life. In order to reinforce patriarchal power, Hutterite colonies discouraged the independence of individual nuclear families, fearing that they would weaken loyalty to communal goals. Consequently, women were not permitted to marry a man from the commune from which they originated as it was believed that this could strengthen familial bonds at the expense of community solidarity. As Hostetler suspects, however, this often had the opposite effect because women tended to maintain kin ties:

> When women become powerful in intracolony politics, it is usually through an emphasis on the consanguineal family [i.e., related by blood] rather than in terms of the interest of the colony as a whole. When a leader is said to be strict, it usually means that he is strict in keeping women in their place. This is said to contribute to the smooth functioning of the colony as a unit, protecting the society from self-centered, competing family groups. (Hostetler, 1974: 272)

Hutterite colonies were characterised by the strictness of their rules, many of which were directly aimed at avoiding the 'vices' of the emerging consumer culture in the USA. For example, one Hutterite rule stipulated that colonists should 'start no new styles'. Younger members of the community reacted against this in a limited way. For example in 1936, younger Hutterites started to wear pith helmets simply because it was the only type of hat that was not prohibited. Hutterite elders banned a range of garments, fearing that by wearing them, younger women's and men's faith could be weakened by temptation. In 1933, for example, it was demanded that 'sweaters...[be] summarily gotten rid of, since they do not belong to our world and only lead to improper dealings...He who does not obey shall have his taken away and burned, and the violator shall be punished' (Eaton, 1973: 517). This is not to say that the colonies were entirely successful in socialising children and young people. As Hostetler notes, 'With colony affluence, there emerges what Hutterites call "girl power" – the tendency for girls to put off marriage for a number of years in order to enjoy the conveniences of their own colony' (1974: 269). The independent spirit of younger women should not be overestimated, however; sometimes it amounted to no more than insisting on the use of perfumed 'toilet soap' instead of the traditional brown colony-made 'laundry soap'.

Some religious communities which migrated to the USA and established colonies did not adhere (like most nonconformist religious societies) to the principle of patriarchal authority. The Shakers, for example, involved both women and men in decision-making processes. It has been argued, however, that this challenge to conventional patriarchal authority hastened the decline of these communities in the twentieth century because men were no longer prepared to remain in the colonies. In 1900 women outnumbered men by 70 per cent in Shaker colonies in the USA, and this had risen to

88 per cent by 1936 (Stein, 1992: 257; see also Brewer, 1986). For many men and women the discipline required by the colonies must have been intolerable. Women and men were obliged not to meet at shops, on staircases, in the fields, or even in the meeting houses because it had a 'tendency to naturalise' the believers and to open 'a door for disorder' (Stein, 1992: 96). Awareness of the temptations of wider American society must have made it all the more difficult to adhere to the principles of Sylvester Graham, the influential health reformer and minister, who demanded that colonists denied themselves sex, alcohol, meat, coffee, tea, highly seasoned foods, chocolate and even refined flour (Stein, 1992). Some could not resist temptation. Brother John Deming left the Hancock Church Family colony in 1821 for committing an act of sexual impropriety. He explained his weakness to act as a deterrent for others:

> The truth is, that the vehement affection which I have to Minerva has undone me. I have had to struggle for life, but fondly hoped that some change would take place which would save my credit – Her excessive kindness still increased my disease ... being unwell, I went to lay down, and she came in and sat on the bed and put her face to mine, and I flung my arm around her neck and kissed her! But nothing else took place at that time, neither have I gone any further since ... O brethren and sisters instead of being stumbled take warning by my fall! O God, O God, what shall I do? (cited in Brewer, 1986: 94).

Not all communes in the nineteenth and early twentieth centuries were established on the basis of the religious devotion of all members of the community. Utopian socialists, including the Owenites, attempted to form communes on egalitarian principles. Like some nonconformist colonies they believed that, as Robert Owen put it, the 'family' and 'private property' were 'essential parts of the existing irrational system. They must be abandoned with the system' (in Rigby, 1974: 34). In most cases, the entrepreneurs who planned and built model villages had no intention of producing democratic or egalitarian communities. Instead, these paternalistic ventures aimed to 'improve' the health and morals of the working classes and, of course, to make them into useful workers. In most model industrial villages of this type, the philanthropic owner was deeply concerned about the moral education of his workers and their families. And so they provided chapels, schools, sports fields and technical institutes, but built no dance halls, pubs or gin palaces in order to wean their workers away from the perils of drink and lust (Creese, 1966; Noyes, 1973). Certainly, the efforts of Salt, Cadbury, Leverhulme and

Rowntree, in Britain, were well meaning; but the imposition of their will on the lives of their workers was often oppressive (Fishman, 1977; Girouard, 1985).

Owen founded two substantial industrial communities which adhered to his utopian socialist principles in New Lanark, Scotland, and New Harmony, Indiana. He and his disciples also established seven Owenite communities in England, Scotland and Ireland between 1821 and 1825 (Pearson, 1988). It was planned that the first of these communities at Clerkenwell, London, would accommodate 250 working-class families, although only 21 families actually joined. Robert Owen's egalitarianism failed to address women's and men's inequitable domestic duties, although he did attempt to tackle the burden of women's domestic work. The aim, according to an *Economist* report of 1822, was for women to undertake domestic tasks collectively and thereby save time to enable 'females either to be profitably employed, or to command a considerable portion of leisure for rational pursuits and innocent recreations' (in Pearson, 1988: 4). The Owenites provided well equipped kitchens to reduce women's labour. In one community, Manea Fen in the Isle of Ely (which was founded between 1839 and 41), prospective members were told that 'The food will be cooked by a scientific apparatus; thus saving an immense labour for the females... Machinery, which has hitherto been for the benefit of the rich, will be adopted in the colony for lessening labour' (in Pearson, 1988: 4). In spite of the good intentions of the Owenites, the projects were not popular amongst working-class women. This is not surprising as the communities represented for women a significant loss of independence.

In the wider working-class community, women worried about losing their sense of self-reliance and had an overriding suspicion of the advisory interventions of the self-professed 'do-gooding' middle-classes. This was a period in England when the working classes had become accustomed to resisting the interference of evangelical Christian missionaries expressing a desire to cure the ills of the 'great unwashed' masses (Hewitt, 1999). H. G. Wells, who is best known for his early science fiction novels including *The Time Machine* (1895), and *War of the Worlds* (1898), also envisaged a utopian world free from conventional domestic arrangements, and he campaigned for alternative patterns of household design and organisation. But, like many of his contemporaries, he had serious doubts about the ability of the working classes – or even the lower middle classes – to aspire to and achieve his high expectations

(J. Carey, 1992). Even though he was himself born in a poor lower middle-class family in London, he stated that his 'associated homes' would not be suitable for everyone because, as he put it: 'I doubt if one could get average working men's wives or clerk's wives into such a place; they would be suspicious of each other, they would quarrel and refuse to speak, and do all sorts of nervous, silly, underbred things' (in Pearson, 1988: 100). This quotation makes the mutual suspicion of the working classes and the upper middle classes all the more explicable.

In the late nineteenth century there were several experiments with new types of architecture and design to overcome the presumed irrationality and waste of labour involved in maintaining and servicing individual households. Clementina Black, for example, proclaimed that the design of houses was wholly inappropriate because it was 'so built and arranged as absolutely to create a waste of labour' (1918: 30). She was one of the first writers to state that most domestic work was a waste of time:

> Labour that develops nothing was recognised ages ago as punishment. Sisyphus rolling up his perpetually-returning stone, the Donaids, for ever pouring water into their sieves...the houses we inhabit and in which we wish people to work for us, create, in one department after another, a necessity for labour of the deadening sort: for penal servitude in fact. (Black, 1918: 40)

Black's radical alternative aimed to challenge 'our extravagant individualism' (1918: 49) which militated against any measure of *co-operation* between households. The advantage of co-operative housekeeping, she believed, would be great, including 'Space, Food, Service, Privacy, Tranquillity, Leisure, Family Happiness' (1918: 87). She proposed that houses should be built around a block of central services including laundry, store, kitchen and dining room which were managed by a professional housekeeper and her staff who would do all the shopping, provide meals, maintain and clean houses inside and out including the polishing of brasses 'until the spread of general intelligence eliminates such labour' (1918: 67). The staff would be well paid, have good accommodation and free leisure time, but they would also be uniformed. Black promised, in sum, that 'With these processes will disappear the whole *batterie-de-cuisine*...No cooking range and washing-up sink...no baker's, butcher's, fishmonger's, grocer's nor greengrocer's boy; no books of any of these tradesmen' (Black, 1918: 67).

Black's manifesto for change may not have come to much in terms of concrete examples of successful communal housing for families, but there were several attempts at producing co-operative housing from the middle of the nineteenth century for single middle-class women. Waterlow Court, which was opened in Hampstead Garden Suburb in 1909, for example, was built for unmarried professional women. Designed by M. H. Baillie Scott, the building was a cloistered quadrangle of 50 flats set around a central lawn. The flats were served by a central dining room, common room and kitchen. Although each flat had a cooker and scullery, it was not assumed that professional women would undertake their own domestic duties. In 1919, for example, a voluntary worker with a private income admitted that she could not cook very much: 'She could boil an egg – if pressed' (in Pearson, 1988: 106).

Since Waterlow was built at a time when it was presumed that marriage was the only route to respectability for women, as has already been shown in Chapter 3, it is not surprising that the moral behaviour of single women was closely monitored. As one columnist argued: 'The way ladies live after working hours is of more importance than the question of how or where or when they work.' She went on to state that women who were not married were likely to become careless in their living conditions and suggested that the single woman may fall 'below her natural birthright of a lady; and her companions know it' (Pearson, 1988: 109). To avoid 'carelessness' at Waterlow, strict rules were laid down. Men were not allowed to stay overnight, and even the brother of one resident, who was on leave from the army, had to jump from the window of his sister's ground floor room early each morning.

For less well off independent single working women, options were very much more limited. In recognition of this, The Ladies Dwelling Company was formed in 1888 and the Ladies' Residential Chambers Ltd in 1889 to build homes for independent women (for a detailed architectural history, see Pearson, 1988: 48–55). One of the first residences was built on Lower Sloane Street in West London, but as the rent was high it was occupied by wealthier women who probably could have afforded other forms of accommodation. Life in these better homes was generally popular, as M. V. Hughes, who shared a flat with a friend, commented retrospectively on her experiences in a 1890s Ladies' Residential Chamber:

> Meals gave us no trouble, for a good dinner was served in the common dining room, lunch was either a picnic affair at home, or else taken at a tea-shop, and our gas-ring was enough for breakfast requirements...The evening dinner was always a pleasant interlude, for we met a variety of interesting women, all of them at work of some kind – artists, authors, political workers, and so on. (in Vicinus, 1985: 296–7)

For poorer working women, it was more likely that they would live under philanthropic supervision in boarding houses built by organisations such as John Shrimpton's Society for Homes for Working Girls and the Young Women's Christian Association. The residents were mainly under 30, and it was expected that this was a temporary stay before marriage. The atmosphere in such homes was often characterised by overregulation and their reputation tarnished by the stigma attached to women deemed to have failed to find a husband. Rachel McMillan described her experience in a converted mansion in Bloomsbury, London, in the 1880s.

> It was a toss-up what became of any of us, and no amount of prudence and well-doing might avail. Many prudent, self-respecting and diligent failures were in this very home. The elder women sat in grim circles in the Sahara drawing room, saying little of their dismal past and vanished hopes...The mere thought of them was like a fire lighted in a dim and draughty attic. (cited in Vicinus, 1985: 296)

Because of the strong social pressure to marry, there was limited social opportunity for unchaperoned young women. Women were barred from pubs or chop houses and so, until cafés, temperance restaurants and department stores opened towards the end of the century, there was little for women to do. As Vicinus points out, single women's 'greater freedom also brought greater isolation' (1985: 297). As a shorthand clerk wrote in a letter to the editor of *Golden Gates* in 1891: 'try all I can, I can't take more than an hour to dispose of [tea]...Then if it is fine, I wander around; if it is wet, I lurk about in railway stations, or any place with a roof. In fine weather it has its enjoyments, in wet it decidedly has not' (in Vicinus, 1985: 297).

As it will be shown in Chapter 9, many single women continue to experience a sense of marginalisation in a society that expects them to marry or cohabit if they are to achieve happiness. The difference, of course, is that single women can now gain levels of economic independence through their educational achievement and employment that was unthinkable to most people a hundred years ago.

Gendered practices in hippy communes

The relative affluence and liberal social and political climate of the mid- to late 1960s and early 1970s produced a number of challenges to the values that underpinned the nuclear family. Reacting against the staid conformity of family life in the 1950s, some radical writers and activists openly criticised the lack of opportunity for self-actual-isation in conventional relationships (Laing, 1965, 1971; Cooper, 1971). As the anthropologist, Edmund Leach, stated in his Reith Lecture of 1968:

> Today the domestic household is isolated. The family looks inward upon itself; there is an intensification of emotional stress between husband and wife, parents and children. The strain is greater than most of us can bear. Far from being the basis of the good society, the family, with all its tawdry secrets and narrow privacy is the source of all discontents. (cited in Abrams and McCulloch, 1976: 122)

The achievement of self-actualisation, some argued, could be enhanced through drug use. This idea was not entirely new. Aldous Huxley had championed the view that society limited individuals' scope for self-exploration and argued that in a world of 'overpopulation and over organisation…a fully human life of multiple relationships… [has become] almost impossible' (in Rigby, 1974: 30). Huxley sought to achieve his mystical aim of discovering his inner self or the 'Divine Ground' or 'Ultimate Reality' through the use of hallucino-genic drugs. Intertwined with ambition to achieve self-actualisation and relationship experimentation was the rise of sexual permissive-ness amongst women who gained control over their fertility through the use of newly available oral contraceptive pills.

The challenge to social convention in the 1960s and 1970s also included attacks on an emergent consumer culture. Leading radicals argued that capitalism was encouraging the spread of shallow, meaningless or base desires for consumer goods and for popular culture (Marcuse, 1964). This was accompanied by an assault on the work ethic itself, on the grounds that people were working harder and harder in order to buy goods and services that did nothing to improve their lives. Finally, there developed a radical critique of conventional politics which, it was argued, produced a conspiratorial relationship between the state and capital. Anti-war campaigning was at the heart of this movement which called for love and freedom in opposition to military violence and neo-colonialism.

The emergence of the commune movement was a culmination of these factors, where predominantly young middle-class people in America (and Britain to a lesser extent) withdrew from the 'rat race'. One study of communes in the late 1960s quotes Aaron, a young long-haired Californian, who said that he had dispensed with his electric toaster and coffee maker and 'dropped out'. Living in a rural commune, he explained what he expected to gain from communal life:

It's an entirely new evolutionary branch. The premise of all these places is that we love one another. And people have to experiment in order to figure out what that means. All the communes, all the families, are facets of the same thing, but no one knows exactly what that thing is, or what it should be, so we all go about it a little differently... What we're really doing here is a pilot study of a life style for the newer future. We're trying to slow down, to remember what this whole trip's about. We're simplifying, getting rid of all those things that just get in the way. We're retribalizing, and when we get it all together, the vibes are so high we know we're doing something right. And like so many people are getting turned on, it's the beginning of a whole new age. (cited in Melville, 1972: 12–13)

Abrams and McCulloch's study of British commune dwellers shows that many sought to make a new start. As one man argued: 'My whole life so far has been fucked up by my family, there's got to be an alternative' (1976: 122). Or, as another stated: 'They say "I love you", but they mean "I own you" – that's what I'm against' (Abrams and McCulloch, 1976: 124). In another British study, one respondent was confident about the advantages of establishing new and open relationships:

The nuclear family is a repressive and horrible institution... where there are only two people, then misunderstandings can arise, you only get a restricted view of each other – in a commune there are others there to give an 'objective' account of their perceptions, clear the air, and so enable you to become more fully aware of each other as humans, clear up the misconceptions that develop through distorted perceptions. (1974: 266–7)

A driving force in many communes was to replace kinship ties and replace them with genuinely egalitarian relationships. Contemporary sociologists (Kanter and Halter, for example) argued that the commune offered opportunities for 'dehousewifing women' and 'domesticating men'. Their research, which reported upon a study of 21 communal households which comprised 175 adults and 27 children, led them to these optimistic conclusions.

1 Equal performance of central household functions and equaliza-
   tion of influence, undifferentiated by sex, can occur immediately
   with the decision to collectivise a household.
2 Since the primary household activities and reasons for forming
   a commune involve nurturance, support, and emotional expres-
   siveness, both men and women tend to learn these behaviours,
   and they show the least differentiation by sex; other sex role
   stereotypes do not differentiate strongly between commune men
   and women.
3 Behavioural, stylistic, and characterological differences between
   men and women remain in those areas (a) not defined intention-
   ally by the group as areas for collective effort and therefore left
   to 'natural' (i.e., socialized) preference and skill; (b) least rele-
   vant to matters of routine concern to the house; and (c) most
   strongly related to stereotypes supported by external institutions.
4 Child rearing remains the primary responsibility of mothers,
   although the burden of childcare is greatly reduced (Kanter and
   Halter, 1974: 199).

Group decision-making was judged to be important in communes,
as Kanter and Halter show: 'The norms and ideologies of the groups
we have studied, in fact, make them resist the idea of power and
leadership, and when asked directly "Do you have leaders?", most
informants respond "no"' (1974: 205). Being 'flower children', they
could hardly be expected to say 'yes' for this would directly contradict
their stated belief in equality. As Kanter and Halter conceded, 'even
in the most ideologically egalitarian groups...some people have
more influence than others', but they insisted that 'women are just
as likely to be represented among the influential as men' (1974: 205).
As they conclude:

> Urban communes threaten to wipe out the housewife, but not in the same way as
> day care, built-in vacuum cleaners, and frozen foods – all of which make the job
> obsolete. Instead, in urban communes homemaking has become a valid part-time
> collective preoccupation of both men and women. (Kanter and Halter, 1974: 202)

Many communes encouraged communal child rearing. Kibbutzism,
for example, promoted *chaverim*: that is, 'the creation of a social
order characterised not so much by the fragmentation of its members into isolated nuclear family groups, as by the brotherhood of
man as a whole' (Rigby, 1974: 270). As one of Rigby's respondents
stated:

A major function of the family is to promote respect, obedience and conformity. In return it provides 'security' and indoctrinated the children with the required responses. All this is damaging to the child if it restricts his free development as an individual...Infants in their helpless state need the care and devotion of a mother. However, it is necessary for their development towards maturity that they be weaned from this state as soon as possible...it is our intention to substitute questioning for blind acceptance and participation for obedience. In doing so we shall be conditioning the children for freedom. (cited in Rigby, 1974: 271)

While many communes openly expressed a desire to nurture children collectively, in most communes parenting fell mainly to women. Similarly, domestic practices often developed along conventionally gendered lines. One example of this is Stoneall's study of the pseudonymous 'Hidden Valley', a free-land rural commune in the northwest USA which was composed of about 60 people, about one-third of whom were children. Conceived by anti-war, anti-consumerists in 1965, the commune was bound together by unwritten but shared values of egalitarianism, non-violence, tolerance of nudity and drugs, and the freedom to 'do your own thing'. Attempting to achieve self-sufficiency meant co-operative hard work by women and men, after which the commune's resources were shared equally between those who had put in the work. But the commune's method of auditing the contribution of each member was gendered, as Stoneall notes:

Only the hours that the women worked in the garden counted toward getting a share; this was exclusive of the time they spent picking vegetables for their own family's meals. All their other activities – cooking, child care, washing, and cleaning – did not count as time for the co-op. On the other hand, almost all the men's activities of working in the garden, herding goats, repairing fences, working 'outside' by baling hay or harvesting wheat, or construction such as making an addition to the school, did count toward getting a share from the co-op. Men also were the ones who made saddles and sandals, the best selling products of the co-op. (Stoneall, 1979: 200)

In theoretical terms, the idea of eschewing consumerism and living a more simple existence sounds like an attractive idea, but in reality it led to more work for women. Not all women were contented with the hardship of living a 'pioneer' subsistence culture that required the making of fires for each meal, food preparation from scratch and the responsibility for food preservation. As one woman said, 'It's no hippy trip to me to do my own canning and everything. My mother did that and I thought my life would be better than hers' (Stoneall, 1979: 201). With only one exception, at Hidden Valley, it was men who had persuaded their partner to join the commune, so it is not surprising that many women were disappointed that traditional sex roles remained unchallenged. As one woman explained:

> My husband and I tried to overcome some of these sex roles. We tried to share the household work. One week I would cook while he would do the dishes and the next week we would reverse. We thought we could share other jobs similarly. But I was not strong enough to chop wood; also my husband would often get opportunities to go fence-repairing or hay-baling with the other men. This left me at home to take care of our two small children and help the women with pickling and canning. I was not freed from traditional feminine roles but carried them out with all the hardships of primitive conditions. (Stoneall, 1979: 204–5)

The Hidden Valley commune adopted the language of gender equality but not its practice, but other communes openly sanctioned patriarchal power structures. J. Wagner's study of the pseudonymous 'Haran' logging community in a remote area of the Ohio River valley in the early 1970s provides an extreme example. Held together by 'Samuel', a charismatic, who claimed that God had told him that 'all evil, greed, competition, war, capitalism, and violence stem from the carnal mind, which is also called the "Woman Mind" or simply "Her"' (1979: 193), Samuel saw women as the 'beast, the flesh, the enemy of divine wisdom and spirituality'. He had little time, either, for liberal-minded (or rather 'Woman Minded') men who had fallen prey to a 'mother dominated upbringing and the pressures of matriarchal society'. The lot of women in Haran was unremitting service to men. As Wagner reports:

> Women are supposed to do as they are bid and to accept what their men tell them. All servile and traditional female tasks are reserved for the women, but women are not allowed to do 'men's work', since they are not thought to possess the necessary mental and physical capabilities. Women open doors for men, run errands for them, cook and serve their meals, and even fetch the objects at a man's fingertips. Women are officially allowed no say in the political decisions of the community. (1979: 194–5)

As a consequence of these practices many women 'split' (i.e., left) the commune, which resulted in a sex ratio of two men for every woman. Because Samuel abhorred both homosexuality and adultery and would not allow either practice in the commune, many single men also left. Not all communal leaders were misogynists, like Samuel, but some were both misogynists *and* sexual predators. Some leaders, especially if they owned the property, demanded complete sexual freedom. This led one woman to say this of her hippie community experience in America:

> The talk of love is profuse but the quality of relationship is otherwise. The hip man like his straight counterpart is nothing more, nothing less, than a predator ... the idea of sexual liberation for the woman means she is not so much free to fuck but free to get fucked over. (cited in Rigby, 1974: 285)

Equality between the sexes, it must be remembered, was not necessarily the principal aim of commune dwellers; as Abrams and McCulloch argue:

> although communes *could* do away with sexual divisions there was no sense in which they *had* to do so. Communes, that is, do not provide a social structure in which a reworking of gender relationships along more egalitarian lines is in any way unavoidable, a component of the structure. The most they provide is a precarious area of freedom in which people who are sufficiently determined to rework gender relationships can, under certain conditions, do so. These conditions in turn are closely linked to the relationships developed between any given commune and the outside world. And looked at it this way, it will be seen that communes are not really all that different from ordinary families. the important difference seems to be that unscrambling a 'commune' ... is a little easier than unscrambling a 'family'. (1976: 126: original emphasis)

The strong belief in achieving individual self-knowledge and self-actualisation, while at the same time establishing relatively egalitarian working and living arrangements, produced tensions in communes. Most communes failed to achieve this because, as Rigby argues, there were too many ways in which strains could manifest themselves.

> The propensity for secular communities to be split by dissensions has usually been heightened by the fact that a large proportion of the members of such communities have been attracted to such experiments as believers in individual freedom and liberty, ends which they have sought to attain through communal living. Such people, who have traditionally found the constraints of life in conventional society irksome, would be unlikely to accept without question the demands of the communal leaders. (1974: 283)

Communes collapsed for many other reasons too, including arguments over property, clashes over the leadership of the commune, over money, work (or laziness), and the degree of openness of the group which may involve outsiders taking advantage of the permanent members and so on (see, for example, Houriet, 1973; Yaswen, 1973; Hall, 1978). But at root, the main problem was a desire for communal life without compromising the autonomy of individual self-interest.

The convenience of convention

As this chapter has revealed, resisting convention is hard work. The principal reason for this is that by being 'different', people lay themselves bare to the disapproval of the majority. Widespread social disapproval of alternative life-styles can lead to the stigmatisation of individuals and also increases the likelihood of social sanctions being levelled against them. Being conventional (or at least giving outward impressions of conventionality), by contrast, allows people to maintain a higher degree of privacy so that they can get on with their lives without interference. This chapter has also shown that living alternative life-styles can actually mean that people's lives are much more rule-governed than in wider society. Religious communes, for example, owe their longevity to the discipline and commitment to a belief system that involves the sublimation of self-interest to the values, objectives and authority of the community.

Without a strong belief system, communes have little chance of success. Industrial communes failed because workers could not be convinced that they should submit themselves wholeheartedly to the values and strictures of a company or entrepreneurial family whose ultimate aim was to make a profit out of their labour. Hippy communes also failed to survive because their participants' key objective was to achieve individual self-fulfilment within an enclave of similarly free-thinking people. In practically any social relationship, it seems fair to assert, it is a recipe for disaster if everyone is encouraged to do their own thing.

Established cultural values impinge to some extent upon the most isolated community. As this chapter has shown, even in hippy communes convention played its part in the sense that gendered domestic practices proved themselves to be culturally resilient. Male commune dwellers, in other words, were more free to exercise their individual volition than women. The number of people who participated in hippy communes represents only a tiny proportion of the populations of Britain and America in the late 1960s and early 1970s. Most people continued to live in conventional nuclear family households. The idea of living in a commune was then, and remains still, anathema to the majority. This is partly because the cultural pressure to conform to conventional roles dissuades the majority from the idea of choosing to be different. The relatively liberal social environment of the 1960s and early 1970s may not have produced a widespread preference for communal living, but the emphasis on radical alternatives to convention did change attitudes. Many people were deeply shocked at that time by the products of the 'permissive society' such as the preference for cohabiting amongst many couples, rising divorce rates and the increasing number of single parent families, and open experimentation with alternative sexualities. In the next two chapters, I will explore the impacts of these challenges to convention by turning attention first to the increased awareness of cultural and sexual diversity in society, and then concentrating upon the domestic practices of the growing number of people who remain single for longer periods of time.

8

Resisting Convention

Adapting and resisting culturally defined roles

In the last chapter, it was shown that communal alternatives to conventional domestic practices have, with the exception of religious communities, generally failed to endure. The reason for this failure is that counter-cultural domestic practices require the establishment of more strictly rule governed behaviour than in conventional households. By definition, it is easier to fall into line with conventional domestic practices because the principles that underlie them are deeply embedded and are therefore constantly reinforced through cultural, personal, economic and political life. But of course, not everybody fully shares this cultural script in Western advanced industrial societies. Clearly, these nations are multicultural societies which means that there are several cultural scripts on gendered domestic practices operating in unison and sometimes in opposition. Furthermore, contemporary Western societies are now characterised by a raised tolerance of alternative sexualities. Gay, lesbian and bi-sexual relationships differ from heterosexual relationships in the sense that many of the features of conventional domestic practices are inevitably and openly challenged.

Challenging convention by practising different values is often met with prejudicial and discriminatory responses from members of a dominant culture and from the state and its institutions. There is a voluminous sociological literature on patterns of discrimination, prejudice and social exclusion of ethnic minority cultures and alternative sexualities. In the case of ethnic minority groups, most research centres on 'social problems' including housing inequalities, racism and discrimination in the workplace and the community (see Skellington and Morris, 1992; Goering and Wienk, 1997; Bulmer and Solomos, 1999; Boal, 2000; D. Mason, 2000), and the implications for social policy of issues surrounding, amongst others, marital violence, divorce and single parenthood (see Engram, 1982; McAdoo, 1988a, 1988b; Davis, 1993; Logan, 1996; Toliver, 1998). Instead of being diverted by a detailed review of that literature, this chapter focuses much more specifically on the way that people adapt to or resist convention in the establishment of domestic practices.

In the next section, the process of acculturation will be addressed by considering how migrant ethnic minority groups adapt conventional domestic practices from their home culture in a Western context. Here I adopt M. Smith's (1986) definition of ethnicity as 'a population whose members believe that in some sense they share common descent and a common cultural heritage or tradition, and who are so regarded by others' (in D. Mason, 2000: 12). This is an issue of such complexity that it is impossible to do much more than scratch the surface of the diverse experiences of different ethnic groups. But by discussing recent experiences of migration among black Caribbeans and South Asians to Britain, it is anticipated that some general conclusions can be drawn about problems of cultural assimilation and adaptation or resistance to culturally dominant domestic practices. As this section of the chapter will show, experiences of migration may differ substantially depending on the cultural milieu from which migration has taken place. South Asian cultures, for example, have a clearly defined and strictly observed set of values on marriage which tend to produce a higher degree of gender segregation in domestic practices than is now found in the majority of white, Anglo-American, culturally (if not practising) Christian households. Black African and Caribbean households, by contrast, tend to have a less rigid cultural adherence to the model of the nuclear family than both South Asians and white Anglo-Americans, which in turn has produced a more diverse set of family forms and gendered domestic practices (Staples, 1999).

The third section of this chapter explains how gay and lesbian couples challenge the cultural conventions of heterosexual domestic practices. It is demonstrated here that gay and lesbian couples tend to emphasise the importance of equality in domestic practices compared with the 'equal but different' model that is commonly adopted by heterosexual couples. While lesbian and gay couples do aspire to achieve a higher level of equality in relationships, the concluding section indicates that the configuration of social class, education and personal factors also impacts strongly on the experience of domestic life. In common with heterosexual couples, in sum, it is argued that the work that must be done to maintain a household is essentially similar and can produce arguments and resentments over disproportionate contributions to domestic work.

Migration, ethnicity and difference

One of the most significant problems migrants experience when moving from a home culture to an alien culture is that physical environments differ markedly. The built environment in any culture, as was argued in Chapter 2, symbolically represents and reinforces particular domestic practices. The Anglo-American cultural model of what constitutes a 'successful' home is therefore represented in a particular type of household form. To the indigenous population of any society, house design can seem to be an entirely functional process to afford shelter, warmth, comfort and facility. But, as was also shown in Chapter 2, conceptions of 'functionality' are fundamentally shaped by cultural expectations about issues such as decency, hygiene, status, and so on. Conventional domestic practices in one culture, in sum, can stand in opposition to those of new migrants. Taking just one example, the Western model of kitchen design does not necessarily meet the cultural expectations of all ethnic groups. As one British study reports:

> Both the type and the volume of cooking taking place in the kitchens of many cultures demands an air change which is very high relative to the average provision in housing, and higher than the improved standards of the [1992] Building Regulations... Bangladeshi, Caribbean, Chinese, Indian, Pakistani, Tamil and Vietnamese cooking all involve large amounts of fat and oil. Some Greek and Turkish Cypriot households may use a charcoal grill. Chinese cookery can involve simmering for seven to eight hours. In many Jewish households, food cannot be prepared on the Sabbath and therefore Saturday lunch has to be cooked beforehand and kept warm on a low flame. In these cultures as well as others, like the Somali, cooking for the family or as an act of hospitality is a large part of the life of the household. (National Federation of Housing Associations, 1993: 29)

Different expectations exist also in the storage space required for frozen or dry goods, plumbing and drainage systems, or the cooking space required for large pots. Similarly, 'pollution rituals' (see Douglas, 1973, 1999) demand that only running water can be used, or that different sinks are used for food preparation. Established gendered practices in the home are also a critical indicator of cultural differences. Conventional British house design, in the form of terraced houses, semi-detached houses and apartments, does not necessarily accommodate the gendered domestic practices of other cultural groups:

> Amongst many minority ethnic groups separation of men's and women's space in the home is the norm. There are many degrees of such separation. In a number of Muslim households, women do not enter the men's space when guests are present. In strict Orthodox Jewish households women and men will not socialise together or take part together in religious observance. In many households of other cultures, such as Hindu, Rastafarian and Sikh, the tendency is for men and women to socialise separately. (National Federation of Housing Associations, 1993: 18)

Even when housing associations or local authorities are aware of different design needs, sometimes problems of resale or rent, objections to prohibitive cost or infringement of building regulations block the building of appropriate designs.

The process of settling in an alien culture requires a degree of 'acculturation' by both the migrant and indigenous population. A social psychologist, Berry (1994), defines acculturation as 'a culture change that results from continuous, first hand contact between two distinct cultural groups' (in Singh Ghuman, 1999: 27). Berry usefully highlights the point that migrant groups must necessarily address an 'other' culture in an active way (whether this leads to assimilation or separation or some point between the two). But of course this is not a one-way process, as Singh Ghuman points out:

> The decision to integrate or not to integrate does not entirely rest on the immigrants and their descendants but also – perhaps more so – on the reaction of the host society. If the institutions of the judiciary, the police, the civil service and employers are prejudiced, there is little incentive for the offspring of the immigrants to integrate. (1999: 27)

Problems of adaptation to a new country are compounded by racism and discrimination, poverty, poor employment prospects and sub-standard housing, together with separation from family, language difficulties and, in many cases, social isolation (see Castles and Miller, 1998; Koser and Lutz, 1998). Singh Ghuman argues that the process of acculturation is likely to occur over several generations, with the original immigrant group finding the process the most difficult.

First generation economic migrants may resist the process of acculturation because they expect to return home later in life (Fog Olwig, 1999). In this sense, first generation migrants can occupy a 'liminal' world which is neither 'here nor there'. As Berger *et al.* have put it: 'Modernity has indeed been liberating…It has opened up for the individual previously unheard of options and avenues of mobility…However these liberations have had a high price. Perhaps the easiest way to describe it is…as homelessness' (in Western, 1992: n.p.). This use of the term 'homelessness' suggests an absence of a sense of place. But this may be an overexaggeration because it gives the impression that a sense of home has been entirely lost. As P. Somerville's (2000) study of a Manchester West Indian community shows, the concept of home itself is defined in a wider variety of ways by migrants than an indigenous population. For migrants, home can mean 'current dwelling', 'area of residence', 'country of residence', 'country of origin', or 'continent of origin'. Consequently, migrants develop multiple strategies to deal with their unusual situation. In her study of black Caribbean economic migrants who moved to England in the 1950s, Fog Olwig shows how such strategies manifest themselves:

> Some Nevisians developed multiple attachments to home, and eventually came to feel at home in several places, moving frequently between their several homes. Some returned to Nevis, usually to create a new home based on their multi-local experiences of home. Yet others became emotionally attached to a home abroad and even relocated the family left behind on Nevis to this new home, thus reconstituting their childhood home abroad. (1999: 83)

Living in another country for long time periods of time changes the manner in which the country of origin is constructed in the imagination. This can lead to confusion and even disappointment when people renew their acquaintance with the old country and find that it fails to meet nostalgic recollections or romanticised expectations. Western's (1992) study of Barbadians' migration to England in the 1950s to work for London Transport shows how the complex relation between home of origin and a new home interact. As two of her respondents stated:

> But it depends on context. I mean, um, I like to think of here [this house] as home. Funnily enough, if I stayed in Barbados for any length of time, I might refer to England as home, I've spent so long living here. It depends on who's asking too! Life's a paradox, really. (1992: 265)

> My gut feeling is it's Barbados – emotionally. Yes this is where I live – structurally. If we won the pools tomorrow, if we could afford it…I'd buy a nice detached house with a nice bit of lawn, a nice four bedroom house…near Surbiton tennis courts. (1992: 264; see also Byron, 1994)

Rather than asserting that first generation migrants find themselves in a permanently dislocated situation (that is, in a liminal world), it is perhaps better to frame our analysis in terms of people's ability to adapt to new situations by making constant reference to cultural origins and destinations.

Maintaining cultural traditions in a new country is often challenged by migrants' second or third generation offspring. Research on South Asians in Britain shows that patterns of acculturation can vary depending upon the cultural mores of different ethnic groups. While it is clearly not possible here to provide a detailed account of the differing cultural constructions of men's and women's attributes and roles in South Asian culture, it is useful to assemble some clues about the differences in gendered domestic practices in Hindu, Muslim and Sikh households. Traditional Hindu culture strongly emphasises the role of women as dutiful wives who should be obedient to their husbands, be economically dependent upon them and accept that their principal role as a wife is to bear children, especially sons. Consequently, parents see it as their responsibility to arrange a suitable marriage for their daughters (see also Caplan, 1985; Ghadialli, 1988). While Hindu marriages in India are generally arranged, there is an expectation that love and intimacy may develop later, although it is parenthood that is thought to be the foundation stone of a successful marriage in a culture where motherhood is revered.

Muslim culture is infused with patriarchal Islamic ideology. Indeed, religion and culture are virtually inseparable in Muslim culture. The Koran provides clear guidance on the place of women and men in society. As Sinha notes: 'Although created spiritually and intellectually equal in the eyes of God, man and woman were also made differently so they would complement one another. This would be reflected in their differing characteristics, capacities and dispositions, and the roles of both sexes in the traditional patriarchal family' (1998: 30). Girls are prepared for marriage from a young age through a socialisation process in which they are taught to be dependent, modest, obedient and passive. Young men, by the same token, are encouraged to be protective towards wives (see Raza, 1993). Marriage is generally arranged: girls and young women are formally expected to give their consent, although the social pressure placed upon them to do so is significant and difficult to resist. Polygamy is practised in many Muslim states, but in Pakistan monogamy is the norm and permission to take more than one wife has to be sanctioned by the state. Once married, it is expected that men's sphere of activity is primarily in the public domain, while women are largely confined to the private sphere of household and family.

Sikhism is also a patriarchal culture, but Sikh women generally enjoy a higher status in a marriage than in Muslim or Hindu culture. As Sinha notes, 'A woman in Sikhism is looked upon as a man's helpmate, and as vital to his spiritual growth and morality' (1998: 37). Dependence upon and obedience to her husband is anticipated; however, there is also an expectation that husband and wife will move together towards a common set of goals or interests (see also Helweg, 1986; Sambhi, 1989; Hiro, 1991, 1980). While making broad generalisations about South Asian women's educational opportunities, work roles and family responsibilities can be problematic, it is generally more acceptable for Sikh women to pursue higher education and professional careers (Bhachu, 1985) than is the case for Muslim women who are more likely to be expected to work for family business (Shaw, 1988).

Each of these three ethnic groups clearly differs from the others in important ways; but there are some common factors that are embraced in all three cultures which differ markedly from the West. The most important of these is that collectivism is more important in Asian society than individualism. Indeed, the kind of individualism that is championed by the West is met with general disapproval. This in turn underpins the different context within which marriage is established between Asian and Western society. As Singh Ghuman comments:

> Asians tend to equate individualism with selfishness. The system of arranged marriages is but one example of this. The chief aim of arranged marriages is not to help realize the pleasure and happiness of the marrying couple, but to enhance the social prestige and economic circumstances of a family through an alliance with another family of equal or higher status. The institution of marriage is still viewed, unlike in Western countries, as a regulator of 'sexuality' and valued for the stability and continuity it provides for the continuity of lineage. (1999: 24)

This produces strains between the more traditional older generations in Britain and younger generations. As Singh Ghuman shows, common practices among young white and African-Caribbean people, such as dating, are strongly disapproved of in young people from South Asian families:

Asian communities in Britain and elsewhere strongly disapprove of dating, although they are prone to turn a blind eye if it is their sons who are 'going out' with white girls. Their hope is that boys will grow out of such transient relationships and eventually return to the fold and marry within their own community. This fundamental difference of personal relationships, between home and host society, is one of the major points of inter-generational conflict and tensions in Asian families, especially with young girls. (1999: 47)

In one British study, as reported by Singh Ghuman, one-fifth of South Asian girls were shown to be secretly dating, sometimes involving drinking alcohol in pubs (Drury, 1991).

The relationship between generations is rarely a clear cut case of out and out conflict between tradition and assimilation. As Elliot points out, young South Asians in Britain make 'compromises that enable them to move between parallel cultural worlds and/or to develop a lifestyle that is a synthesis of Anglo-Saxon and Asian values' (1996: 55). Parental expectations about the maintenance of traditional gender roles in British Asian communities have been changing for some time as is evidenced, for example, by the increased number of young British Asian women who are now entering higher education and employment. While the research evidence is limited at present, there are indications that this, in turn, is impacting upon traditional gendered domestic practices (see also Ballard, 1979; Stopes-Roe and Cochrane, 1989). Cases of parents with deeply held traditional values forcing conformity upon their children are commonly reported in the British press, giving a false impression that such stories are not exceptional. But, for the most part, parents recognise the need for compromise too, understanding that traditions cannot wholly be maintained in a new cultural context.

Transplanting one set of domestic practices that have been long established in one culture into another inevitably forces cultural compromise. To illustrate this point, it is useful to present a brief overview of one case study which compares traditional Muslim households in Pakistan with Muslim households in Oxford, England. Shaw's study of traditional housing in the Faisalabad district of Pakistan shows that house design there is radically different from the terraced properties that Pakistani families generally occupied in Oxford. Village houses were set in a large walled compound area. The main house comprised a large indoor family room with an open roof terrace above, which was accessible via an outdoor staircase. In wealthier houses, there was a second room off the main room, called the Baithak, which was reserved for the use of men only. Often this room was accessible from outside the walled courtyard by a separate door so that male visitors could gain access to the house without coming into contact with women. In smaller houses, this was achieved by separating off a part of the main room by a curtain. This gendered division of domestic space met the requirements of Purdah (that is, that women should not come into contact with men other than those to whom they were directly related). This domestic design clearly signals a very different cultural perspective on domestic space from conventional Anglo-American houses because there are few options for householders to gain any privacy from each other. It should not, though, be assumed that this arrangement was such because families could not afford to build larger houses. Indeed, as Shaw demonstrates:

> These features of a village house show that it is designed for sharing. There is no 'Western' concept of privacy: generally, no individual or couple regards a room as their own; each room is everyone's room. Usually all family members sleep in one room, although sometimes the men of the household sleep separately in the Baithak. This arrangement is not an indication of poverty, for in many cases separate rooms could have been built if the family considered it necessary, and often there were additional and unused rooms. Rather the whole family expects and usually prefers to sleep in one room. (2000: 80–1)

Shaw's earlier study of Pakistanis in Oxford terraced houses in the 1980s shows that some of the practices established in traditional village houses were transposed on to British homes. The front room was used in much the same way as the Baithak, or at least when receiving male visitors, as women and children spent much of their time in the back room. Families often chose to sleep together in the largest room, although a young married couple may have a room of their own (unlike in the village houses where, a few nights after a wedding, everyone would sleep together again in the main room). This practice evinced a shocked response from the indigenous white British population who misunderstood the practice as overcrowding by ruthless Pakistani landlords. But in reality, families chose to sleep in the largest room and, indeed, Pakistani children were horrified by the prospect of sleeping alone, as was the practice among their white school mates. This arrangement did, however, allow families to take in lodgers in spare bedrooms and increased the income of the household. Pakistani households put great emphasis on property ownership in Oxford (instead of land ownership in Pakistan), and it was a mark of status within the community to own two or more houses.

While it is the case that cultural values strongly affect gendered domestic practices in South Asian households, it is important not to assume that practices are merely transferred from one culture into another. As Werbner (1988) shows from her study of a Pakistani community in Manchester, stereotypical assumptions about rigid social segregation of the sexes within Muslim households should not be made. While it is often the case that the day-time domestic world of the Pakistani Manchester community is predominantly female because the men are at work, it does not necessarily follow that relationships in the household are rigidly defined or that social life is formalistic. On the contrary, when men are at home domestic life is informal. As Werbner notes, a husband:

> usually joins his wife and her friends in the back room, in a strikingly informal and relaxed manner. Men make cups of tea for guests, casually and unselfconsciously. Indeed, demonstrations of masculine superiority or of a clear-cut conjugal division of labour in domestic matters are conspicuously absent. The conversation during these daily visits usually flows easily, as people debate momentous topical events and often wax enthusiastic, interrupting each other in loud voices. There is a great deal of joking, gossiping and arguing. The spontaneity and conviviality of relations are clearly distinguished from the formality of behaviour towards strangers. The latter are inevitably ushered into the front room, in the exclusive company of their own sex. (1988: 184)

It remains the case that segregated gendered domestic practices in Muslim communities are more clearly defined, especially on formal occasions, than in most white households. But this does not necessarily signal direct conflict between partners; rather, it provides a backdrop against which negotiation between men and women operates. As Werbner concludes:

> the actual roles fulfilled by a woman, and her domestic influence, vary over her lifetime, and the domestic household division of labour is pragmatically negotiated. Stereotypes, enduring values, and actual roles remain in some tension. But on formal and sacred occasions the strict separation between the worlds of men and women is upheld. Thus the image of a dual, segregated world persists, anchored in enduring cultural notions regarding the 'natural' attributes and proper roles of men and women. (Werbner, 1988: 200)

The above discussion suggests that migration between cultures produces uncertainties and even conflicts about gendered domestic practices because men and women are faced on a day to day basis with alternative perspectives on how to organise their lives and relate to each other. Such problems may be exacerbated when women and men from different cultural backgrounds marry or cohabit. As was shown in Chapter 5, most married couples or cohabitees share similar characteristics of class, age, religion, education, race and ethnicity. Homogamy is a common practice because couples recognise a clearly established cultural script on how to behave, and what to expect of each other in a relationship. Furthermore, homogamy tends to make life easier for families, neighbours and mutual friends in the sense that they need not make any special effort to understand cultural differences, assimilate new ideas or overcome discriminatory or racist feelings.

Voicing racist attitudes about inter-racial marriage is socially unacceptable now, but it is clear that only a few decades ago, such views were more likely to be openly expressed. The term 'miscegenation', once used by the state to describe mixed race marriage, as Alibhai-Brown and Montague comment, is 'infused with opprobrium and with the implication that something not quite the norm, something deviant, is being described' (1992: 2; see also Wilson and Johnson, 1995). In America, 30 states had laws prohibiting inter-racial marriages until the 1930s and it was not until 12 June 1967 that the Supreme Court acted to end this practice (Jacobson, 1995: 357). Indeed, as Rosenblatt, Karis and Powell (1995) note, as recently as the 1970s white families in the USA sent their daughters to psychiatrists and even mental hospitals if they dated blacks. Institutional racism continues to impact on the social, economic and domestic life of mixed race/ethnicity couples in many ways, ranging from racism by estate agents, housing authorities and associations, by religious organisations, employers, the police, and from members of both white and black communities (Macewen, 1991; Dhillon-Kashyap, 1994; Parker and Song, 2001).

When women and men enter into mixed-race or mixed-ethnicity relationships, establishing consensus in domestic practices can be challenged by deep seated cultural differences. It would be a mistake to assert that the impact of such conflicts can be articulated as a coherent and predictable set of responses to broad cultural differences. On the contrary; as in all relationships, personal attributes, circumstances and preferences also impact heavily on what is considered as desirable and tolerable in a partner's behaviour. And so, while disagreements are explained partly by referring to significant cultural differences in, say, manners, religion or politics, they are also generated by unique interpersonal factors. For example, one study of marriages between white British women and black Yoruba men shows that cultural differences in attitude can impact on domestic relationships. As one white British woman stated:

> I've not been to Africa, I've never seen him in his own context. I know he's not typical. People who uproot themselves aren't typical...he must have adapted a tremendous amount, but I only see the ways in which he hasn't adapted...he's terribly forthright, rude really – he never opens doors for me or carries a parcel, he's very firm about 'I'm the man and you're the woman' although he won't treat me as a second-class citizen...We have many different assumptions but I don't think it's all cultural. We're both very awkward people. (S. Benson, 1981: 78)

Another British study of cultural conflicts between black West Indian and white British couples provides evidence to suggest that the interaction between personal foibles and cultural differences is openly articulated by couples in a variety of situations. As one white British woman argued in response to a question about different leisure patterns:

> It takes a bit of getting used to. [West Indian] men expect a lot of time to theirselves, it isn't like an English bloke who'll do a bit around the house...Michael's off out all the time if I let him. Linton [Michael's] cousin is the same. Beverley [Linton's West Indian wife] isn't like me, though, she couldn't care less, she's out every night herself. (cited in S. Benson, 1981: 82)

Benson's study revealed patterned differences in cultural attitudes about factors such as the upbringing of children, work patterns, the management of money and kin relationships. But of course there were exceptions too; as one white British woman stated of her husband: '[He's] A great family man, which is very surprising for a Jamaican...they aren't often like that, from what I can see. Warren has always preferred to be at home – any free time he has he spends with us' (1981: 92). The fact that respondents in Benson's study emphasised cultural differences and yet constantly referred to their own exceptional behaviour presents a common analytical problem not just for sociologists of race and ethnicity, but of relationships in general. Indeed, Benson shows that couples deal with, and account for, cultural differences in many ways. While some couples argue that they have both become incorporated into the host country, others claim to make compromises. Insightfully, Benson recognises that some couples accept each others' different attitudes, preferences and beliefs by developing 'working misunderstandings' (1981: 93). In such cases 'the fragile consensus predicated upon the ignoring of important differences in outlook and interest could be threatened by changing circumstances' (1981: 93), the most important of which was disputes on whether to remain in Britain or to move back to the non-British partner's country of origin.

Achieving equality in gay and lesbian households

Patterns of domestic life are largely governed by a cultural script as the previous section shows, which defines the ground rules for domestic practices. Heterosexuality is an inherent part of this culture which, on the one hand can reinforce gendered inequalities but, on the other, can provide couples with the security of knowing what is expected of them. As Dunne points out:

> Within the context of institutional heterosexuality, women and men are drawn into relationships with each other as socially, symbolically and materially different persons. Their relationships are negotiated with reference to a framework of materially shaped, pre-existing gender scripts which guide interaction. Informing these differential scripts are dominant beliefs about the complementarity of feminine and masculine identities ... The analysis of lesbian partnerships is important because it provides visions of divisions of household and market labour which are not structured by dichotomous gender scripts. (1997: 179)

Sociological research on gay and lesbian domestic practices suggests that couples are less likely to conform to a prescribed set of gendered cultural cues on what roles should be played. As Peplau and Cochran's (1990) study of the USA shows, one of the most valued aspects of lesbian life-styles is the achievement of an egalitarian relationship: 97 per cent of lesbians identified with the idea of equality in an ideal relationship, and 59 per cent believed that they had achieved this (from Dunne, 1997: 180). Similarly, Johnson's study of 108 lesbian relationships in America that had endured for at least ten years shows that more than 90 per cent of couples believed that they had gained equality in their relationships.

In these studies, equality should not be taken to mean parity of power and esteem in every aspect of domestic life, of course, but instead represents a recognition of the *freedom to negotiate* over aspects of domestic practices as the principal definitional benchmark of equality. As one woman, who had been in a relationship for 12 years, remarked:

> Equality is – was certainly a biggie for us in the beginning. Everything had to be equal, from reciprocal backrubs, to money, to the last piece of cake. However, that got old when we realised how much energy it took to keep tabs. Each of us

now knows that we will get what we need from this relationship when we need it. (S. Johnson, 1990: 123)

Or as a woman from a 15-year long relationship commented:

I used to believe that we, as partners, should equally share expenses, chores, and should do all things together. But over the years I have come to accept that we each have strengths and weaknesses at different – and sometimes the same – times, and we must learn to draw strengths from each other when weak, and be willing to share when strong. (S. Johnson, 1990: 123)

Unlike heterosexual couples, who are more likely to extol the virtues of the 'equal but different' partnership, a lesbian couple's emphasis on absolute equality is a tall order. High ideals can lead to disappointment and dissolution of relationships; and so long-lasting relationships – as both Johnson (1990) in the USA and Dunne (1997) in Britain show – tend to be those where a balance of power has been successfully negotiated (see also Weeks, Heaphy and Donovan, 1999, 2001).

The dynamics of lesbian relationships is often made complicated because one or both partners may have been previously married and bring with them a particular set of expectations on what makes relationships succeed or fail. The reasons why heterosexual relationships fail are many, but those which are considered to be most important by lesbian women foreground differences in power which are embedded in patriarchal culture, differences in income or status of employment, and unequal contribution to domestic work, parenting and caring. As one of Dunne's respondents stated:

I just see that there is very little equality in heterosexual relationships – in like the definition of a man and a woman, the man is the one with the power. There is no definition of who takes the lead or the power in a lesbian relationship . . . It is in 99 per cent of the cases the man that will earn more money, he will make all the decisions, well, most of the decisions. (1997: 181)

Similarly, a divorced woman in Dunne's study, who had recently come out, emphasised the point that she had felt obliged to play prescribed roles in a heterosexual relationship. In contrast, she argued that lesbian partnerships 'are just so much more relaxed, there's no obligation to fulfil a role, you make your own. You make your own position comfortable that fits round you, whereas, I mean in most heterosexual relationships, there's no way that people can ignore the set roles, the set expectations, and it's restricting' (in Dunne, 1997: 182).

Entering into a relationship that did not have built-in gendered expectations about roles offered a new kind of freedom to many lesbian women. As one woman from Dunne's study argued: 'There aren't any stereotypical images like in a man/woman relationship... There is *nothing there* at the beginning to influence thoughts on how things should be done' (1997: 183: my emphasis). In reality, there *is* something there: by rejecting one form of relationship an implicit assumption is made about what *is* wanted. Indeed, the belief that there were no pre-set expectations brought its own problems and, as Dunne makes clear, required 'unusual amounts of creativity' to overcome in-built factors that impacted on the power relationship between women. As we have already seen in Chapters 1 and 5 of this book, power differentials in heterosexual relationships are made tolerable by the establishment of an ideology of breadwinner and homemaker roles that generally gives more economic power and leisure opportunities to men, but more power to women over patterns of household organisation, spending and parenting. In gay and lesbian relationships, the absence of a justification for inequalities of power meant that many other factors could produce different tensions in relationships. Differences of power could arise from a number of factors including age differences, differences in income, home ownership, educational achievement or job status, although these factors could impact in surprising or contradictory ways. As one woman pointed out to Dunne:

> I think there are lots of power factors. She sometimes had power because she was older, I sometimes because I was younger. She sometimes had power because she had money, I because I was an academic. There were lots of power factors, none of which were overriding. Fluctuating power but no wild fluctuations, with a middle line of equality. (1997: 184–5)

While studies of lesbian couples suggest that equality is more likely to be achievable than in heterosexual relationships because of immunity from ideological factors, it needs to be recognised that this is often achieved through the selection of a partner who has similar attributes. Unlike most heterosexual relationships, in lesbian couples both partners are generally employed full-time which reduces the likelihood of one being economically dependent on the other. Because of this strong emphasis on equality in lesbian relationships, imbalances in income could create tensions whereas, in heterosexual couples, such imbalances are expected and can be accommodated in other ways. The demand for equality could lead some couples to be quite pedantic about getting the details right; as one woman told Dunne, 'she pays half the mortgage, as far as day-to-day things we split it down the middle, but for big purchases we split it according to our respective salaries; it works out at 12/17th or something silly like that [laughter]' (1997: 195).

Another important source of imbalance was unilateral home ownership which could emphasise feelings of dependence among those who did not share home ownership with their partner. In some cases, women feared that they would be left with nothing if the relationship broke down while in others, problems arose from feeling like a guest in someone else's house and the inability to make choices about furnishings or decoration. As one woman stated:

> There are very few things in this house on display that are actually mine. The house shows [my partner's] personality rather than mine. She just bought the house when I started to live here, and I get frustrated because nothing in the house is mine ... It suddenly dawned on me one day, all I needed was one room to call my own, so I decorated it and put my things in it. And I don't ever really use it, but I know that I can. (cited in Dunne, 1997: 199–200)

The allocation of household tasks also required negotiation. Unlike heterosexual couples, the evidence suggests that lesbian couples had very much more equitable arrangements. But as Blumstein and Schwartz (1985) show, lesbian couples stated that they had lower standards of housework and consequently spent less time on this activity. Dunne's research reinforces this view, leading her to conclude that 'home life was rarely ruled by the tyranny of being house proud, perhaps because their identity and self-worth were not seen as being derived from a demonstration [of] domestic excellence. Consequently, some may have had low standards of household tidiness' (1997: 205). Anecdotal evidence suggests that the reverse may be the case among gay men, but this has yet to be fully researched.

Changing perceptions of domestic practices

While the principal focus of this book is to analyse the impact of gender on patterns of domestic life, it has become clear from this and previous chapters that other factors (including social class differences, race and ethnicity, sexuality and radical political or ideological movements) can make a considerable difference to the way that gendered practices are perceived, relationships established, and households are organised. What has also become apparent, however, is that gendered ideology on what constitutes home is a background variable that all household forms must accommodate to, to a greater or lesser extent. While gender is a hugely important factor in understanding how households are organised, it also needs to remembered that whether domestic practices are undertaken along conventional lines or not, the tasks themselves still have to be done. In sum, it is important to recognise that some issues that require negotiation between partners run across all relationships. As Carrington points out:

> like most other American families lesbian and gay households face the struggles of balancing work and family commitments, of managing the stresses and strains of waxing and waning sexual desires, of maintaining open and honest communications, of fighting over household responsibilities, and, most frequently, of simply trying to make ends meet. (1999: 4)

Carrington's study of lesbian and gay couples adopts the term 'lesbigay' which is gaining currency in the USA to take account of an increasing number of people who define themselves as bi-sexual, and as a way of showing that the experiences of gay and lesbian households are in many respects similar. This approach, though contentious, is justified on the basis of his argument that gays, lesbians and bisexuals all have to 'do' family life. As Carrington puts it 'a family, any family, is a social construction, or a set of relationships recognised, edified, and sustained through human initiative. People "do" family' (1999: 6). Through his week-long ethnographic analyses of four gay and four lesbian households, together with in-depth interviews in 52 households in the San Francisco Bay area, Carrington shows that while homophobia at an interpersonal or institutional level is significant in the experience of domestic life, issues of class impact more heavily on domestic experience. In the poorest households, he argues, the main concern is making ends meet and not political struggle, and that being poor produces conflict in all households whether they are gay, lesbian or straight.

> True equality, measured with a plumb line, eludes many of these families, but that has little to do with the families *per se*, and much more to do with the character and quality of employment opportunities that avail themselves to these families. If the reality is that only one member of the family can make money in a fulfilling way, then lesbigay families adjust to that reality... If all of the family must toil at unpleasant and poorly compensating work in order to make ends meet, they do,

and they try to fit domesticity in where they can. Of course, these are the families
that often don't make it, and that should not be so surprising because without the
resources, time, and energy to create family, it withers. (1999: 206)

Carrington's study demonstrates that domestic practices inevitably
require negotiation, compromise or acceptance of economic, time
or skill inequalities, or tolerance of irritating foibles of partners. As
we all know, arguments in the domestic sphere can range from
heated debates on issues of political principle to equally volatile
arguments on why one member of the household refuses to clean
the shower or bath after they have used it. Like all other households,
Carrington argues, gay and lesbian couples also experience conflicts
over the detail of domestic life. Following the lead of De Vault (1991)
whose work explores the social aspects of food in the household,
Carrington explores the conflicts created over who cooks, who cares,
and what to eat. The following examples, first from a gay and then
a lesbian couple, help illustrate this point.

We continually fight about it. I am more conscious of fat and calories content and
seem to have to remind Richard constantly about it. He prepares great meals, but
I am trying desperately to stay in shape. He gets upset because sometimes I just
won't eat what he made or very much of it. I don't see why it's so hard for him to
make low-fat stuff.

Yeah, she doesn't want me to fry things because it makes such a mess and she has
to clean it up. She would rather that I stir-fry and make more vegetables. She likes
my cooking because it tasted good, but she would rather eat healthier than I
would. I think my cooking sort of reminds of her growing up. She partly likes that
and she partly doesn't because it reminds her of being poor and I think the food I
make sometimes, she thinks she's too good for it, that she should eat like rich
people eat. I try to keep her happy though. (1999: 36–7)

On the basis of his findings, Carrington questions the idea that
lesbian and gay households are necessarily more able to achieve
equality in their domestic practices in comparison with heterosexual
households. Contentiously, Carrington argues that:

Many have argued that because there are not both men and women in lesbigay
families, the traditional assignment of domesticity on the basis of gender cannot
take place, and therefore lesbigay families must negotiate domesticity, which
leads to a more equitable division. This is simply not the case among longer-term
families... My research seriously challenges the effort to place the lesbigay
family in the vanguard of social change, a model of equality for others to emulate.
Such assertions are based on the ideology of egalitarianism, not on its actual
existence, and on the invisibility, devaluation, and diminishment of domesticity.
(1999: 218)

As Table 2.2 demonstrated, there are several tasks that must be undertaken in the household, whatever their composition. In adult couple households, one such task is the provision of caring and emotional support to partners. In heterosexual households, as was shown in Chapter 5, this task is often presumed to fall mainly to women (see also Hochschild, 1983, 1989; Duncombe and Marsden, 1993). But in lesbian and gay households too, Carrington argues, one person generally takes principal responsibility for caring which, in turn, involves monitoring the household and ensuring that things get done. In one long-term lesbian couple Carrington studied, for example, one partner admitted that she used strategic nagging to get her way.

> *Nag* is the word I use. I can be and have been a real nag. I have given it up. It doesn't seem to work. The house cleaners help. But I am much more crafty about it now. I have learned how to read Cindy for moods and I know when I can get her to do stuff and when I can't. It's sort of a subtle negotiation. I don't know if she realizes that I am scanning the moments waiting to ask her to clean out the fireplace or hose out the garage, but that's what I do. I sort get in tune with the rhythm of her life now and it seems to work. (1999: 79)

In a gay couple, a similar pattern emerged:

> Yes, I have to prod him, 'bitch at him' is what he would say. I have found it difficult to figure out ways to bring up the condition of the house without creating too much of a fight. I sort of have learned that there are certain times to bring it up. I especially try to avoid bringing things up when he just gets home from work. I find he is more willing to help, or at least to hear it, later at night. Or course, he doesn't see any of this, it's annoying, nor does he recognise what an effort it is to get him to help. (1999: 80)

As Carrington points out, an emphasis on 'doing family life' helps to show how many gay and lesbian couple relationships survive. Many couples recognise this; as one of his respondents stated, 'We are just like all the other families, maintaining our yard and building [our family]' (1999: 106).

I am doing Carrington's work a disservice if an impression is being gained that gay and lesbian households operate entirely in the same way as heterosexual households. As has already been shown in Chapter 4, conventional patriarchal power relationships continue to underscore domestic practices in heterosexual households. This means that some men have the opportunity to choose to leave some aspects of domestic work to their partner which remains a significant focus for women's dissatisfaction in heterosexual couple households. Carrington's study, by contrast, helps to show that even if tasks are undertaken inequitably, many lesbian and gay couples *feel* that they have achieved equality in their relationships.

The purpose of this chapter has been to recognise that diversity in family and household form can produce particular conflicts of interest and particular strategies to accommodate to new situations. People who migrate between cultures, it has been shown, must re-evaluate the way home is conceived in an abstract sense. While this renegotiation of identity requires enormous energy, gender conflicts over the way that home is organised are not subsumed or eradicated by these wider issues. On the contrary, exposure to new ideas and new identities can raise challenges to conventions about domestic practices, especially by younger generations born in a new country. It has also been shown that people who marry or cohabit with partners from another culture, race or ethnic group can face a kind of double jeopardy. Not only must cultural differences be reconciled in the process of constructing a manageable pattern of domestic life but, in addition, couples have to manage adverse reactions from friends, family and the community.

This chapter has also revealed that gays and lesbians in long-term relationships are freed to some extent from those aspects of a patriarchal ideology that define masculinity and femininity in relation to primary breadwinner and primary homemaker roles. As a consequence it has been possible to challenge the rigidities of gendered domestic practices and the inequities of power that these can produce (see Heaphy, Donovan and Weeks, 1999). In gay and lesbian households, domestic practices often do become differentiated over time depending upon the skills or preferences of individuals, rather than accepting predetermined cultural ideas on what men and women *can* or *should* do. That said, this chapter demonstrates that lesbian and gay households cannot ignore some of the pressures that heterosexual couples also face. Social class remains a significant factor in this respect because those couples who lack the resources of time, money and live in stressed communities can be put under the kinds of pressure that would test any relationship.

9

Single People

The culture of coupledom

Over the last 25 years there has been a steady increase in the number of single person households. In Britain it is expected that by 2006 there will be 8.43 million single person households (including 1.25 million single parent family households). This represents an increase of 26 per cent over a period of 15 years (Department of the Environment, 1995). The proportion of men living alone has also grown significantly from 35 per cent of all single person households in 1980 to 41 per cent in 1998. In total about 2.76 million British men lived alone in 1998, and it has been predicted that this number will have risen by 14 per cent to 3.33 million men by 2003 (MINTEL, 1999). There are three principal reasons for the rising number of single person households. First, increased life expectancy means that there are more older widowed people in society. The second reason is because more younger people delay marriage or cohabitation. And finally, rising divorce rates have led many middle-aged people, and especially men, to live alone (MINTEL, 1999).

While the domestic situation of single women and men has not, as yet, been extensively researched by sociologists, it is clear that the position of single people in society is rising on the political agenda. There are several reasons for this. One of the most important is that governments are becoming increasingly concerned about the growing number of single people who may become dependent on the state later in life. Furthermore, governments have recognised that increased divorce rates or the breakdown of long-term cohabiting couple relationships is producing higher levels of state dependence for single parent families. Finally, governments have been alerted to the fact that the breakdown of relationships can produce social problems including marital violence, homelessness, alcohol and drug abuse, which has put more pressure on law enforcement, housing and health services.

The rise in the number of single person households may represent a significant change in social attitudes about domestic practices. The business community has certainly responded positively to the growth of single person households. Indeed, single people represent a very significant and lucrative market for a whole range of goods and services. The housebuilding industry, in particular, is benefiting from an increase in demand for metropolitan apartment blocks for affluent younger single people for whom living alone for longer periods is now an established life expectation, and for post-divorcees who break up family homes and move to separate houses and apartments.

Nevertheless, as this chapter shows, being single can still be experienced as problematic in a society where heterosexual couple-dom is still regarded as the cultural norm. As the next section of this chapter shows from an analysis of changing social attitudes to bachelors and spinsters since the nineteenth century, people who live alone have often been pitied or even feared by wider society. Living alone may no longer be exceptional but, as this section also demonstrates from a case study of the contemporary media, the social pressure to cohabit or marry remains considerable. The third section of this chapter will explore the subjective experiences of women and men who live alone. This analysis demonstrates that only a minority of single people live outside relationships in the longer term. Indeed, many people who live alone are currently in long-term relationships, have recently ended a relationship or have regular but short-term relationships. Perceptions of home and the way that domestic life is practised may differ for single people because of their stronger reliance on friendship networks than may be the case among couples. In the final section on post-divorce households, it will be shown that living alone can be a significant problem for many people at critical points in their lives. But it will also be argued that, even if living alone in such circumstances can be an isolating experience at first, it is for the majority a temporary and transitional phase.

Bachelors and spinsters in the nineteenth and twentieth centuries

Getting married has traditionally been a crucially important rite of passage for women and men. As was shown in Chapter 3, marriage was the principal means of gaining social respectability for the majority of women in the eighteenth and nineteenth century because they were effectively debarred from most other routes to independence and social status. As Jane Austen demonstrated in her novels, the politics of a competitive marriage market were complex and led parents to take desperate steps to successfully and beneficially marry off their daughters. As she cleverly observed in the opening line of *Pride and Prejudice*, 'It is a truth universally acknowledged, that a single man in possession of a good fortune, must be in want of a wife' ([1813] 1972: 51). But as Austen knew only too well, in this market the odds were stacked in men's favour because bachelorhood was much less restricting than spinsterhood (see M. Anderson, 1984).

As Perrot suggests, in the nineteenth century, 'Bachelorhood was a happy time, at least as embellished in memory, a time of fleeting love affairs, of travel, of camaraderie, and of free wheeling relations with other men ... it was also the age of "sentimental education" and sexual experience, when everything was permitted' (Perrot, 1990: 248). Indeed, many middle- and upper-class Englishmen embraced the idea of maintaining their independence and sought adventure instead of succumbing to what many considered to be the dullness of domesticity (Tosh, 1999). The imaginations of young men were fuelled by writers such as Kipling. Born in 1865 in India, his jingoistic accounts of imperial adventure became hugely popular reading in Britain and later in America (A. Wilson, 1997). Other writers, including G. A. Henty, romanticised travel beyond England's shores. Henty produced over 80 story books for boys with stirring titles such as *With the Allies to Pekin* (1904) and *Held Fast for England* (1892). The books followed the familiar formula of a brave young British boy meeting a friend and then setting off on an overseas adventure where they would meet some great mysterious 'foreign' historical figure. In their adventures they would be captured, then escape; perhaps rescue a 'girl' from a fate worse than death; and by the last chapter she would fall for the hero (Newbolt, 1996).

Public boarding school education also promoted the idea that young men should be independent and patriotic. Following the tradition of Dr Arnold at Rugby, public school boys were instructed to embrace the spirit of 'muscular Christianity' which demanded good manners, physical courage, comradeship and a passable degree of intelligence (P. Mason, 1993: 163). The education of British boys in the public school system may have been a brutalising experience, but many gained the confidence and emotional resilience to emigrate in large numbers via the army, navy, or colonial administration. As Tosh shows, the Empire:

> occupied an unprecedented place in the masculine imagination ... it had become an imaginative space where male comradeship and male hierarchies found their full scope, free from feminine ties. Almost all the popular paragons of imperial manliness at this time were men who either never married (Gordon, Kitchener, Rhodes) or else married very late (Baden Powell, Lugard, Milner). (Tosh, 1991: 68)

Bachelorhood in later life could signify failure. Older bachelors in France were ridiculed and were known as 'dry fruit', for it was assumed that they were celibate or perhaps even impotent. Flaubert caricatured bachelors (*célibataire*) in his *Dictionary* as 'all selfish and debauched. They ought to be taxed. A sad old age lies in store for them' (in Perrot, 1990: 247). Many bachelors understood that their status in the eyes of others was diminished, even if they wanted to remain unmarried. In 1831, for example, Gustave de Beaumont wrote in a letter to his brother, Achille, about the model of family life in America, which he believed would soon also become the norm in France: 'I fear that we shall arrive at a state of affairs in which bachelors will find themselves in an untenable situation and only fathers with families will enjoy any security at all' (in Perrot, 1990: 247).

Men in Victorian society, as has already been shown in Chapter 3, had many more options open to them than women because of better education, employment opportunities, social and economic independence, and political citizenship. While the position of women in society did begin to improve towards the end of the nineteenth century, they remained heavily dependent upon the institution of marriage if they were to gain any measure of security and status in adult life. The low status of unmarried women in the nineteenth century was not a new phenomenon. On the contrary, for centuries unmarried women had been generally perceived as a threat to the social order and had been subject to accusations of emotional, social and sexual incompleteness by church and state. In seventeenth-century New England, as Chambers-Schiller has shown, remaining unmarried was regarded as:

> a sinful state, an evil to be exorcised from community life because solitary women menaced the social order. Rather than allow women at liberty, most communities required the unmarried to live in families headed by respectable, property holding,

church affiliated men. Family supervision ensured virtue and orderliness, and
prevented licentiousness and sin. (Chambers-Schiller, 1984: 11)

Unmarried women were known as 'spinsters' because it was expected
that they must work to support themselves. And if they had not
married by the time they reached the age of 26, women became
known as 'thornbacks' which was a derogatory reference to a sea skate
with spines on its back and tail (Chambers-Schiller, 1984; see also
Hufton, 1984; Watkins, 1984; Cavallo and Warner, 1999).

Concern about the plight of single women in nineteenth-century
Britain and America grew because of widening demographic imbalances. In Britain in 1851, for example, there were 20 per cent more
unmarried women aged over 40 than men (Shoemaker, 1998: 140).
In New England, similarly, women outnumbered men by some
20,000 (K. Brown, 1996). This presented a real problem for single
women as there were few opportunities to establish themselves on
an independent economic footing. As Zimmeck notes: 'Victorian
society found it difficult to countenance the spectacle of "distressed
gentlewomen" suffering gross physical hardship, loss of class or a
fall into prostitution, which would otherwise have been their fate'
(1986: 157). The search for 'fresh modes of activity' for this surplus of
young middle-class women by well-meaning philanthropic married
ladies often bordered on the ridiculous. In one article published in
Cassell's Family Magazine in 1883–4, for example, Elizabeth L.
Banks proposed a range of possible occupations such as 'art needle-
work, table decoration, breaking-in new boots, shopping for country
folk, specialist cleaning of delicate furniture and china, and dog
walking (for those of "bashful, shrinking dispositions")' (in Zimmeck,
1986: 157).

Attitudes began to change by the end of the nineteenth century in
England due to the increased economic activity of middle-class single
women, especially in the growing field of clerical work together with
the more established occupations of school teacher, governess and
nurse. As the *Westminster Review* commented in 1894, the single
woman was 'a new sturdy and vigorous type. We find her neither the
exalted ascetic nor the nerveless inactive creature of former days'
(in Bland, 1986: 125). Clerical work, in particular, was thought to be
a particularly suitable job for young women. According to Lady
John Manners, the wife of the Postmaster General in 1882, clerical
work did not lead to the loss 'of those feminine graces, of dignity,
of delicacy, of reserve, which are the essential characteristics of

English gentlewomen' (in Zimmeck, 1986: 158). Men were generally successful in keeping women out of the professions by blocking educational opportunities and from skilled manual work through trade union action, as was shown in Chapter 3; but clerical work was the exception. In Britain, the number of women clerks grew from 2,000 in 1851 to 166,000 in 1911.

Most clerks were young unmarried women and it was expected that theirs was a temporary stay in the labour market. Indeed, in Britain and America, the idea that women could be married and work at the same time was deeply shocking to most middle-class men. Supposing himself to be funny, G. K. Chesterton wrote, 'I do not deny that women have been wronged and even tortured; but I doubt if they were ever tortured so much as they are tortured now by the absurd modern attempt to make them domestic empresses and competitive clerks at the same time' (in de Silva, 1990: 110). Consequently, there were few opportunities for promotion (Jordan, 1996), and in most companies and the civil service women had to leave employment once married (see Martindale, 1938).

The assumption that all single women were, in some sense, incomplete or failures was not universally accepted. Some commentators argued that marriage stifled the free spirit of women and that the law robbed them of all independence. As the American suffragette, Susan B. Anthony, wrote to her friend Lydia Mott in 1867:

> In the depths of my soul there is a continual denial of the self-annihilating spiritual and legal union of two human beings. Such union, in the very nature of things, must bring an end to the free action of one or the other, and it matters not to the individual whose freedom has thus departed whether it be the gentle rule of love or the iron hand of law which blotted out from the immortal being the individual soul-stamp of the Good Father. (Chambers-Schiller, 1984: 52)

Anthony was brought to trial in 1873 for illegally voting in an election. Women were not allowed to vote at that time because the common law principle of coverture had yet to be abandoned. Under this rule, women were legally judged to be dependent upon and subordinate to their husbands. Anthony attempted to defend herself by arguing that she should be protected under the fifteenth Amendment of the Constitution which had abolished slavery:

> I submit if the deprivation by law of the ownership of one's own person, wages, property, children, the denial of the right as an individual, to sue and be sued, and to testify in the courts, is not a condition of servitude, most bitter and absolute, through under the sacred name of marriage? (cited in Coltrane, 1998: 146)

In the same year, the Supreme Court denied women's access to the legal profession on the grounds that their natural role was in the family. As the Court stated:

> The civil law, as well as nature herself has always recognised a wide difference in the respective spheres and destinies of man and woman. Man is, or should be, women's protector and defender. The natural and proper timidity and delicacy which belongs to the female sex evidently unfits it for many of the occupations of civil life. The constitution of the family organisation, which is grounded in divine ordinance, as well as in the nature of things, indicates the domestic sphere as that which properly belongs to the domain and functions of womanhood ... The paramount destiny and mission of woman are to fulfill the noble and benign offices of wife and mother. (cited in Coltrane, 1998: 147)

It is hardly surprising under these ideological and legal conditions that women's refusal of marriage produced alarmist responses. Indeed, the growing number of women choosing to live independently from men fuelled speculation about the medical origins of their pathological fear of marriage. Wilhelm Stekel's *Frigidity in Women in Relation to Her Love Life*, for example, had this to say about 'marriage dread'.

> Marriage dread and aversion to childbearing affect particularly our 'higher circles'. Increasing numbers of girls belonging to the upper strata remain single. Women of culture withdraw more and more from their roles as mothers and wives. They are 'emancipated'; they are growing self reliant, self sufficient and, economically too, they are becoming more and more independent of the male. They are accustoming themselves to get along without love, or they pander to love 'without issue'... What is the result? ... The Spiritual aristocracy of the race is dying out. The progress of humanity is being halted. (cited in Chambers-Schiller, 1984: 200; see also Hartley, 1924)

Some American women intellectuals chose not to marry in order to maintain their independence but, as a consequence, they often remained dependent upon their fathers. As Chambers-Schiller has shown, even successful women writers of the calibre of Emily Dickenson achieved independence only by remaining in her father's home (1984: 105).

Employment opportunities for single women improved considerably from the last quarter of the nineteenth century in Britain and America, but society remained unaccepting of the status of the single woman. Simon's oral history study of 50 American older single women born at the turn of the twentieth century shows how women managed their 'deviant' status in a society where the vast majority of women married. Drawing upon Goffman's (1968) analysis of stigma,

Simon argues that single women had three options available to them: first, to remedy the situation by marrying; second, to behave as 'normal' by, perhaps, devoting her energies to working with children; or third, to challenge convention and celebrate their unorthodox status. While some vacillated between these three positions, most of the single women Simon interviewed emphasised the 'positive marginality' of their ambiguous situation. The following quotation illustrates one woman's ambivalence:

> Marry? Why would I marry? As a single woman, I had my freedom all of the time. Some relatives hinted every now and then that there was something wrong that I had not ever married. But I wasn't odd. I dressed lacier than a lot of married women I saw on my block. I spent more time with my brothers' kids than a lot of my married neighbours spent with their *own* children. And, I can assure you, I had nothing whatsoever to do with women who didn't like men. (in Simon, 1987: 14)

This woman makes a considerable effort to show that she is not abnormal in any way. She takes trouble to emphasise that she is feminine by referring to her lacy clothes, she shows that she is just as capable of caring for children as her neighbours, and that she is not a lesbian. Her defence shows that she is well aware of the commonly held prejudices about single women in America at that time. For black women, the situation was more complex. Many poorer black women in America in the early part of the twentieth century also chose to avoid marriage, or at least recognised that it was not at the top of their list of priorities. As Simon shows, black women generally had to take the lowest paid and dirtiest jobs, and they were often victims of sexual and racial harassment. One of the older black single women in Simon's study recalled:

> About once a day my parents (tenant farmers) spelled out what I should become. They talked about me studying to be a school teacher and painted quite a clear picture of the alternatives. If I didn't go to college, I would become a tenant farmer, starving like they were. Or I would become a maid who cleaned up after white people's dirt. Or I would become a 'woman of Satan', someone who slept around and drank cheap bourbon on Sunday mornings. I don't remember my folks worrying about my getting a husband. That was way down the list of what they cared about. (cited in Simon, 1987: 8)

Another black woman, born in 1896, shows why she refused to be 'swallowed up' by their family or by her husband:

> My momma was a slave in South Carolina, so I know about what that word means. I never wanted to be anyone's slave, not a white man's and not a black man's. I didn't marry because that looked dangerously close to slavery to me. Neither did

I let my father or sisters push me around after I was a full grown woman . . . I told them I would have to see each time if I could give the kind of help they wanted. You see, I won't be anyone's 'nigger', not my boss's, not my poppa's and not some other man's, just because he stood in front of an altar with me one Sunday morning when we were still too stuck on each other to know better. (in Simon, 1987: 33)

Black women from middle-class families were expected both to achieve at college and marry. By contrast, Hispanic women in Simon's study spoke of 'extreme pressure' from church, family and community to marry early and have children (1987: 8).

Pressure on women to marry and become a homemaker at the turn of the last century was intense because there were few other options for most women. At the beginning of the twenty-first century it is clear that women have gained greater political and economic independence, and yet the social pressure to marry appears not to have abated, especially in the USA where over 90 per cent of the population still marry (Coltrane, 1998: 48). In Europe, the popularity of marriage has declined by comparison, with about 80 per cent of British people marrying, compared with about 70 per cent in France and Germany, but only 55 per cent in Sweden (Elliot, 1996: 15). The decline in the popularity of marriage does not, however, signal a progressive abandonment of the idea of coupledom.

The contemporary media, in particular, tend to highlight the problematic status of single people. Take, for example, the rash of films (*Bridget Jones's Diary, Four Weddings and a Funeral*), television comedy series (*Sex in the City, Ally McBeal, Friends*), together with novels, magazines and newspaper articles which focus on what Gordon has defined as single people's 'existential angst' (1984). Given the constraints of space, I will restrict myself to one case study drawn from a British newspaper, *The Observer*, to illustrate this point. *The Observer* devoted an entire issue of its Sunday magazine to 'The Singles Issue' in November 2000, ostensibly to show that being single was no longer a stigmatised condition. The editor presented the special issue as follows:

In this week's magazine, we celebrate the single life. For the first time, being single is a proactive lifestyle choice, like the car you drive, the food you eat, or the books you read. People are no longer willing to settle for settling down . . . There's been a significant shift in attitude, a feeling that singletons may be alone, but they certainly aren't lonely. Again and again, the people in this issue use the word 'freedom' to describe their lives. They've got the financial control, the network of friends, and the confidence to be independent . . . The single stigma has faded away (the more there are, the less likely they are to be pitied). Friends are the new family. (*The Observer Magazine*, 5 November, 2000: 1–3)

The text of this introduction is revealing in a number of ways. To begin with, it obviously attempted to flatter its readers and thereby reassure them that this special issue was going to make them feel good about themselves. But at the same time, the introductory text also sows seeds of doubt in readers' minds by suggesting that they are '*less* likely to be pitied': thus signifying that this status is not yet fully legitimate.

The majority of the feature articles exposed a tension between the freedoms afforded by the single life and anxieties about not being in a 'normal' relationship. Some articles emphasised the fun single people had, but did so very much in the context of a period of transition before settling down. These articles did not confine themselves to the advantages of being a young eligible bachelor, as would have been the case only a few decades earlier. Instead, many articles directly addressed the young affluent single woman on issues such as the advantages of owning a sports car or having raucous 'girls' nights out'. For example, under the banner headline 'Sex and the single woman', the strap-line read, 'They drink too much, smoke too much and if they feel like it, they have sex too much. Women today know what they want and are happy to go and get it.' Interview quotations were chosen to show that women could, perhaps must, be as callous in love as men are often stereotyped to be. As one woman said, 'The men I sleep with don't have much to say. I met the current one when he came to do odd jobs. He is a bit of rough, which is perfect ... I call it shagging without ironing' (*The Observer Magazine*, 5 November, 2000: 31). By contrast, an autobiographical piece entitled 'Table for one', by a well known chef, suggested cheerful resilience:

> Speaking as someone who is (now) devoutly single, I often find myself eating alone – though in practice not as often as I would like – and highly recommend the solitary supper ... There is untold pleasure to be had in cooking for yourself. We should do it whenever we can, basking in the luxury of having only ourselves to please. There is no one to regale us with tales about their day or to quiz us about ours, no children, no one to serve, no one to fuss over. At last a meal in which we have only to consider our own satisfaction. Yet no one should regard this as an act of selfishness. Cooking for yourself is simply a matter of self-respect. (*The Observer Magazine*, 5 November, 2001: 70)

While the newspaper claimed on the one hand that being single was a legitimate status, most articles carried a strong advisory emphasis on 'how to' resolve problems. Indeed, many articles focused on providing help in finding true love and escaping from loneliness. The feature titles illustrate this: 'Before the fall', 'The cost of being alone', 'The dating game', 'The perfect chat-up line' and inevitably, a quiz which asked 'Just how single are you?' This brief case study demonstrates how anxieties about being single are reinforced with a subtle in-between-the-lines message which stated that 'this *is not* what you *really* want'.

Why do people live alone?

Government statistics on single people generally refer to 'single person households', but it is important to recognise that when individuals are defined as single in terms of housing tenure, it does not necessarily follow that they are not in long-term relationships (often referred to as 'living apart together'), have regular casual relationships or have recently been separated, divorced or widowed. British market research suggest that only a minority of people who live alone have not had a relationship in the last five years. Younger single women and men in Britain are much more likely to be in a medium to long-term relationship according to this research; indeed, only 8 per cent of men and 5 per cent of women aged under 35 have had no relationship over the past five years. In the middle-aged cohort of 35–54 year olds, women were more likely than men not to have had a relationship; that said, about one-third of both women and men seem to have been in steady relationships. Only amongst the over 55 year olds did this research reveal that more than one-third have had no relationship for five years. The MINTEL (1999) project also suggests that only 24 per cent of men and 18 per cent of women preferred being single. A similar proportion of men and women stated that they preferred being in a relationship where they lived separately from their partner. Although this research sample was only relatively small, it is notable that 43 per cent of single women aged 35–54 stated a preference for living apart. Perhaps less surprising is the finding that about 40 per cent of men compared with 35 per cent of women expressed a preference to live together as a couple given the advantages that many men expect to gain from living with a women, as was shown in Chapters 4 and 5.

The above discussion suggests that a significant minority of women and men prefer to live alone, but it is not safe to assume that this was a principled choice. Gordon's (1984) study of single women aged over 35 from Finland, Britain and the USA shows that few of her respondents chose to remain single. Indeed, many of the women she interviewed were surprised by their situation. As one Californian woman in her study stated:

> I always thought I would be married with a family... but every time I thought about it I thought, well, gee, I'm not ready for it. And then I got older and older and probably the last ten years or so I've started thinking, well, what's... wrong with me? There's some reason why I'm single. (1984: 49)

The likelihood of remaining single may not be purely a matter of chance because, as was shown in Chapter 5, women with high levels of educational achievement and established careers are more likely to delay marriage because they commit longer periods of time to study and the establishment of a professional career. The marriage market is weighted against such women because men with a higher occupational and educational status are more likely to choose a younger marriage partner who is of a lower occupational status than themselves. Furthermore, when women gain financial and professional independence, the imperative to marry in order to gain financial stability and security is significantly diminished, which means that women can afford to be more choosy about prospective partners.

Ethnicity, similarly, can have an important impact upon women's likelihood to marry or avoid marriage. More black British and American women remain single than white women, Hispanics or South Asians (see also hooks, 1982; Elliot, 1996). While marriage rates are getting lower in many Western societies, patterns of cohabitation suggest that long-term monogamy is most people's preferred option. This option is less achievable in black Britain and especially in black America. Indeed, as Staples (1999) has recognised, for black Americans, the chances of establishing a stable heterosexual family relationship is becoming increasingly limited. In America, the majority of black women who have married eventually divorce or separate and, indeed, 39 per cent of women never marry at all. One reason for lower marriage rates is the shortage of eligible males, as Staples has argued:

> Unless there is a reversal of present trends in post-industrial America, the black family of the 21st century will be a unit headed by women and children trying to survive on an income below the poverty line. The man she might have married has been institutionally decimated, by the forces of racism and a chaotic, exploitative economy. Thus, he is in prison, the military, ravaged by drugs and alcohol, or gone

to an early grave. Any male child she bears faces a similar fate. Although these same economic forces are directing White families into a similar form, many of the causes are as much cultural as economic. A substantial number of White women have defined the traditional nuclear family as oppressive and have achieved the economic independence to explore alternative forms. Blacks simply find themselves in a struggle between the aspiration to have a traditional family life and the structural conditions that render those hopes futile. (1999: 287)

Black American women's prospects of marriage are also affected by their tendency to outperform black men in the education system and increasingly to gain middle-class jobs too. Black women college graduates outnumber men by two to one, and nearly 19 per cent gain managerial or professional work compared with only 13 per cent of men. Marrying non-black men is an option only 2 per cent of black women take, while twice as many black men marry white women (1999: 355). By contrast, 90 per cent of highly educated black men with middle-class jobs marry in some states (Staples, 1999: 286–7).

Being in long-term or intermittent relationships may have an impact on perceptions of domestic life. For example, the boundaries of home are conceptualised differently by women and men in single person households when compared with couple households. Single people may compensate for the absence of a partner to some extent by developing strong friendship networks, and this can impact upon the way that homes are used (Adams and Bliesner, 1992; Bien, Marbach and Templeton, 1992; Nutt, 1999). According to Gordon, single women spend a great deal of their time away from home and, the more time they spend away from home, 'the more likely they were to consider its appearance as secondary' (1984: 86). Younger single men, by contrast, are reported to be more interested in the appearance of their homes than men in relationships, although they seem to be more relaxed about untidiness and dislike housework (MINTEL, 1999).

The eating habits of single women also seem to differ from women in couples and families. As one Californian woman in Gordon's study stated: 'I hardly ever cook meals for myself...I think that last year I must have cooked around...five times. I don't cook full meals unless I have some people over...I just, I can't. Maybe it's just growing up in a large family...Who wants to cook for one?' (Gordon, 1984: 88). Sociologists have tended to ignore single people's domestic eating habits because most analyses of food and eating centre on social aspects of eating (see Lupton, 1996; Germov and Williams, 1999), leaving open a fruitful avenue for future research.

Recent market research suggests that gender differences in attitudes towards cooking amongst younger single people may not be as pronounced as in older generations. Indeed, one study shows that 44 per cent of single men and 49 per cent of single women claim to 'love cooking'. That said, the same study reveals that among these men, 40 per cent of their food spending was used on convenience food, restaurants and take-away meals compared with only 24 per cent for women (MINTEL, 1999). Nevertheless, the popularity of cooking among single men seems to be rising, as suggested by the popularity of the well known British television chef, Jamie Oliver, who is positioned in the media as a role model for younger men. As Brunsdon *et al*. (2001) argue, Oliver is successful on both sides of the Atlantic because his approach differs dramatically from established television cooks whose expert presentation is precise, educational and middle class. In his BBC *Naked Chef* series, by contrast, Oliver's 'manner and language is hard and cheeky, punctuated with words like "bash", "smash" and "throw" ... the camera work is rough, edgy, out of focus and continually trying to keep up with events' (2001: 38). Oliver seemed to demonstrate that for single men, being a good cook is a useful source of social capital that can help cement friendships and relationships; and, of course, he is married now.

The experience of living alone

The term 'home', as was shown in Chapter 1, has many positive connotations in Western culture which incorporates the notion of a peaceful haven away from the pressures of the outside world. But popular images of ideal home life generally focus on couples enjoying intimacy, privacy and security within the communion of family life, rather than as single people. In the analysis that follows, I will draw on two studies which explore the experiences of single American men (Waehler, 1999) and single British, Finnish and American women (Gordon, 1984) in their thirties and forties. Although neither study was directly concerned with the domestic life of single people, a critical reading helps to provide comparisons between single and couple households.

Waehler's study suggests that men perceive a number of disadvantages of living alone. These included the lack of opportunity to share experiences on a daily basis, periods of loneliness and the inability to plan for the future in a positive way. Men in Waehler's study often stated that they felt lonely sometimes living alone, but would not elaborate on this. In Gordon's study, about half the women said they considered loneliness as a problem and were more open about their feelings. Whether they felt lonely because they lived alone is difficult to determine because it is, of course, possible to experience extreme loneliness when surrounded by other people in, say, a boarding school or military academy, just as it is possible to experience loneliness in marriage. Loneliness is not, then, caused by being alone, so much as lacking intimacy or yearning for intimacy. A key difference is that when single people are lonely the problem can be compounded when family and friends fail to recognise that. As Gordon shows, married people often assume that single people have a more exciting life than they do because they are less pressured by financial, relationship and parenting problems. One of Gordon's Californian respondents illustrates this point:

> I don't like people to feel sorry for me so I don't tell them about it, you know, that I'm lonely or I'm depressed, you know...I just don't talk about it, I keep it to myself...I figure it's my problem...nobody can do anything about it, right? Yes, I tell my cousin that I'm tired of this life, you know, it's so lonely, and then she goes: 'Oh, you're lucky!' (in Gordon, 1984: 91)

The men in Waehler's study stressed the advantages of living alone. Most importantly, they emphasised the importance of personal freedom, keeping their options open and avoiding relationship problems. Many of the men in this study had been in relationships with women in the past, but reacted against a tendency they saw in women to make them change their behaviour.

> I perceive women as wanting to change me. If I could find a woman who said, 'you're okay the way you are', I think I would just be enraptured by that. But I have never found that in real life; I have just found women who said, 'Well if you would change your hairstyle, or your clothes, or the way you live, then you'd be okay'. They want to remake me. I do not want to do that. I don't want to become a camper in my own house. Any woman who wants to share my life had better know that I am my own person. (in Waehler, 1999: 65)

Some women in Gordon's study recognised that they had a tendency to idealise potential partners. This is illustrated by the following quotation:

> If I ever find somebody that I really think that I could share everything, yeah, that I share political opinions, that I share the same goals in life, that is prepared really

to put others before himself, that he's prepared to give of himself to what he
believes, perhaps then I could say I might consider this person. But I haven't.
(in Gordon, 1984: 112–13)

Complete refusal to compromise in relationships is not necessarily
the most attractive feature in a prospective partner. And of course,
lack of compromise on one side effectively forces compromise on
the other, unless a couple is almost miraculously well matched!
As Waehler shows, however, only a minority of the bachelors in his
study were so deeply entrenched in their attitudes.

While men tended to express the avoidance of relationship
discord as one of the best reasons for living alone, single women in
Gordon's study emphasised the importance of financial independence,
taking care of themselves, being in control of their own destiny, and
of emotional and mental independence (Gordon, 1984: 161–5).
That said, some women were concerned about becoming too
comfortable with their single status and worried that they may be
conforming to an 'old maid' stereotype. As one of Gordon's British
respondents stated: 'Probably I shall become more like that stereotype, I'm sure. Get more cranky as I get older [laughs], gather
more cats around me and – you know, all the usual cranky stuff'
(1984: 130).

Waehler's study, similarly, shows that many men had 'nagging
uncertainties' about missed relationship opportunities or not experiencing fatherhood. About a quarter of the men in this study were
described by Waehler as 'conflicted bachelors', many of whom were
too inflexible in their attitudes to adjust to their situation, but not
settled enough either to entrench themselves in a relatively satisfied
role as a confirmed bachelor. As one man stated: 'For me the worst
part of being single is the self-incrimination and self doubt that I
wonder about. It doesn't grab me very often, but sometimes I wonder if I'm not intimate with anybody because I can't be' (1999: 74).
In extreme cases, as the next section will show, some men can fall
into a self-destructive spiral because of their inability to deal with
conflict in relationships.

Living alone after divorce and separation

There is clear evidence that some men are at greater risk than others
of losing control over their lives when they are unable to achieve or

lose their traditional masculine role of breadwinner, husband and father. The increased incidence of divorce in Western societies has been shown to produce enormous emotional turmoil for most men and women, but men are often reported to suffer higher levels of anxiety, anger and confusion than women for longer periods of time after divorce and separation. The principal source of such confusion, many studies show, is that men fail to recognise as legitimate the complaints women have about maintaining conventional breadwinner and homemaker roles in the home (especially when women have jobs too). And further, many men fail to live up to women's expectations in terms of communication, intimacy and emotional engagement (Gerson, 1993 Mapstone, 1999). Many studies show that women feel a sense of 'release' when they lose the responsibility of maintaining relationships and undertaking principal caring roles. As a woman from one study typically stated: 'I feel like I'm living again, I feel like I was dying a slow death in that relationship. There's joy in my life ... I feel energised and liberated. I feel a real emotional release' (Reissman, 1990: 165–6).

Arndt (1989) argues that many men suffer higher degrees of stress after divorce because they fail to understand why the relationship ended, and further are often ill-equipped to find a way of negotiating the terms of separation reasonably successfully. As Jordan (1985) notes:

> The responsibility for the emotional stability of the relationship is placed in the woman's hands very early in the relationship ... When responsibility for nurturing and maintaining the relationships is given to the wife, also goes with it the power to end the relationship ... Many men being unaware of the *power* and responsibility their wives have are shocked at the separation. Such men feel let down by someone they trusted with their marriage, and so they believe and feel it has all been done to them. (in J. Wilson, 1990: 61)

The loss of the social status of responsible husband, father and breadwinner forces men to reconfigure perceptions of themselves (see Alvarez, 1982; Ambrose, Harper and Pemberton, 1983; Simpson, 1999). As one man from Cauhapé's study of American divorcees suggests:

> For a man, divorce can be sort of an inverse suicide. Instead of one's being dead – almost everyone *else* is. The divorced male is almost a ghost. He ceases to exist as far as most of his former world is concerned. You lose the primary Other, and the kids, and the house, the furniture, the friends, the life-rounds, and the total life pattern. (1983: 28)

For many men, the loss of responsibility and power causes anxiety and stress. As one man from Reissman's study of British and American men stated: 'I had a power base, I felt very good about myself. Now, you know, I'm different now. I just came out of a broken marriage. I don't have any real power base' (1990: 183).

Not all men feel or become dysfunctional after divorce, of course, although a number of studies demonstrate that the loss of day to day contact with children can have unforeseen and dramatic impacts on men's sense of well-being even if they chose, for whatever reason, to walk away from the marriage (Kruk, 1983; Fox, 1985; Hetherington and Hagan, 1986; Myers, 1986; Lund, 1987). Some men are more susceptible to serious life crises following relationship breakdown than others for psychological reasons. These problems can be compounded by other factors, such as their level of education, employment status, income, kinship and friendship support networks.

Higate's study of homeless ex-servicemen 'on the road' in Britain shows that these men's rejection of home for the 'freedom on the open road' is more closely linked to relationship crises than difficulties in taking responsibility for themselves after long-term subordination to military organisational authority. Relationship problems often preceded their departure from service and were linked to long periods of absence from their partner and an aggressive culture of masculinity that made it hard for men to communicate their feelings. Being in the army led many of the ex-infantrymen in Higate's study to seek clear cut solutions to problems rather than enter into negotiation with their former partner:

> Though participants varied in their experience of relationship breakdown, all tended to leave the home with few possessions and little regard for their own financial well-being. This may have reflected their inability to calmly negotiate the terms under which they would leave, rather they reported 'cracking up' and 'walking out'. (Higate, 2000: 335)

Men who become homeless closely associated home with conflict and claimed that being on the road was a kind of defence from emotional attachment and the consequent conflicts that they associated with relationships. As a result, many expressed satisfaction with their situation, affecting a romantic evocation of life on the road whilst concealing 'unspoken distress'. Voluntary homelessness is, in a sense, a rejection of the idea of home rather than just the lack of permanent housing. As Dovey notes in her discussion of the distinction between home and homelessness, 'Home...involves a commitment not of money but of time and emotion. It is the place where we invest dreams, hopes and care' (1995: 53–4; see also Dehavenon, 1996; Kennett and Marsh, 1999; for a discussion of women and homelessness, see Wardhaugh, 1999).

The feeling of transition is a common experience among people who have recently divorced or separated because their sense of home has been undermined by their marginalisation from previously held roles, responsibilities and routines and a sense of incompleteness by lacking the companionship of a partner, even if they were no longer happy in that relationship. While many men are unable to continue to have day to day contact with their children, an increasing number of men engage in co-parenting relationships with their former partners (Smart and Neale, 1999) or become custodial parents in their own right. J. Wilson (1990) shows that early studies of single parent fathers tended to emphasise the dysfunctional characteristics of such families, while later studies place a more positive emphasis on the coping strategies that single fathers adopt. Experiences vary depending upon a range of factors such as income, the circumstances under which custody of children was gained, level of involvement with their children's care prior to divorce, and the pattern of participation in parenting by their ex-wife. Studies tend to report a number of positive aspects of being a single father which included the satisfaction of seeing their children grow, the love and companionship they had with their children, their sense of self-reliance, successful parenting and their children's achievements. Loneliness was the most commonly defined problem, together with the problem of balancing the demands of work and family life, difficulties of adjustment to their new role, money problems and insufficient time to do everything (Greif DeMaris and Hood, 1993; Hood, 1993). Many lone fathers felt isolated but did not want to form a new relationship because of its potential impact on their children (Winn, 1986; J. Wilson, 1990).

Studies of women single parents generally show that women adapt more easily to their new situation because they have not changed their principal social status as a mother and are also supported by complex friendship and kin networks (see, for example, Kiernan, Land and Lewis, 1998; Dickerson, 1995). Men's friendship marital friendship networks are more difficult to sustain because their wives maintained these connections. Married men's independent male friendships are often less well developed and are of a different character from women's because they tended to centre on work or separate men-only leisure activities rather than family based leisure. As one male single parent in O'Brien's British study commented:

> Your friends drop away and all my friends were workmates, especially being in the print. They rarely live in your neighbourhood... Pub friends don't tend to be a lot of good. They only want to know you for a drink or a game of darts, so when you stop going down the pub they drop you out. (1987: 237)

Fathers' successful acquisition of homemaking and parenting skills can produce unwelcome reactions. As one man in Hipgrave's British study reported: 'A lot of people are sympathetic, but I'm not struck on them being too sympathetic. A bit of sympathy's all right, it boosts your ego a bit, but if they come out and say "You're coping very well, but it's a pity", it sort of clashes, doesn't it? You're saying the opposite of what you mean' (1982: 178; see also Hanson, 1985; Marsiglio, 1995; Coltrane, 1996; A. Burgess, 1997).

While women single parents tend to have stronger kin and friendship network than men, they also have to learn new skills, roles and to manage on low incomes. And yet many studies show that women in this situation prefer this to marriage, as a woman in Hardey's study stated:

> Looking back, I think I must have been mad all those years making a home for my ex. Even when Joe [her son] came along the home would be all nice and tidy and a meal would be on the table when he [the husband] came home. We had all this furniture that I never really liked but David [her ex husband] wanted it. So I just thought 'Oh that's all right then'. Now this is my home and I decide what goes in it and how tidy it is. I think it's great to have some toys around the floor and things. I could never have had all these plants in the house when I was married but I like them and it is now up to me to decide how I want to decorate the house. I always used to have to fit in with how David wanted things to look but now it's all up to me. The whole house is mine, not just the kitchen! (1989: 134).

Studies show that women claim to be more satisfied living alone or with their children after divorce. This is borne out by the a fall in the number of remarriages in Britain, although this is less pronounced in the USA (McRae, 1999). However there has been a concomitant increase in the number of divorcees who cohabit which, in turn, suggests that these feelings of satisfaction when living alone may be short lived (Elliot, 1996: 20).

Recent divorcees may not feel that they can or want to establish another relationship, but the evidence suggests that many of them will. This further reinforces the main point of this chapter: that living alone is for a growing number of people a temporary, transitional and often recurrent feature of their lives. Coupledom, whether it involves living together or living together apart, has an enduring appeal despite all of the problems it seems to engender. In this sense, as Gordon has put it, established cultural expectations about marriage 'cast a long shadow' and people who live alone walk a tightrope between 'separateness and connectedness', and between 'independence and intimacy' (Gordon, 1984: 194).

10

Domestic Practices After Retirement

The principal emphasis of this book has been to explore how changing patterns of breadwinning and homemaking have affected gendered domestic practices. As a consequence, most chapters of this book have concentrated upon the experiences of adults who are of working age. This chapter takes a different point of view by addressing older people's expectations and experiences of domestic life. It is widely accepted in the sociological literature, as this chapter will show, that because older couples are more likely to subscribe to traditional views on gendered domestic practices than younger people, the process of transition to retirement can be problematic. Such explanation is often justified on the grounds that women often find it difficult to accommodate to the idea of their husband being at home all the time. And in turn, because the routines of domestic life have been determined to a large extent by women over many decades, men often find it difficult to identify a role for themselves. This chapter shows, then, that the relationship between ideas about masculinity and femininity continue to affect the way that domestic practices are negotiated after retirement.

Social class and the ageing process also have a significant impact on domestic practices. As this chapter will show, social class influences financial planning prior to retirement the level of choice people have over the process of retirement, financial well-being after retirement, and can also affect patterns of caring later in life. By contrast, the impact of ageing on people's experiences of domestic life is less predictable. While social stereotypes of older people categorise them as socially unproductive, infirm and dependent on others, the reverse is most often the case. Most older people retain independence throughout their lives; they remain key players in family life and often in wider social life too through voluntary work or by remaining in paid work well into later life. Even when facing physical disabilities or illnesses, it does not necessarily represent infirmity or dependence. Younger onlookers often assume that medical conditions produce specific personal responses but, as Gullette argues: 'A given and named condition is not thereby *your* condition. Your condition is your reaction, your living with your changed body, and the new state you and it make together. It's really a narrative issue: how do I want to fit this into my life story?' (cited by Hepworth, 1999a, 143; see also Cole and Gadow, 1986; Thompson, Itzin and Abendstern, 1990).

While the ageing process and class differences are important, the primary focus of this chapter is to argue that gender differences are a crucial indicator of social, physical and economic well being later in life which, in turn, shapes domestic practices. This chapter will be divided into four sections. The first demonstrates that retirement planning is a gendered process which can result in serious economic problems for women in later life compared with men. The second section assesses the impact of retirement on gendered domestic practices by explaining how conventional breadwinner and homemaker roles are reconfigured and renegotiated. The third section considers how gender affects domestic practices in later life. The final section considers the impact of the ageing process on patterns of caring and assesses its consequences for the experience of home in later life.

Gender and planning for retirement

Making generalisations about different approaches people take to retirement planning is a complex process. Many households are able to plan their retirement very carefully by, for example, entering into savings or pension plans, by reducing commitments to paid work incrementally, or by taking part-time employment after retirement. Others plan less well. This can be due to the inability to save or enter into pension schemes because of low pay, a distrust of the pension industry or an individual preference for (or cultural tendency to) live for today and not for tomorrow. Gender is an important variable when analysing retirement planning. Married women, as will be revealed below, are particularly vulnerable to economic problems in later life because they depend upon their husbands to make financial

arrangements (Pienta and Haywood, 2002). If they are widowed or
divorced, this can have a dramatic impact on their financial well-
being. While many people do prepare for retirement carefully, the
best laid plans can suddenly and unexpectedly be disrupted by the
failure of company pension schemes, bad advice from the private
pension industry, redundancy, ill health, or because they have to
care for their parents or spouse (Ekerdt *et al.*, 2001; Dentinger and
Clarkberg, 2002).

In the first half of this section, where the retirement of men is
discussed, it will become apparent that patterns of retirement are
affected by a number of 'push' and 'pull' factors. In contractual
terms, retirement age is less clearly prescribed now than in the
mid-twentieth century. In Britain, for example, 31 per cent of men
and 44 per cent of women retire between the ages of 55 and 59
(Hilbourne, 1999). In the past, the model of middle-class and skilled
working-class men serving a life-long career until they reached
retirement age in one occupation or industry held fast for many, but
this has been undermined over the last two or three decades by a
number of factors that tend to push older people out of work. These
factors include, first, the economic restructuring of a wide range of
industries resulting in an employer preference for increasingly
flexible working practices and shorter-term employment contracts
(R. Brown, 1997). Second, employers often recognise the financial
advantages of replacing more highly paid older people with lower
paid younger people when preparing voluntary redundancy packages.
Finally, many employers indirectly discriminate against older workers
by adopting 'ageist' notions that younger people, or 'new blood',
make a more valued creative contribution than older people, which
has led to the development of employer-led early retirement
schemes.

Retirement can be viewed in a positive light too. Upon retirement,
many men can expect to be reasonably well off, even though they
have given up work, because this is a time in their lives when the
mortgage is paid, they have most of the things they need in the home
which have been accumulated over the years and their children are
independent and much less demanding financially. Furthermore, as
E. Thompson's (1994) analysis of men's retirement in America
indicates:

> Older men, compared to older women, would also seem to be at a quality-of-life
> advantage even though they are at a mortality disadvantage ... later life for older

men presents fewer troubles...elderly men are much more likely than elderly women to live with their spouses. Nearly three quarters of elderly men today are both married and living with their spouses...Aging does not oblige many older men to recast their lives and go it alone after the death of a spouse. (1994: 10)

The experience of men is not uniform, of course. Class impacts heavily on men's mortality rates, for example. Furthermore, race and ethnicity can impact on men's experiences. As Thompson's study suggests, for example, older black men are much less likely to be married than white or Hispanic men. Indeed, amongst the 65–75 age group 58 per cent of black men, compared with 79 per cent of white men and 77 per cent of Hispanic men, are married (1994: 11; see also Szinovacz, DeViney and Davey, 2001; for general discussion of men and retirement see also Parnes, 1981; S. Parker, 1982; Parnes *et al.*, 1985).

Many men and women approach retirement relatively optimistically from a financial point of view but, in reality, men often have considerably more pension wealth than women. As Anderson *et al.* (2000) reveal from a study of British retired people, such optimism is strongly affected by class position and marital status. As Table 10.1 clearly demonstrates, working-class people recognise that their prospects in retirement will be much less comfortable than their middle-class counterparts. While single people are reasonably certain that they will be catered for well enough financially in retirement, they are less optimistic than couples. The most significant feature of this

Table 10.1 *Expectations of comfort in retirement in Britain (%)*

	Comfortable	All right	Difficult	N
Men	48	38	14	63
Women	49	34	16	67
Couples	51	33	16	104
Living alone	38	50	12	26
Middle class	58	33	9	45
Intermediate	41	47	12	17
Working class	44	35	21	68
Income (top quartile)	69	31	0	42
Income (2nd quartile)	49	44	8	39
Income (3rd quartile)	48	26	26	27
Income (lowest quartile)	9	46	46	22

Source: adapted from Anderson *et al.* (2000: 458), Table 7.

table is the close match between men's and women's expectations of achieving a comfortable life after retirement. Anderson *et al*. report that 45 per cent of men in their sample, compared with 49 per cent of women, felt that they had prepared adequately for retirement. In reality, many of these women's positive outlook may be misplaced.

Women's financial prospects after retirement can be considerably less positive than men's (Richardson, 1999; Vartanian and McNamara, 2002). Dailey's (1998) study of baby boom women's retirement prospects in America anticipates that women will continue to lag behind men in terms of pension provision. This is due to women's shorter period of time in the labour market, a tendency for their career advancement to be limited by interruptions for child rearing or care for elderly parents, and a tendency to be concentrated in low paid jobs. Women are also likely to be less well off financially because they have worked in industry with poorer pension cover, may receive lower social security benefits and may have accumulated lower assets and savings (1998: 121). This is illustrated in a recent British study of pension wealth of women and men. Warren, Rowlingson and Whyley (2001) show in Table 10.2 that amongst the middle classes, older women are substantially less well catered for financially compared with men. While this may be offset if they are married to a man with good pension provision, many women approaching retirement age are single, divorced or widowed.

The economic situation for women who have never married can be daunting although, as Simon's study of older American women who never married indicates, almost half of her sample of 50 women claimed that their lives had improved after retirement. These single

Table 10.2   *Pension wealth of women and men in Britain aged 55–64*

	Median total pension wealth (£)		Percentage of income from occupational pension	
	Women	Men	Women	Men
Middle class	22,587	87,723	58	66
Intermediate	3,940	81,697	56	66
Working class	0	50,844	37	51
Average	2,559	56,223	54	57

Source: *Family Resources Survey* (1995/6), adapted from Warren, Rowlingson and Whyley (2001: 481), Table 7.

women had planned carefully and looked forward to retirement on their own terms. For the rest of her sample, however, retirement was an unwelcome life transition. As one woman stated:

> The worst part of it is the dishonesty involved. My bosses kept talking about my 'golden years' and my 'well deserved rest'. What they weren't saying is what they really thought – that they wanted to make room for younger people whom they could pay less and hoodwink more. One day I'm the brains behind the operation. The next day I am expendable because my birthday came and went. (in Simon, 1987: 146)

The economic reality of retirement hit hard many of the single women in Simon's study, with 44 per cent living below the poverty line. In anticipation of retirement and the financial challenges that entailed, most women in Simon's study chose to live with someone else. This did not necessarily lead to harmonious or companionate relationships especially when living with siblings, as the following quotation suggests:

> Fear of poverty in my last years led me to ask Kate [a younger sister] to live with me. I thought I had weighed carefully all the pros and cons. Most of them I foresaw... However, what I forgot to calculate was the cumulative effect of living with someone who whines instead of talking. When we were kids, I could not stand Kate's whining. But back then Momma usually made her stop. Nowadays, there is no Momma to get her back on track. I try my best, but usually she just whines more when I object to her complaining tone of voice. I am a good Christian, so I try to live and let live. Some days, though, I just want to put her possessions out on the street and change the locks. Only a louse would actually do that, but what a fine fantasy it is. (in Simon, 1987: 156)

There is currently only a very scarce literature on men's sibling relationships in old age (see Matthews, 1994, for a review), but the limited research that is available suggests only a patchy support system, especially amongst male siblings.

While labour market conditions have impacted negatively on many older people's financial prospects, there are also several factors operating in their favour. There is much evidence to suggest that many middle-class men look forward to finishing work earlier than in former generations. The development of a leisure and consumption oriented life-style amongst well off older people (or 'woopies', as market researchers often call them) has led to positive imaging of the 'third age'. Such attitudes to retirement are reflected by the growing market for glossy niche-market magazines, sales promotions and advertising brochures where later life is presented as a time of creativity, health and happiness (Featherstone and Hepworth, 1995). Financial planning for retirement is affected by the intensive activity of banks and companies that sell private pensions and other forms of retirement savings.

Advertisements for such financial products tend to focus on one particular niche in the market, however, and that is relatively affluent white middle-class men. As Ekerdt and Clark (2001) argue, they tend to portray their typical customer as 'habitually hard working, discerning, responsible ... disciplined, and serious. According to one ad, "You'd do anything for your children. You'd do anything for your parents. But sometimes you ask – are you doing enough for your own retirement?" (2001: 59). Advertisers also focus on the presumed strategic financial and social orientation of middle-class men by emphasising the importance of their 'time horizons', 'risk tolerance', 'investment objectives' and 'unique financial goals' (2001: 59). But advertisers of retirement plans do not just pander to the middle-class men's sense of family and financial responsibility; a strong play is also made about their potential to enjoy themselves once they have finally given up work. As Ekerdt and Clark argue:

> When it is shown [in advertisements], the leisure of retirement is active and healthy, so depicted by models fishing, surfing, water skiing, on a swing, on a bike, as volunteer carpenters, chasing penguins, or leaping in the air. Ad texts said that retirees have 'fun,' 'fuller, more active lives,' and 'lust for life.' They 'play' during 'a second childhood,' being 'whatever your cholesterol-free, fully aerobicized, ever-loving heart desires'. (2001: 62)

In some advertisements, men were explicitly informed, 'now it's your turn' for leisure, having been a responsible husband and parent for the whole of their adult life. As one man was reputed to have stated in one advertisement, 'I've spent 40 years building up a nest egg, 30 years paying off a mortgage, 20 years saving for college. I've WORRIED enough. Now I want to LIVE' (2001: 62). As was revealed in Chapters 4–6, married men with families do not generally deny themselves leisure opportunities (see also Deem, 1985; Green, Hebron and Woodward 1990) but, by playing on the ideology of the breadwinner's presumed magnanimity in their disposal of their incomes to meet the needs of others, advertising pitches such as these help to justify investing in their own future. That said, advertisements of this kind also reinforce commonly held ideas about the breadwinner's responsibility to plan for the family's financial security in the future, and not just be a provider in the immediate term.

Many couples approach retirement optimistically as an opportunity to change their lives. One such strategy, especially among older married couples, is moving home. Often this process of moving home reflects a scaling down of the space requirements of home as grown-up children have established themselves on a fully independent footing. The absence of children is often framed in a positive light, as J. Mason argues:

> Ageing and retirement, and the reconstitution of the membership of the home, contributed to an emerging ideal image of the home: it was to be about relaxation, leisure, or at least non-work. It was to be secure, safe, comfortable and 'ours', and to provide an environment conducive to a gentle process of ageing. (1989: 116)

Many couples plan retirement moves over longer distances (Longino, Perzynski and Stoller, 2002). Among wealthier households this is sometimes referred to by sociologists as 'amenity migration' (Walters, 2002b). Amenity migration means that people move to a new area in search of a better climate and an environment that is more geared up for leisure activities. It is now becoming more common for British people to move abroad for their retirement (Karn, 1977; King, Warnes and Allen, 2000), while in America the practice of moving long distances to a more pleasant climate to live a holiday-style existence became well established early on in the last century. Indeed, there is a wide range of self-help books published in America on successfully managing moves in retirement (Goodwin, 1999; Howells, 1999; Savageau, 1999; for a useful review of the academic literature see Walters, 2002a). In recognition of the demand for retirement migration in the USA, there are several business corporations that build retirement communities for the 'younger' old. These organisations place strong emphasis on the opportunity to live energetic and healthy lives, and tend to play down discussion of ill-health and ageing. The following quotation is drawn from the website of Sun City retirement communities.

> Welcome to Sun City Communities® by Del Webb,™ where active adults age 55 or better live the life of their dreams... You'll learn that we aren't your typical retirement community, and that the active adult lifestyle we offer is second to none. It's no wonder, then, that when looking for active senior housing, Sun City is universally regarded as the premier destination... At Del Webb, we understand that you've worked hard, played equally hard, and achieved many goals along the way. Now your time is your own. We welcome you to discover dream homes and locations, amenities second to none, and interesting people just like you. Let this be your first step toward living the lifestyle of your dreams. (http://www.delwebb.com/activeadult/index.shtml: 2002)

The marketing material presented on the Sun City website emphasises the opportunities for meeting people, staying fit and healthy in a fitness centre, being involved in clubs, meeting at a café or restaurant, or using garden terraces outside the larger houses and apartments. Sun City sites are spacious and the architecture opulent and expansive, which produces a strong impression of a status-giving and success-driven move rather than a retreat into old age, ill-health and dependance. As Laws has argued, developments such as these are 'geared to a very particular embodied identity' (1997: 97) which meet the needs of an affluent ageing population. This represents a transformation over the last three or more decades where traditional images of ageing have been challenged and life-styles produced to resist a premature decline into 'old age' (see Featherstone and Hepworth, 1995). Whether or not such positive images of ageing are translated into experience is the subject of the next section.

The impact of retirement on domestic practices

While retirement is viewed more positively than in the past, there is some evidence to suggest that many men approach this life transition with some trepidation. This is especially likely to be true of men who have invested so much energy in their work that other avenues of activity (such as friendships, leisure, education or voluntary work) have been neglected. Men who have enjoyed very high incomes and high status jobs can be vulnerable to worries about what their lives will be like without work. Sonnenfeld's (1988) study of retired chief executive officers (CEOs) in the USA demonstrates why men can be uneasy about their loss of privilege and power. As Irving Shapiro, former CEO of DuPont, suggested:

> All the perks of office, not the material perks but all the psychological perks of office that you don't realise you have really takes hold of you, become a very important part of your mind-set, and the day they're gone, you recognise that you've got to learn to live in a different way. (1988: 173)

These men's expectations and experiences are, of course, untypical as they had many opportunities for new avenues of work or influence after retirement. David Rockefeller, former CEO of Chase National Bank, for example, was involved with a wide range of organisations including the New York City Partnership, the American Society, and Rockefeller University.

For my own part, I seem to continue to be as busy as ever... Perhaps I have been more fortunate than some others in having these opportunities, but my retirement has been a very rich and rewarding experience. Certainly, any fears of sitting at an empty desk waiting for only the phone to ring have proved unfounded. (1988: 199)

Even though new opportunities came their way, former bosses of large corporations still felt uneasy about their loss of social status. This is a common response amongst life-long career men from across the spectrum of occupations, because work and conceptions of masculinity are so closely entwined. As Gradman argues, adaptation to retirement is difficult because:

Work supports a sense of masculinity both overtly and in ways that are not acknowledged consciously. Throughout adulthood, men work to obtain extrinsic (monetary and social) and intrinsic (self-expression and fulfilment) rewards. Work supports a man's perception of his status, ability and worthiness... Work creates multiple opportunities for a man to see himself as powerful, self-reliant, and competent. In general, work enables a man to meet the social norms for masculine attitudes and behavior. (1994: 105)

The transition from a work oriented sense of identity to that of retired man, as many commentators have suggested, can produce feelings of emasculation. In extreme cases, some men appear to overcompensate for their loss of status by claiming to be working even harder than they were when in employment. As Solomon and Szwabo have commented:

Some men maladaptively respond by becoming increasingly socially withdrawn so that others do not see them in an 'unsuccessful' mode. Others try to maintain the external accoutrements of their past success, even as their domestic situation deteriorates. One of our patients, a 78 year old retired business executive, suffered a series of severe financial setbacks. Although he continued to belong to exclusive clubs, remain active in community affairs, dress impeccably by buying new and stylish clothes, and eat at the community's finest dining establishments, his 150 year old mansion was literally falling apart. (1994: 57)

Such was the condition of this man's house that the roof was falling in, rubbish was strewn everywhere, and he could not afford to pay for personal and nursing care for his wife who suffered from dementia. As Solomon and Szwabo comment, 'He bought new clothes (which he could not afford) rather than do any laundry. Both he and his wife began to drink heavily. Only the intervention of an astute attorney saved him from bankruptcy' (1994: 57). It is clear, in this case, that this man simply could not adapt to his circumstances. Solomon and Szwabo argue that in extreme cases men can enter a private world of 'existential hollowness' (1994: 58) where they are unable to establish leisure interests or gain any sense of inner satisfaction as all their efforts are tirelessly focused on achievement.

It would be a mistake to assume that all men find adaptation to their new retired status a serious psychological problem, but it should be recognised that, for married men in particular, their retirement impacts on domestic practices for the simple reason that they are at home more of the time. This in turn requires a renegoti-ation of the way that the routines of domestic work and leisure are configured. Responsibility for organising domestic practices, as was argued in Chapter 6, generally gives women more authority in this domain over the setting of standards, the establishment of routines and the right to monitor and comment on the contribution of the husband to domestic tasks. As Gradman points out, 'A man's entry into his wife's domain, and loss of his own, can result in uncertainty about appropriate masculine behaviour. Many married men express concern that they will be criticized by their wives once they can be observed more closely' (1994: 106).

Cliff's (1993) study of recently retired men in Britain graphically illustrates the kind of problems men and women can experience. His respondents routinely used the phrase 'getting under their wife's feet' to account for their invasion of their wife's space and for inter-rupting her routines. One couple expressed their situation as follows.

> *Husband*: It's a big change for your wife. More for her than me, that's the biggest area. It was a joint decision [to retire early] but it was the most significant change in our marriage since having children. She's had to change. She could please her-self during the day. Now if she wants to go for a coffee with her friends I don't restrict her. You've got to live your own lives to some extent. The first few months took a bit of adjustment.

> *Wife*: He got under my feet at first. He had to be retrained in doing things and accept that I wasn't going to just drop all my activities because he was at home. There has to be a lot of give and take on both sides. (in Cliff, 1993: 36)

While this couple had started to come to terms with their changed situation, it is clear that conflict had arisen over issues of who con-trolled aspects of domestic practices. While the woman clearly resisted change to her routine and demanded that her husband fit-ted into doing things her way by 'retraining' him, the man clearly felt that he had some control over her leisure activities. By stating that 'I don't restrict her', he clearly recognises that he could do so if he chose to. Other couples proved themselves to be less adept at changing their attitudes after retirement, as this couple's comments clearly illustrate.

> *Husband*: My wife always leaves important decisions to me but I think that she feels that ... well, that I obviously show discontent. She feels I should have stayed with the company. She says that I was happiest there. Our relationship has changed. My discontent rubs off on her. She's discontented. We've had quite a few words to be quite honest. It's caused an awful lot of problems.

> *Wife*: I suppose I do blame him really. He was very happy with the chemical company and he's been that upset and bad tempered since. He's come to terms with it more these last six months but there's no doubt it's affected us. We've definitely rowed more and we've had nastier rows. (in Cliff, 1993: 38)

Cliff argues that the level of involvement men had in domestic work had an impact on the ease of adaptation to men's retirement. Men who had low involvement prior to retirement clearly had more difficulty in adapting to retirement than men with high involvement in domestic life. But many men also changed their pattern of involvement in domestic practices after retirement which could be related to issues such as their wife continuing to work or their wife's illness. Often when men did become more involved, they were aware that their role was subordinate to their wife's. As one man stated:

> I've increased my share in housework. We didn't exactly draw up a contract but it was part of the agreement that if I took early retirement I would become more involved. It was apparent that burdens ought to be shared more equally. Mind you I'm very definitely second fiddle. As far as I'm concerned she's the boss and I'm the helper. But the garden's a different issue. I sort of pushed her nose out there but not to the point of fisticuffs. (in Cliff, 1993: 40)

A number of studies on marital quality after retirement suggest that men's increased or full-time presence in the home produces a higher degree of anxiety and dissatisfaction (Kulik, 2002). This is especially pronounced in couples where women continue to work (Moen, Kim and Hofmeister, 2001), although relatively few women remain in full-time paid employment beyond their husband's retirement. This can partly be explained by different statutory retirement ages for women and men in some countries, but a more convincing explanation is that traditional ideas about the male breadwinner role means that women's employment is usually regarded as secondary to their husband's. Consequently, a married woman generally accommodates to her husband's retirement in much the same way as her pattern of employment was shaped by his career and her care for their children (J. Mason, 1989; Zimmerman *et al.*, 2000). But this process of accommodation does not, as this section has revealed, necessarily stretch as far as to yield their control over domestic practices.

Anxieties about husbands retiring often emerge before retirement because, as Dorfman (1992) argues, retirement can 'open up previously unresolved power conflicts between couples' (cited by Hilbourne, 1999: 167). One British study of 309 men and 300 women following pre-retirement classes supports the view that both men and women were concerned about the potentially unsettling impact of retirement on their domestic lives and their personal relationships. The study demonstrates that highly career focused male executives or senior managers were accustomed to working for more than 60 hours a week, they often worked at home in the evenings and weekends and they regularly travelled on business. Their wives generally had lower levels of commitment to and success within careers, or else were full-time homemakers. The concerns of these soon-to-retire career men and their partners differed quite markedly, however. The men tended to worry mainly about bereavement, illness and loneliness, while wives were more concerned about the invasion of their space. Both men and women had ambivalent feelings, however, as Hilbourne reports:

> Women hope that they and their husbands might 'grow closer together' and have a 'different kind of marriage'. Also, unlike the men, they looked for an improvement in the emotional and sexual side of their relationship. They expected to 'find a friend and confidante in their husband', to 'rediscover and maintain romance', to 'have a little more intimacy, tenderness and attention', and to 'have a good sex life – afternoon fun'. (1999: 174)

These positive feelings were countered by worries about getting on each other's nerves, boredom, irritating habits, or taking each other for granted. Women also emphasised worries about communication, sharing problems and honestly divulging deeper feelings, suggesting that they had not previously had much opportunity to do so due to their husband's career demands.

In sum, this section has demonstrated that retirement can bring to the fore old tensions and introduce new ones; as Hilbourne notes: 'Tension between the opportunity for greater companionship and more shared time on the one hand, and the threat to personal space and independence on the other, was much in evidence' (1999: 175).

When women have invested a great deal of time and emotional energy in the establishment, organisation and running of the home, the arrival of a retired husband on the scene can disrupt patterns of domestic work, leisure and use of space. Based on her study of women and men in Britain where the male had recently retired, J. Mason comments:

> Many of them were ambivalent about retiring husbands' apparent encroachment into their home. Sometimes their concern was simply about husbands 'being there' at new times, or being in parts of the house previously the wife's domain. Men's help with the housework, where forthcoming, was often perceived by wives (and possibly intended by husbands) as an attempt to take over their domestic routines and organisation. (1989: 121; see also J. Mason, 1987, 1988)

Keith's (1994) study of a sample of 448 American men and 352 women aged over 65, which was drawn from the National Survey of Families and Households, for example, demonstrates that while women emphasised the importance of sharing their lives more closely in retirement, they were less enthusiastic about an egalitarian approach to housework. Indeed, men's involvement reduced their satisfaction with their relationship with their husbands. Men, on the other hand, seemed to be more satisfied with their marriage after retirement. This surprised the researcher because 'It had been anticipated that men in marital relationships characterised by disagreement and inequity would assess the household experiences more negatively, but they did not' (1994: 151). Men generally express more satisfaction in marriage than women, as has already been argued in Chapters 3–6, because they gain more tangible benefits in terms of the care they receive and the support and service wives provide in the home. The above analysis seems to suggest that this pattern is sustained into and beyond retirement.

Gender and home in later life

This chapter has revealed that planning for retirement and retirement itself is a gendered process. By concentrating upon the experiences of older men and women who have considerable control over the management of their lives, the chapter has sought to counter younger people's tendency to stereotype older people as dependent upon others. In this concluding section, the analysis will be pushed one step further by examining how the ageing process can result in

a loss of independence. In so doing, it is not my aim to provide a
general overview of the sociological literature on ageing and dependence. Instead, I intend to focus specifically on the way that the domestic
practices of older people become constrained by the expectations
and strictures of other family members or professionals, and to
indicate how gender interacts with this process.

Arber and Ginn's (1992) research reveals that ageing has a strong
impact on people's ability to carry out a range of domestic tasks. In
so doing, they demonstrate that gender becomes a less important
factor in defining who has difficulty in undertaking particular tasks
as women and men grow older. They find, for example, that 32 per cent
of men over 75 years have problems with laundry work compared
with only 14 per cent of women. This distinction is accounted for on
the basis that women are more experienced in undertaking such
tasks. The gender gap narrows substantially with age, however.
Amongst the under 75s, only 1.5 per cent of women (compared with
8.6 per cent of men) had difficulty cooking a main meal but, in the
case of the over 75s, these figures were 10 per cent for women and
13 per cent for men (Arber and Ginn, 1992: 173).

When people become less dextrous or less confident in undertaking
personal or domestic tasks, a common strategy is to seek additional
help from professionals or family members so that they can remain
in their own home. Others take a different approach by entering
sheltered accommodation which provides additional security and
facility for older people in a managed environment. Levels of support
in sheltered accommodation can differ significantly. Some centres
provide general management of security, building and garden maintenance only, while others provide leisure facilities, catering and
medical support in a health care centre (Silverstein and Zablotsky,
1996; Krout *et al.*, 2002). Sheltered accommodation is an attractive
option for many older people because they can maintain a higher
degree of independence than living in a care home or remaining in
their original home which has become unmanageable. While sheltered accommodation does provide more freedom and independence than in a care home, there exist subtle constraints on older
people's behaviour. For example, the design of sheltered accommodation tends to reflect professional discourse on older people's
needs in terms of space, facility and leisure. In England there are
around 465,000 sheltered homes, usually occupied by poorer older
people who do not have the option of paying for help in their own
homes or the cost of moving to more suitable private accommodation.

About 10 per cent of sheltered houses and apartments are privately owned, around 300,000 are owned by local authorities and 120,000 by housing associations (Balchin, 1995: 264). The designers of sheltered housing schemes such as these tend to work within tight budgetary constraints, and so a premium is placed on reducing space. This means that residents must make difficult choices on what furniture they can take with them. Fairhurst's study of sheltered housing in Manchester shows that reduced space distressed some residents. As one older woman stated:

> [sheltered housing] might be all right for one but for a couple, I mean they're so inadequate. What are you going to do with all your things? The things I've got over the years. They're not just material possessions. They're memories... I've got things [my sister] bought me, what the children have bought over the years. My collection of Toby jugs which has taken me years. What am I going to do with those things? Things I've brought back from holiday as souvenirs. I can't throw memories away. (in Fairhurst, 1999: 106)

The artefacts people surround themselves with to build up an image of home can be crucial for all generations to present a sense of selfhood to significant others (Czikszentmihalyi and Rochberg-Halten, 1981; Chapman and Hockey, 1999). Scaling down treasured possessions can be frustrating and upsetting for many people, but not all older people feel this way. As one woman in Fairhurst's study commented: 'Some things I've had for donkey's years... I want everything away, everything new and I'm going to have it if it kills me. I just want the remaining time we've got to have a bit of comfort which we've never had' (1999: 106). Limited space could, however, restrict social life because residents had too little room to cook and serve a meal for visiting friends and family, or put them up for the night. Often the only option was to socialise in open communal lounges which restricted privacy.

Facing infirmity without professional or family care leads many older people to enter residential care homes. In Britain, about 5 per cent of the population aged over 65 live in such institutions, 9.7 per cent of the over 75s and 23.7 of the over 85s (Hockey, 1999; see also Gurney and Means, 1993; Dupuis and Thorns, 1996). Such homes are organised to manage the process of bodily deterioration. As Hockey points out:

> There are extensive laundry facilities and removable carpet tiles in anticipation of double incontinence. There are also spaces specifically dedicated to illness and death, the 'sickbay' and the 'morgue'. However, just as the exclusion of very

elderly family members from the domestic home undermines the ideal of home as
sanctuary, so the accommodation of deterioration within the residential 'home'
must be carried out discretely, if the premises are to be viewed as a living space
rather than a charnel house. (Hockey, 1999: 110)

While efforts are made to provide a homely atmosphere, residents'
behaviour tends to be supervised closely, especially when older
people choose to behave in 'inappropriate' ways. Definitions of inap-
propriateness are often determined with reference to stereotypical
images of old age. As Hepworth argues, images of ageing are produced by 'a narrative process [which] provides us with a wide range
of spurious links between the variable biological changes which take
place as the body ages internally and externally and the result is a
series of stereotypical images of what it means to be an old person'
(1999a: 142).

Stereotypical images of 'normal' adulthood tend to stigmatise
sexual or newly established loving relationships amongst older
people because it is wrongly assumed that sex is something that only
younger people do (Marsiglio and Donnelly, 1991; Marsiglio and
Greer, 1994). Such relationships are often frowned upon and, as
a consequence, as Higgins points out, 'the chances of [maintaining]
any relatively "normal" relationships between the sexes, especially
of a physical nature, are extremely remote' (1989: 166; see also
Clough, 1981; Wilkin and Hughes, 1987; Willcocks, Peace and
Kellaher, 1987). Anecdotal evidence suggests that younger people's
negative attitudes to older men and women establishing sexual and
loving relationships is also shaped by their fear of losing an expected
inheritance. And furthermore, younger people are often in a powerful
enough situation to impose behavioural norms on elderly parents
and relatives with the support of the caring and medical professions.
In institutional care older women and men are less able to signify
a sense of personal identity and ownership of space; instead, as
Higgins puts it, they are portrayed as 'a homogeneous group of "old
people" lacking personal identity or individuality' (1989: 169). Many
researchers continue to neglect the issue of self-identity and self-
worth amongst older men and women. Instead, the research agenda
has been driven by the notion that older people are a 'problem'
for the state in terms of the costs of caring, or for families (and
younger women in particular) who carry the 'burden' of caring (see
Elliot, 1996).

By emphasising the 'burden' older people are presumed to
impose on society and on younger relatives or children, implicit

assumptions are often made about the isolation and loneliness of those older people who live alone (Featherstone and Wernick, 1995; Gannon, 1999). Knipscheer *et al.* (1995) found that 40 per cent of the population in the European Union believe that older people are lonely, and yet only 12 per cent of people over 65 consider themselves to be so. Often it is also assumed that childless older people are more isolated but, in reality, many older people in this situation compensate by developing better sibling relationships and non-kin networks. Knipscheer *et al.*'s study of 4,500 older people in Holland shows that men who 'never married' had the smallest social friendship networks, but on average these men still had 7.8 contacts. Arber and Ginn (1992: 167) reveal that only 11 per cent of widows under 75 never visited friends or relatives compared with 17 per cent of men. This may be partly due to women's greater propensity to gain friendships in the neighbourhood and maintain kin-networks, while men's friendships are often employment related or are associated primarily with non-domestic leisure pursuits such as pubs, sporting activities, hobbies and so on (for more general discussion of friendship, see Oliker, 1989; Adams and Bliesner, 1992; Nardi, 1992; Adams, 1994; Allan, 1996).

For both men and women, however, the ageing process leads to a general reduction in non-domestic (own home, kin/friend's home) leisure activity (for international comparisons on the daily life of older people see Altergott, 1988). Jerome and Wenger's (1999) longitudinal study of older people in Wales suggests that isolation is not just a result of friends or family dying or due to a move to residential care, but expectations about friendship may change:

> a question remains about the nature of the apparent disengagement of some very old people, those who neither have real friends nor want them. Perhaps friendship needs change at the end of life, with an emotional distancing which reflects a reduced need for intimacy. An adult daughter or sister, acting as a confidante, provides emotional security, and friendship activities are not missed. Changing patterns of confiding raise the possibility that this is indeed a developmental stage rather than a product of necessity. (1999: 674)

While it is important to recognise that many older people eventually live in care homes, the majority do not. A more common experience is for older couples to care for each other at home, or indeed to care for relatives in another household.

Until quite recently, it was generally assumed in the sociological literature that older women provided most of the care in such households. This assumption is explicable given that women are more practised in housework and childcaring than men in their middle years, and that women in general are much more likely to survive their husbands. Arber and Gilbert's (1989) analysis of men's caring in later life indicates that this perspective is mistaken. Based on a sample of over 4,000 older people drawn from the British General Household Survey, Arber and Gilbert demonstrated that about one-third of co-resident carers were men. They explained this pattern of caring with reference to the life histories of these men.

> Three-quarters of the men are caring for spouses with whom they have probably lived most of their lives. Love may be the major motivating factor . . . the majority of other male-carers are unmarried men caring for an elderly parent and are most likely never to have moved out of the parental home since they were children or to have returned following a divorce. In all these households, there is likely to be a strong bond between the carer and the cared for. (1989: 113–14)

This situation is mirrored for married women carers looking after their husbands, but women who care for elderly parents are much less likely to have lived with them during their adult lives. Instead, older parents come to live in these married women's homes. This represents a more clear cut case of women bowing to ideological expectations about kinship obligations (Finch and Groves, 1983; Arber and Ginn, 1992). In other words, as Arber and Gilbert put it, 'The responsibility for caring is more likely to be the result of a conscious decision than the result of "drifting into care"' (1989: 114). Arber and Gilbert conclude from their analysis that gender is not the key factor in determining who cares for older people, but the kind of household that they live in.

> Once one has controlled for the level of disability, the major source of variation in the amount of support services received by elderly infirm men and women seems to be not the gender of the recipients or the gender of the carer, but the kind of household in which they live, and, in particular, whether there are others in the household who could take on the burden of caring. Thus infirm elderly people living alone get much more support from formal services than those living with others. Elderly people living with their elderly spouse or with other elderly people get more support from formal services than those in households in which there are younger unmarried members. In all these households, the amount of support does not depend much on the gender of the carer. (1989: 116)

This quotation seems to suggest that gender is not important, but in reality the contrary is the case: gender is important here because their analysis shows that men do contribute so much towards caring.

Gender is not only an issue when one sex does more than the other of a particular household practice.

More recent studies also indicate that men play a very significant role in caring for someone in their own household or someone in another household. As Table 10.3 demonstrates, in Britain women still do more caring for relatives or spouses than men do, but the gap has narrowed over the last ten years. Glaser and Grundy (2002) also found that unmarried men play a significant role in caring for co-residents or people in other households. Around 11 per cent of married and unmarried men provide care in another house compared with about 16 per cent of married or unmarried women. Men's significant participation in caring seems to be contradictory if women generally live longer than men. The reason for this anomaly, of course, is that it is very common for married men to provide much of the care for their wives for many years, but that these same men are survived by their wives, whose care is then undertaken by younger family members, siblings or by professionals.

In sum, this chapter has demonstrated, as others have done throughout this book, that when we look beneath the surface of stereotypes about domestic practices, it becomes apparent that there is much more complexity in the way that gender impacts than

Table 10.3   *Gender and caring amongst older people in Britain 1985–95 (percentages)*

| | Caring for someone in same household | | Caring for someone in another household | |
	1985	1995	1985	1995
Men				
55–9	5	6	10	12
60–4	5	7	10	13
65–9	6	8	9	10
All	6	7	9	12
Women				
55–9	7	7	16	16
60–4	9	7	14	17
65–9	7	6	12	12
All	7	7	14	15

Source: *General Household Survey*, adapted from Glaser and Grundy (2002: 331), Table 1.

may be expected. As the above analysis demonstrates, it is not appropriate automatically to assume that gender roles are played out according to a prescribed script.

Socialisation and gendered domestic practices

Socialisation helps women and men to understand the social world in the sense that values have been internalised about appropriate social behaviour. But, as this chapter has shown, the social and personal circumstances that affect individual lives change over time which can challenge or even make redundant many of those socialised rules and roles. In the concluding section of this chapter, I want to draw upon some of the analytical insights produced by research on old age and turn attention to the other end of the life cycle: childhood. The purpose of this exercise is to highlight the point that gendered socialisation does affect the way that people construct ideas about what is possible and what is not, but at the same time to recognise that social change gets in the way of achieving the objectives for successful adult life that were laid down in childhood.

As this chapter has shown, children tend to control their parents' lives to some extent when they reach deep old age while, at the other end of the age spectrum, parents control the boundaries of infants' and childrens' lives. Sociologists have not yet devoted much research energy into the agency of children in the domestic sphere: that is, their demands in terms of the use of space and their impact on the way that homes are organised and priorities set. This betrays a commonly held adult view that children are *socialised* by parents in a one-way process, even if this does not fit with their own experience of the demanding relationship that children establish with their parents from birth. Up until the 1970s sociologists generally adopted this perspective. Writers who were persuaded by functionalist social theory, in particular, tended to emphasise the importance of the nuclear family in establishing clear adult roles for children.

Girls, it was presumed, through play, through the chores they did, and through formal schooling would learn the right kind of attitudes and skills to perform their adult role of homemaker and mother. Boys, by the same token, were aimed squarely at the role of breadwinner by toning down their emotionality and familial intimacy so that they would have what were presumed to be the right kinds of skills for work. Under this functionalist depiction of the nuclear family, as was shown in Chapters 3 and 4, mothers and fathers were also expected to adopt prescribed gendered roles of homemaker and breadwinner to ensure that their children grew up in the company of role model parents (the subtleties of these processes have been explored extensively in the sociological literature: see Coltrane, 1998: 107–32 for a useful review). The sociological research agenda has yet fully to catch up with events. For example, while there has been much research on gendered play patterns, there remains an implicit assumption of gender conformist outcomes in adult life. Corsaro (1997) has shown, for example, that there is currently little research on parent–child interaction in home or in public, and no real analysis of how toys are used, adapted and symbolically valued. Indeed, Corsaro argues that much of the sociological research on gendered play assumes too readily that playing with specific toys leads to particular outcomes. How true this is remains fully to be explored.

Since there are some serious problems with the notion that child socialisation is something that adults can successfully achieve it is hard to predict how gendered domestic practices will develop in future. Everyone reading this book will be able to identify occasions when, as children, they overtly or secretly undermined their parents' authority; or as adults perhaps they are still openly fighting, or privately deceiving their parents in order to act 'out of role'. Such intergenerational conflicts occur because parents often construct quite rigid rules on what it is to be a successful adult man or woman, while they see childhood as a process of learning these roles.

Qvortrup (1994) has drawn a useful distinction between the conceptualisation of an adult as a 'human being' and the child as a 'human becoming'. Adulthood, or human being, for Qvortrup, represents the achievement of completeness and independence, in opposition to childhood or human becoming which is conceptualised as incompleteness and dependence. In the 1950s doctors, midwives, teachers, politicians, priests, child psychologists and many other professionals who positioned themselves as experts on child rearing tended to sing from the same songsheet about the practice of social-isation. Arguably, such commonality in advice was more authorita-tive then because women's and men's adult roles seemed to be more predictable than they are now. As Lee has argued:

> Against this backdrop of a stable, predictable adulthood, one's early life could be understood as a period in which one built toward that stability, secure in the

assumption that it would arrive. Childhood, then, could be viewed as a journey towards a clear and *knowable* destination. But as we enter the twenty-first century, the experience of adult life is a lot less stable than it used to be. With regard to being 'grown up', we have entered an age of uncertainty, an age in which adult life is newly unpredictable and, in which whatever stabilities we manage to produce cannot be expected to last our whole lives. (2001: 8: original emphasis)

Whereas in the 1950s adult life was relatively predictable, as was shown in Chapters 4 and 5, there are now many uncertainties that adults of all ages face. In the 1950s and 1960s, girls and boys may well have been brought up expecting to conform to conventional breadwinner and homemaker roles in a life-long marriage, but their own lives did not necessarily follow this path.

The salience of theories of parental socialisation should also be questioned because emerging evidence suggests that children have much more agency than previously expected. As James and Prout have argued: 'Children are and must be seen as active in the construction and determination of their own local lives, the lives of those around them and of the societies in which they live' (1997: 8, in Lee, 2001: 47). This is a very modern way of looking at children's lives. It was not until the nineteenth century that childhood itself was fully recognised as a life transition; instead, as was shown in Chapter 2, children were thought of as diminutive adults (see Ariès, 1979; Pollock, 1983; James and Prout, 1990). This is not to argue that children's agency has just been discovered; on the contrary, much of the emphasis on taming children in the past was premised upon the assumption that they would run riot if given a free hand. But the positive attribution of agency to children is a more recent phenomenon. As Lystad (1984) shows, for example, from a study of children's story books published in America between 1700 and 1980, there has been a progressive shift away from the notion of children as hard-working, truthful, dutiful and obedient, to social actors who can engage in self-expression, have greater freedom of choice and more interest in egalitarian personal relationships and in society itself.

Children, like older people, are concerned about the issue of independence. In the case of children, demanding more independence raises parental fears about the perceived dangers of the outside world. As Valentine (1999) argues, parents make judgements about how far to strengthen or weaken spatial boundaries depending on their assessment of children's 'competence' and 'performance' in key social tasks. Competence is defined, as we have already seen, in relation to commonly accepted notions of adult life as a completed state of development, and so adults make judgements on how well children can master the skills required to survive in the outside world. Performance, on the other hand, is defined in sociological terms in relation to the ability of children to play the right role. Following Butler's (1990) study, *Gender Trouble*, Valentine argues that age, like gender, is understood in a similar way because it is 'naturalized through repetition' (1999: 138). As she argues: 'Rather than children's spatial boundaries being rigidly fixed by adults according to a child's biological age, "age" appears to be a performative identity, which is highly contested within households and which is sometimes defined in contradictory ways' (1999: 140).

Any parent and child will have experienced these contradictions as the child or parent insists at one moment that they 'are old enough' to do one thing, but 'too young' to do something else. Older people, as this chapter shows, sometimes use 'performative strategies' to persuade their children that they (the parents) cannot live alone and should live with their children; or, conversely, that they are capable enough 'even at their age' to maintain their independence living alone. Making the performance convincing can depend crucially on the gendered authenticity of the behaviour. Older men may find it harder to persuade their children that they can cope if they have never managed the household affairs and domestic duties themselves, or worse still it is assumed that they cannot because they are men. Similarly, as Valentine argues, girls may be able to perform 'maturity' more convincingly than boys. In her study of children's negotiation of children's boundaries, one mother suggested:

> My son's a bit dizzy [laughter]. He is, he's sometimes not, sometimes he's on another planet, you know, he, he, he's not very responsible at all really, he's [pause] I mean you do say to him 'Don't get into strangers' cars or whatever' but I could see him doing it, I could. She's more sensible. She's quite a dominant person . . . she can take care of herself [laughter]. (1999: 142)

This distinction between boys as 'dizzy' and girls as 'sensible' that is commonly used by parents can reinforce gendered assumptions about what boys and girls can or cannot do. Such meanings change over time. Twenty years ago, girls' advanced maturity was used to explain why they became interested in relationships at an earlier age than boys and did badly at school in some subjects as a consequence, whereas now girls' propensity to outperform boys at school is often explained in the *same* terms.

Just as it is hard to generalise about adult experiences of home, the experiences of children and home are clearly also very varied. The experiences of children in gay and lesbian households, the children of divorcees, children who live in two 'shared care' households, children who are constrained to take paid work, and so on, cannot directly be compared with children who live in conventional two-parent households. Indeed, even if children do live in such households, their experiences are shaped by a plethora of factors such as their parents' occupations, social class background, education, ethnicity, religion and so on. While we must wait for researchers to fill these gaps in our knowledge, the indications are that parents can at best only be partially successful in socialising children into becoming like themselves.

Just because socialisation is an incomplete process and has unpredictable outcomes, we should not abandon the concept completely. Even if society has changed, people still draw upon the social expectations that were instilled into them when they were young. What is important, however, is to recognise that women and men draw upon socialised gendered expectations in an active way to define, control, negotiate or avoid domestic practices. When negotiating who should do what, then, it can be rather like an exchange of incompetences, where women and men tell each other that they are 'useless' at some tasks while on other occasions they perform their own brand of 'uselessness' to avoid something else. The question is, are these gender scripts changing sufficiently to impact upon the experience of domestic life in future? This will be the issue that the concluding chapter of this book will address.

11

Conclusion: Changing Domestic Practices

As this book has demonstrated, domestic practices have been subject to dramatic transformation over the last hundred years. Possibly the most important of these changes is the slow and as yet incomplete shift from a predominantly middle-class model of domestic life, where men as breadwinners and women as homemakers expected to occupy relatively separate spheres of influence in adult life, to the present where gendered domestic practices have become much more fluid, varied and negotiable. Over the last 30 years, sociologists have tended to adopt a negative outlook on domestic life. This position arose from the feminist challenge to the relatively positive functionalist appraisal of the nuclear family that predominated up until the mid-1960s. Feminists came to regard the domestic arena as a principal site of women's oppression and argued that women's emancipation could only be achieved, amongst other things, by gaining economic independence from men through paid employment. Equality of opportunity in the labour market has not yet been achieved, but much progress has also been made. While there remain barriers to women's success, women's lives have been transformed in the sense that it is no longer necessary to marry in order to gain economic security in life and, for women who do marry, many have much more say in the way that their personal priorities are set and objectives achieved. Women may have also recognised, through their experiences in the labour market, that the advantages paid work brings in terms of social and economic independence can be offset by the demanding nature of many jobs, both physically and emotionally. The shift from the homemaker/breadwinner household has not been achieved without other costs. For many years, women were expected to shoulder a double burden of work and homemaking, although the evidence suggests that this situation is changing now that men do about one-third of the housework (and, in a small but growing minority of households, they do more housework than women).

Transformations in domestic practices reflect women's raised ambitions in the world of work, but also occur in response to significant changes in men's attitudes towards home and work. Many married and cohabiting men now expect to be more involved in the upbringing of their children than was the case in the past. Furthermore, they are showing signs of becoming much more interested in the project of domestic life through greater engagement in both routine and also in more creative aspects of home life. One of the reasons for this shift in interest may be the progressive breakdown of breadwinner ideology which demanded that men invested most of their emotional and physical energy in life-long careers supporting their family. Clearly, many men no longer expect to have life-long careers in a single profession or industry because the labour market has changed in character. It is now commonplace for men to change career direction, often involuntarily when they are made redundant, but also of their own volition when they see an opportunity to change their lives. Furthermore, the break down of the life-long career has created a tension between the once inseparable relationship between work and masculinity. Conceptions of masculinity are now more fluid. Men do not just adopt a model of manliness which is learned at work, but choose from a range of masculinities.

Conventional homemaker and breadwinner identities may have been challenged but, as this book has shown, cultural notions of masculinity and femininity run deep. Traditional ideas about marriage, for example, continue to produce partnerships where men are older, earn more money and by definition have more say over many aspects of domestic life. And for couples who want to have children, conventional nuclear family forms remain a convenient option for many because the traditional gender script helps women and men to decide who should do what. The outcome for women can be a struggle to establish their career on the same terms as their husband or partner but, by the same token, men find that they cannot be as centrally involved in caring for children or decision-making about patterns of parenting and schooling. The difference, perhaps, amongst younger couples is that there is more scope to choose this life-style rather than to have it forced upon them by the weight of social and family expectations.

As younger couples are more likely to choose marriage from a range of options than in the past, it may be the case that expectations about marriage and cohabitation are now much higher than was once the case. In pre-industrial society, it is generally agreed, women and men entered into marriage with a contractual mind-set. The practicalities of security and survival were at the centre of things, not love. In early modern times, it seems to be the case that a companionate view of marriage emerged. In such relationships, emphasis continued to be placed on the idea that women and men should occupy different roles because they had different temperaments and natural abilities; but, at the same time, it was assumed that their companionship was integral to the success of marriage, and that it may also be defined as a loving relationship even if that love was not present at the outset. The problem with conceptions of modern marriage is that it sets a great deal of emphasis on the communion of minds and bodies, but at the same time expects that both husbands and wives should also achieve individual self-fulfilment. As this book has shown, men have been advantaged in this respect for much of the nineteenth and twentieth centuries in the sense that they have been able to take time and resources from the family to enjoy leisure or other self-actualising activities. Women, on the other hand, were expected to find a kind of contentment by supporting their husbands and children while denying their own interests. The shift in emphasis in family ideology has produced much conflict between the sexes. For the last 30 years, sociologists have tended to characterise domestic life as something of a battle ground. Giddens has caricatured this 'crisis' of gender relationships in the following terms:

> Men's anger against women today in some substantial part is a reaction against women's self-assertion in the home, the workplace and elsewhere. Women are angry at men in turn because of the subtle and not so subtle ways in which men deny them material privileges claimed for themselves. Economic poverty for women, emotional poverty for men: is this the state of play in the relation between the sexes? The self-appointed advocates of men and women on both sides would say so, although each is likely to accuse the other of not fully acknowledging the sufferings of the other side. (Giddens, 1992: 149)

Consequently, it is now commonly recognised that the home can be the site of real struggle between men and women which can result in domestic violence and emotional abuse. Research shows that women are much more likely to suffer from such abuse than men (see Dobash and Dobash, 1998; Dobash *et al.*, 2000; Hague and Malos, 1998; Jackson and Oates, 1998), but some men also suffer from violence and emotional abuse in heterosexual relationships (see Mignon, 1998; Dasgupta, 1999; Strauss, 1999), as do women and men in lesbian and gay relationships (see T. Burke, 1998; Jackson, 1998), which suggests that analysis of dysfunctional domestic power relationships cannot be explained by conventional heterosexual gendered power relationships alone.

This book has steered clear of the 'dark side' of domestic life because its principal aim was to explore patterns of negotiation between women and men that more commonly characterise day to day domestic life. In so doing it has shown that a degree of discord is inevitable in couple households. This is because key issues such as the standards of housework, spending priorities, who should do what jobs around the house, who should make the biggest commitment to work (and so on) have to be sorted out through argument and compromise. Gay, lesbian and heterosexual couple households alike, it has been shown, all have to face up to and sort out these problems one way or another if the relationship is to survive.

Compromise does not, of course, mean the same thing as equality. Indeed, it has been demonstrated that couples can bring a range of powerful attributes to the bargaining table, ranging from economic power, socialised skills, physical capabilities and sets of ideas. In heterosexual households in general, it remains the case that men tend to have more economic power than women, while in gay and lesbian households economic inequalities tend to be less pronounced. This is not because gay and lesbian couple relationships are, by definition, more likely to be more equal than heterosexual couples of course, but instead reflects an interest in achieving equality by choosing partners who occupy broadly similar income brackets and commitment to paid work. Heterosexual couples, by contrast, are more likely to build inequalities into their relationship at the outset because they ally themselves, as noted above, to traditional ideas on what constitutes a good marriage partnership.

While discord in households is inevitable, as is the case in any organisation where resources are limited, it is incorrect to assume that such conflict is inevitably and irrevocably gender based. Indeed, as this text has shown, many of the problems that households face can be the result of class inequalities, age discrimination or institutionalised racism. While these factors create tensions in the home, what often happens is that most of this conflict in heterosexual couple households is interpreted as gendered conflict. This is a particular problem for those sociologists who want to explore conflicts in domestic life dispassionately because women and men respondents all too readily roll out standard explanations and complaints about each other. Gendered conflict, in this sense, is habitual rather than inevitable. In Chapter 6, for example, it was clearly demonstrated that when women earned more money, or had higher status jobs than their husbands, serious gender squabbles could emerge if men and women allied themselves to traditional ideas about gender roles. Couples who had less traditional views, by contrast, argued about how on earth they could both get the work done rather than whose job it was to do it in the first place.

Habitual argument along gendered lines is so deeply ingrained in language that it is very difficult to eradicate. There has been significant movement in that direction, however, over the last 30 years. Men rarely insist that they want to keep their wives at home as home-makers, for example, because it is recognised that there are many advantages of having a dual income family in a society that demands a higher level of comfort, facility and space in the home than was the case in the past. This change in mind set is significant in the sense that notions of masculinity have changed: men do not feel that they have to rule the roost economically to feel like men. This is not to say that all men, or even most men, think that they must play an equal part in doing the domestic chores, but instead the majority of men still leave much of the work for their wife or partner to do. The important point, however, is that men gain social capital from the housework they do, which can only encourage more men to participate more fully.

Since different generations, social classes and ethnic groups may change attitudes at different paces, it is very difficult to make gener-alisations about transformations in the way that people think about gendered domestic practices. What we can do, however, is to show that there is a strong likelihood that men's and women's interests in domestic practices may be characterised by a closer proximity of interests than has been the case in the past. Just because women and men *are* now sharing many similar experiences at home, work and leisure, it does not necessarily mean that they want to empathise with each other when arguments arise between them over tasks they *do not want to do*. On the contrary, they are likely to reach out for their gendered dodge-books which contain a long lists of excuses for not doing that work. But when conflicts arise about tasks that they both *do* want to make a significant contribution to, the situation changes. In sociological circles, it is quite radical to suggest that women and men may compete with each other in this way but, in many households, anecdotal evidence suggests that such competition may be quite common. The value of this assertion clearly requires further research. It may be the case, however, that more men are not prepared to defer to their partner when she interrupts the process of him cooking a meal or bathing children, just as men telling women how to do work-a-day DIY jobs can produce adverse reaction.

As women and men become more practised in a range of activities that were formerly divided between the sexes, it has become more common for both partners to recognise that most household tasks have both positive and negative qualities. Table 11.1 lists each of these practices and provides some clues about the relative worth of each in a primitive (but I hope instructive) way which is based on the more closely focused analyses of the preceding chapters. Taking housework first, it seems to be clear that many such tasks are not just integrative and creative, but can also give satisfaction if the person doing it is in the right mood. Furthermore, housework can be experienced positively because it affords influence over the way that home-life is imagined and structured and also gives one power over others through the knowledge gained from undertaking tasks. And yet the opposite can at the same time also be true because the work that is done can seem invisible to other members of the household and, as a consequence, housework can quite literally be experienced as a thankless task. Worse still, it can become a significant source of criticism from other householders when they become the object of nagging for messing up what has just been done. In sum, housework cannot be defined precisely as positive or negative because it can encompass both qualities simultaneously.

The same can be said of all the other domestic practices listed in Table 11.1. Parenting can be enormously fulfilling but also extremely frustrating. Domestic life is full of such paradoxes. Taking leisure collectively as a family can be a source of personal delight when everyone partakes in the activity with generosity and enthusiasm. Of course, such moments of family communion can be quite fleeting because, even when at leisure, there are disputes over time, money and preferred activities. Similarly, leisure can be very tedious or stressed when we feel obliged to 'perform' happiness in an activity that in reality bores us, even if it is a burden we willingly take on to

Table 11.1 *Illustrations of positive and negative aspects of domestic practices*

Domestic practices	Illustration of positive aspects	Illustration of negative aspects
Housework	Opportunities to develop skills, creativity, impose order, gain knowledge about and control over other household members, etc.	Routinisation of repetitive work, doing dirty work, achieving no thanks for work, invisibility of work to other household members, unavoidability of hated tasks.
Parenting	Personal fulfilment, entertainment and opportunity to play, helps to put other pressures into proportion, feelings of love, responsibility and security, etc.	Unable to enjoy former leisure patterns, limited time, pressure on financial resources, negative impact on career, puts pressure on relationship with spouse, etc.
Leisure	Opportunities for relaxation, enjoyment, creativity; to develop skills, explore personal interests, develop and maintain relationships, etc.	Facilitating other household members' leisure, involvement in other members' activities, too close relationship between leisure and housework, etc.
Providing income and wealth	Gain esteem from wider community, gain power over financial decision-making, resources to fund household and family events, opportunities to escape from household work, etc.	Negative impacts of paid employment such as stress, tiredness, boredom, low income, repetitive work, low esteem, others' financial dependence, partner's refusal to contribute to income, wealth.

Table 11.1 (*Continued*)

Domestic practices	Illustration of positive aspects	Illustration of negative aspects
Planning	Satisfaction from shaping household priorities, maintaining order and continuity, gaining/ensuring security, negotiating, etc.	Priorities not being shared by members of the household, insecurities created by household members' failure to comply with agreed priorities, feeling disempowered by other householders' priorities, etc.
Managing money	Successfully managing money, achieving objectives, maintaining security, facilitating plans, etc.	Insecurity created by lack of control over finances, running from crisis to crisis, disagreements about priorities, lack of knowledge about income, sense of failure gained from inability to manage money, etc.
Caring	Maintaining harmonious relationships, investing in children's/partner's futures, successfully managing wider kin relationships, etc.	Feeling like the only person who makes sacrifices, worries not being taken seriously, unfair accusations of nagging and bullying, being mean with money, etc.

please others. Consequently, people sometimes really enjoy leisure when they leave others behind or leave jobs undone; the pleasure comes, in other words, from stealing free time.

What of future generations? Making prophecies about the future is a perilous step for sociologists because, by their very nature, predictions require a kind of certainty and simplicity of message that can defy understanding of the complexities of social life. Making qualified judgements about emergent trends is a different matter. The clear message of this book is that there may be some scope to be more positive about gendered practices because women and men can make more choices about their domestic life-styles than in the past. In some cases, men and women choose to follow convention and live in nuclear families. Some couples are choosing not to have children. Some couples choose to live in separate households. Some couples choose to invest in the woman's career and to allow the man to invest more energy in their children. Some people choose to live alone, or have multiple relationships while remaining single, rather than committing themselves to someone who does not seem right for them because society insists that they settle down. It is not my intention to give the impression that contemporary society is a relationship free-for-all where everybody can choose to have what they want; serendipity plays its part in everyone's lives. What I am saying, however, is that whether we are lucky in love or not, there are many ways of constructing the way we live our domestic lives. Now that more and more men and women are becoming skilled in undertaking the whole range of tasks that are required successfully to perform the practices of domestic life, they are more likely to be able to empathise with each other's point of view. This may not stop everyday arguments about the unfairness of it all, but the arguments may be based on the facts of the matter at hand, rather than reverting automatically to gendered stereotypes.

Bibliography*

Abbott, M. (1993) *Family Ties: English families 1540–1920*, London: Routledge.
Abrams, P. and McCulloch, A. (1976) *Communes, Sociology and Society*, Cambridge: Cambridge University Press.
Acker, J. (1973) 'Women in social stratification: a case of intellectual sexism', *American Journal of Sociology*, 78:4, 936–45.
Acker, S. (1989) 'The problem with patriarchy', *Sociology*, 23:2, 235–40.
Adam, B. (1995) *Timewatch*, Cambridge: Polity Press.
Adams, R. (1994) 'Older men's friendship patterns', in E. Thompson Jr (ed.), *Older Men's Lives*, Thousand Oaks, California: Sage.
Adams, R. and Bliesner, R. (1992) *Adult Friendships*, London: Sage.
Alibhai-Brown, Y. (2001) *Mixed Feelings: The Complex Lives of Mixed-Race Britain*, London: Women's Press.
Alibhai-Brown, Y. and Montague, A. (1992) *The Colour of Love: Mixed Race Relationships*, London: Virago.
Allan, G. (1996) *Kinship and Friendship in Modern Britain*, Oxford: Oxford University Press.
Allen, S. and Wolkowitz, C. (1987) *Homeworking: Myths and Realities*, London: Macmillan.
Altergott, K. (ed.) (1988) *Daily Life in Later Life: Comparative Perspectives*, Newbury Park, Beverly Hills: Sage.
Alvarez, A. (1982) *Life After Marriage: Scenes from Divorce*, London: Fontana.
Ambrose, P., Harper, J. and Pemberton, R. (1983) *Surviving Divorce: Men Beyond Marriage*, Brighton: Wheatsheaf Books.
Anderson, B. (2000) *Doing the Dirty Work? The Global Politics of Domestic Labour*, London: Zed Books.
Anderson, M. (1984) 'The social position of spinsters in mid-Victorian Britain', *Journal of Family History*, 9:4, 377–93.
Anderson, M., Li, Y., Bechhofer, F., McCrone, D. and Stewart, R. (2000) 'Sooner rather than later? Younger and middle-aged adults preparing for retirement', *Ageing and Society*, 20:4, 445–66.
Arber, S. and Gilbert, N. (1989) 'Men, the forgotten carers', *Sociology*, 23:1, 111–18.
Arber, S. and Ginn, J. (1992) *Gender and Later Life: A Sociological Analysis of Resources and Constraints*, London: Sage.
Aries, P. (1988) *Centuries of Childhood: A Social History of Family Life*, New York: Random House.
Arndt, B. (1989) *Private Lives*, Melbourne: Penguin.
Atkinson, M. (1910) 'The economic relations of the household', in A. Ravenhill and C. Schiff (eds), *Household Administration: Its Place in the Higher Education of Women*, London: Grant Richards.

---

* *[Square brackets] denote first date of publication.*

Attfield, J. (1989) 'Inside pram town: a case study of Harlow home interiors 1951–61', in J. Attfield and P. Kirkham (eds), *A View from the Interior: Feminism, Women and Design*, London: Women's Press.

Austen, J. (1972) *Pride and Prejudice*, Harmondsworth: Penguin.

Bachelard, G. (1958) *The Poetics of Space*, Boston, Massachusetts: Beacon Press.

Balchin, N. (1995) *Housing Policy: An Introduction*, London: Routledge (3rd edn).

Ballard, C. (1979) 'Conflict, community and change: second generation South Asians', in V. Saifullah Khan (ed.), *Minority Families in Britain: Support and Stress*, London: Macmillan.

Barker, D. and Allen, S. (eds) (1976) *Dependence and Exploitation in Work and Marriage*, London: Longman.

Barley, N. (1989) *Native Land: The Bizarre Rituals and Curious Customs that make the English English*, Harmondsworth: Penguin.

Barrett, M. (1980) *Women's Oppression Today*, London: Verso.

Barrett, M. and McIntosh, M. (1980) 'The family wage: some problems for socialists and feminists', *Capital and Class*, 11:1, 51–72.

Barrett, M. and McIntosh, M. (1982) *The Anti Social Family*, London: Verso.

Barstow, P. (1998) *The English Country House Party*, London: Sutton.

Barthélemy, D. (1988) 'Kinship', in G. Duby (ed.), *A History of Private Life. II – Revelations of the Medieval World* (trans. A. Goldhammer), Cambridge, Massachusetts: Harvard University Press.

Baxter, J. (1993) *Work at Home: The Domestic Division of Labour*, St Lucia: University of Queensland Press.

Baxter, J. and Western, M. (1998) 'Satisfaction with housework: examining the paradox', *Sociology*, 32:1, 101–20.

Beardsworth, A. and Keil, T. (1990) 'Review article: putting the menu on the agenda', *Sociology*, 24:1, 139–51.

Bebbington, D. (1989) *Evangelism in Modern Britain: A History from the 1730s to the 1980s*, London: Routledge.

Beck, U. and Beck-Gernsheim, E. (1995) *The Normal Chaos of Love*, Cambridge: Polity Press.

Bell, C. and Newby, H. (1976) 'Husbands and wives: the deferential dialectic', in D. Barker and S. Allen (eds), *Dependence and Exploitation in Work and Marriage*, London: Longman.

Bell, L. and Ribbens, J. (1994) 'Isolated housewives and complex material worlds – the significance of social contacts between women with young children in industrial societies', *Sociological Review*, 42:2, 227–62.

Bendellow, G. and Williams, S. (eds) (1998) *Emotions in Social Life: Critical Themes and Contemporary Issues*, London: Routledge.

Bendix, R. (1956) *Work and Authority in Industry: Ideologies of Management in the Course of the Industrial Revolution*, Berkeley, California: University of California Press.

Benson, J. (1983) *The Penny Capitalists: A Study of Nineteenth-Century Working-Class Entrepreneurs*, London: Macmillan.

Benson, J. (1989) *The Working Class in Britain 1850–1939*, London: Longman.

Benson, S. (1981) *Ambiguous Ethnicity: Interacial Families in London*: Cambridge: Cambridge University Press.

Berking, H. (1999) *The Sociology of Giving*, London: Sage.

Berry, J. (1994) 'Acculturation and psychological adaptation: an overview', in A. Bouvy, R. Vand de Vijver, P. Boski and P. Schmitz (eds), *Journeys into Cross-Cultural Psychology: Selected Papers from the Eleventh International Conference of the International Association for Cross-Cultural Psychology*, Liège: Swets & Zeitlinger.

Beynon, H. (1973) *Working for Ford*, Harmondsworth: Penguin.

Bhachu, P. (1985) *Twice Migrants: East African Sikh Settlers in Britain*, London: Tavistock.

Bien, W., Marbach, J. and Templeton, R. (1992) 'Social networks of single-person households', in C. Marsh and S. Arber (eds), *Families and Households: Divisions and Change*, London: Macmillan.

Birdwell-Pheasant, D. and Lawrence-Zúñiga, D. (1999) *Houselife: Space, Place and Family in Europe*, Oxford: Berg.

Black, C. (1918) *A New Way of Housekeeping*, London: Collins.

Bland, L. (1986) 'Marriage laid bare: middle-class women and marital sex, c. 1880–1914', in J. Lewis (ed.), *Labour and Love: Women's Experience of Home and Family, 1850–1940*, Oxford: Basil Blackwell.

Blood, R. and Wolfe, D. (1960) *Husbands and Wives: The Dynamics of Married Living*, New York: Free Press.

Blumstein, P. and Schwartz, P. (1985) *American Couples: Money, Work, Sex*, New York: Pocket Books.

Boal, F. (ed.) (2000) *Ethnicity and Housing*, Aldershot: Ashgate.

Bonney, N. and Love, J. (1991) 'Gender and migration: geographical mobility and the wife's sacrifice', *Sociological Review*, 37:3, 335–48.

Booth, C., Darke, J. and Yeandle, S. (eds) (1996) *Changing Places: Women's Lives in the City*, London: Paul Chapman.

Bott, E. (1957) *Family and Social Network*, London: Tavistock.

Bourdieu, P. (1984) *Distinction: A Social Critique of Judgements of Taste*, London: Routledge.

Bradley, H. (1989) *Men's Work, Women's Work: A Sociological History of the Sexual Division of Labour in Employment*, Cambridge: Polity Press.

Brannen, J. and Wilson, G. (eds) (1987) *Give and Take in Families*, London: Allen & Unwin.

Breitenbach, E. (1982) 'A comparative study of the Women's Trade Union Conference and the Scottish Women's Trade Union Conference', *Feminist Review*, 7, 65–86.

Brewer, P. (1986) *Shaker Communities, Shaker Lives*, Hanover, New Hampshire: University of New England Press.

Briggs, A. (1968) *Victorian Cities*, Harmondsworth: Penguin.

Brindley, T. (1999) 'The modern house in England: an architecture of exclusion', in T. Chapman and J. Hockey (eds), *Ideal Homes? Social Change and Domestic Life*, London: Routledge.

Brod, H. (1987) *The Making of Masculinity*, London: Allen & Unwin.

Bronstein, P. and Cowan, C. (eds) (1988) *Fatherhood today; Men's Changing Role in the Family*, New York: John Wiley.

Brooke, C. (1989) *The Medieval Idea of Marriage*, Oxford: Clarendon Press.

Brown, B. and Altman, A. (1983) 'Territoriality, defensible space and residential burglary: an environmental analysis', *Journal of Environmental Psychology*, 3, 203–20.

Brown, K. (1988) *A Social History of the Nonconformist Ministry in England and Wales 1800–1930*, Oxford: Clarendon Press.

Brown, K. (1996) *Good Wives, Nasty Wenches and Anxious Patriarchs: Gender Race and Power in Colonial Virginia*, Chapel Hill, North Carolina: University of North Carolina Press.

Brown, P. (1988) *The Body and Society: Men, Women and Sexual Renunciation in Early Christianity*, London: Faber & Faber.

Brown, R. (1976) 'Women as employees: some comments on research in industrial sociology', in D. Barker and S. Allen (eds), *Dependence and Exploitation in Work and Marriage*, London: Longman.

Brown, R. (1992) 'World War, Women's Work and the Gender Division of Paid Labour', in N. Gilbert and S. Arber (eds), *Women and Working Lives: Divisions and Change*, London: Macmillan.

Brown, R. (ed.) (1997) *The Changing Shape of Work*, London: Macmillan.

Bruce-Milne, M. (ed.) (1956) *The Book of the Home*, London: Caxton.

Brunsdon, C., Johnson, C., Moseley, R. and Wheatley, H. (2001) 'Factual entertainment on British television: the Midlands TV research group's "8–9" project', *European Journal of Cultural Studies*, 4:1, 29–62.

Bryden, I. and Floyd, J. (eds) (1999) *Domestic Space: Reading the Nineteenth Century Interior*, Manchester: Manchester University Press.

Buckingham, D. (2000) *After the Death of Childhood: Growing up in an Age of Electronic Media*, Cambridge: Polity Press.

Bulmer, M. and Solomos, J. (eds) (1999) *Racism*, Oxford: Oxford University Press.

Burgess, A. (1997) *Fatherhood Reclaimed: The Making of the Modern Father*, London: Vermillion.

Burgess, K. (1990) *The Challenge of Labour: Shaping British Society 1850–1930*, London: Croom Helm.

Burgoyne, C. (1990) 'Money in marriage: how patterns of allocation both reflect and conceal power', *Sociological Review*, 38:4, 634–65.

Burke, G. (1986) 'The decline of the independent bal maiden: the impact of change on the Cornish mining industry', in A. John (ed.), *Unequal Opportunities: Women's Employment in England 1800–1918*, Oxford: Basil Blackwell.

Burke, T. (1998) 'Male to male gay domestic violence', in N. Jackson and G. Oates (eds), *Violence in Intimate Relationships: Examining Sociological and Psychological Issues*, Boston, Massachusetts: Butterworth/Heinemann.

Butler, J. (1990) *Gender Trouble: Feminism and the Subversion of identity*, London: Routledge.

Byron, M. (1994) *Post-War Caribbean Migration to Britain: The Unfinished Cycle*, Aldershot: Avebury.

Cadbury, E., Matheson, M. and Shann, G. (1906) *Women's Work and Wages*, London: Fisher Unwin.

Callan, H. and Ardener, S. (eds) (1984) *The Incorporated Wife*, London: Croom Helm.

Cancian, F. (1987) *Love in America: Gender and Self Development*, New York: Cambridge University Press.

Caplan, P. (1985) *Class and Gender in India: Women and their Organisations in a South Indian City*, London: Tavistock.

Carey, F. S. (1916) *A Profession for Gentlewomen: being some reflections on the philosophy of housekeeping*, London: Constable.

Carey, J. (1992) *The Intellectuals and the Masses: Pride and Prejudice among the Literary Intelligentsia, 1880–1939*, London: Faber & Faber.

Carrington, C. (1999) *No Place Like Home: Domesticity and Family Life within Lesbian and Gay Relationships*, Chicago, Illinois: University of Chicago Press.

Casper, L. and Bianchi, S. (2002) *Continuity and Change in the American Family*, Thousand Oaks, California: Sage.

Castles, S. and Miller, M. (1998) *The Age of Migration: International Population Movements in the Modern World*, London: Macmillan.

Cauhapé, E. (1983) *Fresh Starts: Men and Women after Divorce*, New York: Basic Books.

Cavallo, S. and Warner, S. (ed.) (1999) *Widowhood in Medieval and Early Modern Europe*, London: Longman.

Chambers-Schiller, L. (1984) *Liberty, A Better Husband: Single Women in America: the Generations of 1780–1840*, New Haven, Connecticut: Yale University Press.

Chandler, J. (1981) *Women Without Husbands: An Exploration of the Margins of Marriages*, London: Macmillan.

Chapman, R. (1988) *Male Order: Unwrapping Masculinity*, London: Lawrence & Wishart.

Chapman, T. (1999a) 'Stage sets for ideal lives: images of home in contemporary show homes', in T. Chapman and J. Hockey (eds), *Ideal Homes? Social Change and Domestic Life*, London: Routledge.

Chapman, T. (1999b) 'The Ideal Home Exhibition: an analysis of constraints and conventions in consumer choice in British homes', in J. Hearn and S. Roseneil (eds), *Consuming Cultures: Power and Resistance*, London: Macmillan.

Chapman, T. (1999c) 'You've got him well trained: the negotiation of roles in the domestic sphere', in T. Chapman and J. Hockey (eds), *Ideal Homes? Social Change and Domestic Life*, London: Routledge.

Chapman, T. (2001) 'There's no place like home', *Theory Culture and Society*, 18:6, 135–46.

Chapman, T. and Hockey, J. (eds) (1999) *Ideal Homes? Social Change and Domestic Life*, London: Routledge.

Chapman, T., Hockey, J. and Wood, M. (1999) 'Daring to be different', in T. Chapman and J. Hockey (eds), *Ideal Homes? Social Change and Domestic Life*, London: Routledge.

Charles, L. and Duffin, L. (eds) (1985) *Women and Work in Pre-Industrial England*, London: Croom Helm.

Charles, N. and Kerr, M. (1988) *Women, Food and Families*, Manchester: Manchester University Press.

Cheal, D. (1987) '"Showing them you love them": gift giving and the dialectic of intimacy', *Sociological Review*, 35:1, 130–69.

Cheal, D. (1988) *The Gift Economy*, London: Routledge.

Chinoy, E. ([1955] 1992) *The Automobile Worker and the American Dream*, Urbana, Illinois: Illinois University Press (2nd edn).

Christian, H. (1994) *The Making of Anti-Sexist Men*, London: Routledge.

Clarke, N. (1991) 'Strenuous idleness: Thomas Carlyle and the man of letters as hero', in M. Roper and J. Tosh (eds), *Manful Assertions: Masculinities in Britain Since 1800*, London: Routledge.

Clatterbaugh, K. (1997) *Contemporary Perspectives on Masculinity*, Boulder, Colorado: Westview (2nd edn).

Cliff, D. (1993) '"Under the wife's feet": renegotiating gender divisions in early retirement', *Sociological Review*, 41:1, 30–53.

Clough, R. (1981) *Old Age Homes*, London: Allen & Unwin.

Cobbett, W. ([1830]1980) *Advice to Young Men and (Incidentally) to Young Women in the Middle and Higher Ranks of Life in a Series of Letters Addressed to a Youth, a Bachelor, a Lover, a Husband, a Father, and a Citizen or Subject*, Oxford: Oxford University Press.

Cockburn, C. (1983) *Brothers: Male Dominance and Technological Change*, London: Pluto.

Cockburn, C. and Fürst-Dilic, R. (eds) (1994) *Bringing Technology Home: Gender and Technology in a Changing Europe*, Buckingham: Open University Press.

Cockburn, C. and Ormrod, S. (1993) *Gender and Technology in the Making*, London: Sage.

Cole, T. and Gadow, S. (1986) *What Does it Mean to Grow Old? Reflections from the Humanities*, Durham, North Carolina: Duke University Press.

Coltrane, S. (1996) *Family Man, Fatherhood, Housework and Gender Equity*, New York: Oxford University Press.

Coltrane, S. (1998) *Gender and Families*, Thousand Oaks, California: Pine Forge Press.

Coltrane, S. (2002) 'Research on household labor: modeling and measuring the social embeddedness of routine family work', *Journal of Marriage and the Family*, 62 (November), 1,208–33.

Connell, R. (1995) *Masculinities*, Oxford: Polity.

Cooper, D. (1971) *The Death of the Family*, Harmondsworth: Penguin.

Corden, A. and Eardley, T. (1999) 'Sexing the enterprise: gender, work and resource allocation in self-employed households', in L. McKie, S. Bowlby and S. Gregory (eds), *Gender Power and the Household*, London: Macmillan.

Corsaro, W. (1997) *The Sociology of Childhood*, Thousand Oaks, California: Pine Forge Press.

Coser, L.A. (1977) *Masters of Sociological Thought: Ideas in Historical and Social Context*, New York: Harcourt Brace Jovanovich.

Coyle, A. (1980) 'The Protection Racket', *Feminist Review*, 4, 1–14.

Craib, I. (1995) 'Some comments on the sociology of emotions', *Sociology*, 29:1, 151–8.

Crawford, P. and Gowing, L. (ed.) (2000) *Women's Worlds in 17th Century England*, London: Longman.

Creese, W. (1966) *The Search for Environment: The Garden City – Before and After*, New Haven, Connecticut: Yale University Press.

Creighton, C. (1997) 'The rise of the male breadwinner family', *Comparative Studies in Society and History*, 38:2, 310–37.

Crompton, R. (1997) *Women and Work in Modern Britain*, Oxford: Oxford University Press.

Crompton, R. and Sanderson, K. (1990) *Gendered Jobs and Social Change*, London: Unwin/Hyman.

Czikszentmihalyi, M. and Rochberg-Halton, E. (1981) *The Meaning of Things: Domestic Symbols and the Self*, Cambridge: Cambridge University Press.

Dailey, N. (1998) *When Baby Boom Women Retire*, Westport, Connecticut: Praeger.

Dallos, R. and McLaughlin, E. (eds) (1993) *Social Problems and the Family*, London: Sage.

Dasgupta, S. (1999) 'Just like men?' A critical review of violence by women', in M. Shepard and E. Pence (eds), *Co-ordinating Community Responses to Domestic Violence*, Thousand Oaks, California: California: Sage.

Davidoff, L. (1976) 'The rationalization of housework', in D. Barker and S. Allen (eds), *Dependence and Exploitation in Work and Marriage*, London: Longman.

Davidoff, L. and Hall, C. (1987) *Family Fortunes: Men and Women in the English Middle Class 1780–1850*, London: Routledge.

Davidoff, L., Doolittle, M., Fink, J. and Holden, K. (1999) *The Family Story: Blood, Contract and Intimacy: 1830–1960*, London: Longman.

Davis, R. (1993) *The Black Family in a Changing Black Community*, New York: Garland.

de Silva, A. (ed.) (1990) *Brave New Family: G.K. Chesterton on Men and Women, Children, Sex, Divorce, Marriage and the Family*, San Francisco, California: Ignatius Press.

De Vault, M. (1991) *Feeding the Family: The Social Construction of Caring as Gendered Work*, Chicago, Illinois: University of Chicago Press.

Deem, R. (1986) *All Work and No Play? The Sociology of Women and Leisure*, Milton Keynes: Open University Press.

Dehavenon, A. (ed.) (1996) *There's no Place like Home: Anthropological Perspectives on Housing and Homelessness in the United States*, Westport, Connecticut: Bergin & Garvey.

Delphy, C. ([1970] 1977) *The Main Enemy*, London: Women's Research and Resources Centre.

Delphy, C. (1984) *Close to Home: A Materialist Analysis of Women's Oppression*, London: Hutchinson.

Dennis, N., Henriques, F. and Slaughter, C. (1956) *Coal is our Life: An Analysis of a Yorkshire Mining Community*, London: Tavistock.

Dentinger, E. and Clarkberg, M. (2002) 'Informal caregiving and retirement timing among men and women – gender and caregiving relationships in later midlife', *Journal of Family Issues*, 23:7, 857–79.

Department of the Environment (1995) *Projections of Households in England*, London: HMSO.

Dhillon-Kashyap, P. (1994) 'Black women and housing', in R. Gilroy and R. Woods (eds), *Housing Women*, London: Routledge.

Dickens, C. ([1854] 1969) *Hard Times*, Harmondsworth: Penguin.

Dickerson, B. (1995) *African American Single Mothers: Understanding their Lives and Families*, Thousand Oaks, California: Sage.

Dill, B. (1994) *Across the Boundaries of Race and Class: An Exploration of Work and Family among Black Female Domestic Servants*, New York: Garland.

Dobash, R. and Dobash, R. (1998) *Rethinking Violence against Women*, Thousand Oaks, California: Sage.

Dobash R., Dobash, R., Cavanagh, K. and Lewis, R. (2000) *Changing Violent Men*, Thousand Oaks, California: Sage.

Dolon, J. (1999) 'I've always fancied owning my own lion', in I. Cieraad (ed.), *At Home: An Anthropology of Domestic Space*, New York: Syracuse University Press.

Dongen, M., Frinking, G. and Jacobs, M. (1995) *Changing Fatherhood: An Interdisciplinary Perspective*, Amsterdam: Thesis Publications.

Donley-Reid, L. (1990) 'A structuring structure: the Swahili house', in S. Kent (ed.), *Domestic Architecture and the Use of Space*, Cambridge: Cambridge University Press.

Dorfman, L. (1992) 'Couples in retirement: division of household work', in M. Szinovaca, D. Ekerdt, D. and B. Vinick (eds), *Families and Retirement*, Newbury Park, California: Sage.

Douglas, M. (ed.) (1966) *Purity and Danger: An Analysis of Concepts of Pollution and Taboo*, London: Routledge.

Douglas, M. (1967) 'Primitive rationing', in R. Firth (ed.), *Themes in Economic Anthropology*, London: Tavistock.

Douglas, M. (1973) *Rules and Meanings: The Anthropology of Everyday Knowledge*, Harmondsworth: Penguin.

Douglas, M. (1999) *Implicit Meanings: Selected Essays in Anthropology*, London: Routledge (2nd edn).

Dovey, K. (1995) 'Home and homelessness', in I. Altman and C. Werner (eds), *Home Environments*, New York: Plenum Press.

Dowling, R. (1998) 'Gender, class and home ownership: placing the connections', *Housing Studies*, 13:4, 471–86.

Drabble, M. (1979) *A Writer's Britain: Landscape in Literature*, London: Thames & Hudson.

Drury, B. (1991) 'Sikh girls and the maintenance of an ethnic culture', *New Community*, 17:3, 387–400.

Dryden, C. (1999) *Being Married, Doing Gender: A Critical Analysis of Gender Relationships in Marriage*, London: Routledge.

Duby, G. (1985) *The Knight, the Lady, and the Priest: The Making of Modern Marriage in Medieval France*, Harmondsworth: Penguin.

Duby, G. (ed.) (1988) *A History of Private Life. II – Revelations of the Medieval World* (trans. A. Goldhammer), Cambridge, Massachusetts: Harvard University Press.

Dudden, F. (1983) *Servicing Women: Household Service in Nineteenth Century America*, Middletown, Connecticut: Wesleyan University Press.

Duncombe, J. and Marsden, D. (1993) 'Love and intimacy: the gender division of emotion work', *Sociology*, 27:2, 221–42.

Dunne, G. (1997) *Lesbian Lifestyles: Women's Work and the Politics of Sexuality*, London: Macmillan.

Dupuis, A. and Thorns, D. (1996) 'The meaning home has for older people', *Housing Studies*, 11:4, 485–501.

Dyhouse, C. (1989) *Feminism and the Family in England: 1880–1939*, Oxford: Basil Blackwell.

Eaton, J. (1973) 'The Hutterite accommodation to social change', in R. Kanter (ed.) *Communes: Creating and Managing the Collective Life*, New York: Harper & Row.

Edgell, S. (1980) *Middle Class Couples: A Study of Segregation and Inequality in Marriage*, London: Allen & Unwin.

Eisenstein, Z. (1979) *Capitalist Patriarchy and the Case for Socialist Patriarchy*, New York: Monthly Review Press.

Ekerdt, D. and Clark, E. (2001) 'Selling retirement in financial planning advertisements', *Journal of Aging Studies*, 15:1, 55–68.

Ekerdt, D. Hackney, J., Kosloski, K. and DeViney, S. (2001) 'Eddies in the stream: the prevalence of uncertain plans for retirement', *Journals of Gerontology Series B: Psychological Sciences and Social Sciences*, 56:3, 162–70.

Elliot, F. (1996) *Gender, Family and Society*, London: Macmillan.

Engels, F. ([1844] 1969) *The Condition of the Working Class in England in 1844*, St Albans: Granada.

Engram, E. (1982) *Science, Myth, Reality: The Black Family in One-half Century of Research*, Westport, Connecticut: Greenwood.

Epstein, S. (1991) *Wage Labour and Guilds in Medieval Europe*, Chapel Hill, North Carolina: University of North Carolina Press.

Ereva, P. (2001) *Family Diversity: Continuity and Change in the Contemporary Family* Thousand Oaks, California: Sage.

Erler, M. and Kowaleski, M. (1988) *Women and Power in the Middle Ages*, Athens, Georgia: University of Georgia Press.

Evetts, J. (1988) 'Managing childcare and work responsibilities: the strategies of married women primary and infant teachers', *Sociological Review*, 44:4, 503–31.

Fairhurst, E. (1999) 'Fitting a quart into a pint pot: making space for older people in sheltered housing', in T. Chapman and J. Hockey (eds), *Ideal Homes? Social Change and Domestic Life*, London: Routledge.

Faulkner, W. and Arnold, E. (eds) (1985) *Smothered by Invention: Technology and Women's Lives*, London: Women's Press.

Fava, S. (1980) 'Women's place in the new suburbia', in G. Wekerle, R. Peterson and D. Morley (eds), *New Space for Women*, Boulder, Colorado: Westview Press.

Featherstone, M. and Hepworth, M. (1995) 'Images of positive aging: a case study of *Retirement Choice* magazine', in M. Featherstone and A. Wernick (eds), *Images of Aging: Cultural Representations of Later Life*, London: Routledge.

Featherstone, M. and Wernick, A. (eds) (1995) *Images of Aging: Cultural Representations of Later Life*, London: Routledge.

Ferguson, M. (ed.) (1985) *First Feminists: British Women Writers 1578–1799*, Bloomington, Indiana: Indiana University Press.

Ferris, I. (1864) 'Men of business: their home responsibilities', in J. Alexander, J. Todd, W. Sprague, S. Tyng, I. Ferris and J. Stearns (eds), *Men of Business; Considered in Six Aspects: A Book for Young Men*, Edinburgh: William Nimmo.

Finch, J. (1983) *Married to the Job*, London: Allen & Unwin.

Finch, J. (1989) *Family Obligations and Social Change*, Cambridge: Polity Press.

Finch, J. and Groves, D. (eds) (1983) *A Labour of Love: Women, Work and Caring*, London: Routledge.

Finch, J. and Mason, J. (1995) *Negotiating Family Responsibilities*, London: Routledge.

Firestone, S. ([1970] 1974) *The Dialectics of Sex: The Case for Feminist Revolution*, New York: Morrow.

Fishman, R. (1977) *Urban Utopias in the Twentieth Century*, New York: Basic Books.

Fletcher, A. (1995) *Gender, Sex and Subordination in England 1500–1800*, New Haven, Connecticut: Yale University Press.

Fog Olwig, K. (1999) 'Travelling makes a home: mobility and identity among West Indians', in T. Chapman and J. Hockey (eds), *Ideal Homes? Social Change and Domestic Life*, London: Routledge.

Forty, A. (1986) *Objects of Desire: Design and Society 1750–1980*, London: Thames & Hudson.

Fothergill, A. (1995) 'Living with a teleworker', *European Journal of Teleworking*, 1:4, 20–4.

Fowlkes, M. (1980) *Behind Every Successful Man: Wives of Medicine and Academe*, New York: Columbia University Press.

Fox, G. (1985) 'Non-custodial fathers', in S. Hanson and F. Bozett (eds), *Dimensions of Fatherhood*, Beverly Hills, California: Sage.

Foyster, E. (1999) *Manhood in Early Modern England: Sex and Marriage*, London: Longman.

Frederick, C. (1920) *Scientific Management in the Home: Household Engineering*, London: Routledge.

Freeman, C. (1982) 'The "understanding employer"', in J. West (ed.), *Work, Women and the Labour Market*, London: Routledge.

Friedan, B. (1963) *The Feminine Mystique*, New York: Norton.

Gamarnikow, E., Morgan, D., Purvis, J. and Taylorson, D. (eds) (1983) *The Public and the Private*, London: Heinemann.

Gannon, L. (1999) *Women and Ageing: Transcending the Myths*, London: Routledge.

Gaskell, E. ([1848] 1970) *Mary Barton*, Harmondsworth: Penguin.

Gauldie, E. (1974) *Cruel Habitations: A History of Working-Class Housing, 1780–1918*, London: Allen & Unwin.

Gavron, H. (1968) *The Captive Wife*, Harmondsworth: Penguin.

Genovese, E. (1999) 'The myth of the absent family', in R. Staples (ed.), *The Black Family: Essays and Studies*, Belmont, California: Wadsworth.

Gerber, L. (1983) *Married to their Careers*, New York: Tavistock.

Germov, J. and Williams, L. (1999) *A Sociology of Food and Nutrition: The Social Appetite*, Oxford: Oxford University Press.

Gershuny, J. and Robinson, O. (2001) 'Cross national changes in time use: some sociological (hi) scores re-examined', *British Journal of Sociology*, 52:2, 331–47.

Gerson, K. (1993) *No Man's Land: Men's Changing Commitments to Family and Work*, New York: Basic Books.

Ghadialli, R. (ed.) (1988) *Women in Indian Society*, New Delhi: Sage.

Giddens, A. (1971) *Capitalism and Modern Social Theory*, Cambridge: Cambridge University Press.

Giddens, A. (1982) *Profiles and Critiques in Social Theory*, London: Macmillan.

Giddens, A. (1984) *The Constitution of Society*, Cambridge: Polity Press.

Giddens, A. (1992) *The Transformation of Intimacy: Sexuality, Love and Eroticism in Modern Societies*, Cambridge: Polity Press.

Gilbert, A. (1976) *Religion and Society in Industrial England: Church, Chapel and Social Change, 1740–1914*, London: Longman.

Gilbreth, L. (1930) 'Efficiency methods, applied to kitchen design', *Architectural Review*, March, 291–4.

Gill, G. (1999) *The Third Job: Employed Couples' Management of Household Work Contradictions*, Aldershot: Ashgate.

Gillis, J. (1983) 'Servants, sexual relations and the risks of illegitimacy in London 1801–1900', in J. Newton, R. Rapp and E. Ross (eds), *Sex and Class in Women's History*, London: Routledge.

Girouard, M. (1978) *Life in the English Country House: A Social and Architectural History*, Harmondsworth: Penguin.

Girouard, M. (1985) *Cities and People: A Social and Architectural History*, New Haven, Connecticut: Yale University Press.

Girouard, M. (1990) *The English Town*, New Haven, Connecticut: Yale University Press.

Glaser, K. and Grundy, E. (2002) 'Class, caring and disability: evidence from the British Retirement Survey', *Ageing and Society*, 22:4, 325–42.

Goering, J. and Wienk, R. (eds) (1997) *Mortgage Lending, Racial Discrimination and Federal Policy*, Brookfield: Ashgate.

Goffman, E. (1967) *Interaction Ritual*, Garden City, New York: Doubleday.

Goffman, E. (1968) *Stigma: Notes on the Management of Spoiled Identity*, Harmondsworth: Penguin.

Goffman, E. (1969) *The Presentation of Self in Everyday Life*, Harmondsworth: Penguin.

Goldthorpe, J., Lockwood, D., Bechhofer, F. and Platt, J. (1969) *The Affluent Worker*, Cambridge: Cambridge University Press.

Goodwin, C. (1999) *Making the Big Move*, Oakland, California: New Harbinger.

Gordon, T. (1984) *Single Women: On the Margins?*, London: Macmillan.

Gorman, E. (1999) 'Bringing home the bacon: marital allocation of income-earning responsibility, job shifts, and men's wage', *Journal of Marriage and the Family*, 61 (February), 110–22.

Gradman, T. (1994) 'Masculine identity from work to retirement', in E. Thompson Jr (ed.), *Older Men's Lives*, Thousand Oaks, California: Sage.

Gray, J. (1992) *Men are From Mars and Women are from Venus: A Practical Guide for Improving Communication and Getting what you want in Relationships*, New York: HarperCollins.

Green, E. (1996) 'Women and leisure', in C. Booth, J. Darke and S. Yeandle (eds), *Changing Places: Women's Lives in the City*, London: Paul Chapman.

Green, E., Hebron, S. and Woodward, D. (1990) *Women's Leisure, What Leisure?*, London: Macmillan.

Greer, G. (1970) *The Female Eunuch*, London: MacGibbon & Kee.

Gregson, N. and Lowe, M. (1994) 'Waged domestic labour and the renegotiation of the domestic division of labour within dual career households', *Sociology*, 28:1, 55–78.

Greif, G., DeMaris, A. and Hood, J. (1993) 'Balancing work and single fatherhood', in J. Hood (ed.), *Men, Work, and Family*, Newbury Park, California: Sage.

Grier, K. (1988) *Culture and Comfort: People, Parlours and Upholstery: 1840–1930*, Rochester, New York: The Strong Museum.

Grieshaber, S. (1997) 'Mealtime rituals: power and resistance in the construction of meal times', *British Journal of Sociology*, 48:4, 649–66.

Gunter, B. and Furnham, A. (2000) *Children as Consumers*, London: Routledge.

Gurney, C. and Means, R. (1993) 'The meaning of home in later life', in S. Arber and M. Evandron (eds), *Ageing, Independence and the Life Course*, London: Jessica Kingsley.

Hadley, D. (ed.) (1999) *Masculinity in Medieval Europe*, London: Longman.

Hague, G. and Malos, E. (1998) *Domestic Violence: Action for Change*, Cheltenham: New Clarion Press.

Hakim, C. (1991) 'Grateful slaves and self-made women: fact and fantasy in women's work orientations', *European Journal of Sociology*, 7:2, 101–21.

Hakim, C. (1995) 'Five feminist myths about women's employment', *British Journal of Sociology*, 46:3, 429–55.

Hall, J. (1978) *The Ways Out: Utopian Communal Groups in an Age of Babylon*, London: Routledge.

Halttunen, K. (1982) *Confidence Men and Painted Women: A Study of Middle Class Culture in America, 1830–1870*, New Haven, Connecticut: Yale University Press.

Hammerton, J. (1992) *Cruelty and Companionship: Conflict in Nineteenth Century Married Life*, London: Routledge.

Hamnett, C. (1999) *Winners and Losers, Home Ownership in Modern Britain*, London: UCL Press.

Hanson, S. (1985) 'Single custodial fathers', in S. Hanson and F. Bozett (eds), *Dimensions of Fatherhood*, Beverly Hills, California: Sage.

Hanson, S. and Bozett, F. (eds) (1985) *Dimensions of Fatherhood*, Beverly Hills, California: Sage.

Hantrais, L. and Letablier, M. (1996) *Families and Family Policy in Europe*, London: Longman.

Haour-Knipe, D. (2001) *Moving Families*, London: UCL Press.

Harden, J. (2000) 'There's no place like home: the public/private distinction in children's theorizing of risk and safety', *Childhood*, 7:1, 43–59.

Harden, J., Scott, S., Backett-Milburn, K. and Jackson, S. (2000) 'Can't talk, won't talk? Methodological issues in researching children', *Sociological Research Online*, 5:2, www.socresonline.org.uk.

Hardey, M. (1989) 'Lone parents and the home', in G. Allan and G. Crow (eds), *Home and Family: Creating the Domestic Sphere*, London: Macmillan.

Hardill, I., Dudleston, A., Green, A. and Owen, D. (1999) 'Decision making in dual career households', in L. McKie, S. Bowlby and S. Gregory (eds), *Gender Power and the Household*, London: Macmillan.

Harrison, J. (1969) *Robert Owen and the Owenites in Britain and America: The Quest for the New Moral World*, London: Routledge.

Hartill, R. (1989) *Writers Revealed*, London: BBC Books.

Hartley, C. (1924) *Women, Children, Love and Marriage*, London: Heath Cranton.

Hartmann, H. (1979) 'Capitalism, patriarchy and job segregation by sex', in S. Eisenstein (ed.), *Capitalist Patriarchy and the Case for Socialist Feminism*, New York: Monthly Review Press.

Haste, C. (1994) *Rules of Desire: Sex in Britain World War 1 to the Present*, London: Pimlico.

Hawkins, A. and Dollahite, D. (1997) *Generative Fathering: Beyond Defecit Perspectives*, Thousand Oaks, California: Sage.

Heaphy, B., Donovan, C. and Weeks, J. (1999) 'Sex, money and the kitchen sink: power in the same sex couple relationship', in J. Seymour and P. Bagguley (eds), *Relating Intimacies: Power and Resistance*, London: Macmillan.

Hearn, J. (1987) *The Gender of Oppression*, Brighton: Wheatsheaf.

Hearn, J. and Morgan, D. (1990) *Men, Masculinity and Social Theory*, London: Unwin/Hyman.

Hearn, J., Pringle, K., Müller, U., Oleksy, E., Lattu, E., Chernova, J., Ferguson, H., Gullvåg Holter, Ø., Kolga, V., Novikova, I., Ventimiglia, C., Olsvik, E. and Tallberg, T. (2002) 'Critical studies on men in ten European countries', *Men and Masculinity*, 4:4, 380–408.

Hebron, S. and Wykes, M. (1991) 'Gender and patriarchy in mining communities', in M. Cross and G. Payne (eds), *Work and the Enterprise Culture*, London: Falmer Press.

Heer, F. ([1962] 1990) *The Medieval World: Europe from 1100–1350*, London: Wiedenfeld & Nicolson.

Helweg, A. (1980) *Sikhs in England: The Development of a Migrant Community*, New Delhi: Oxford University Press.

Hepler, A. (2000) *Women in Labor: Mothers, Medicine, and Occupational Health in the United States 1890–1980*, Columbus, Ohio: Ohio State University Press.

Hepworth, M. (1999a) 'In defiance of an ageing culture', *Ageing and Society*, 19:1, 139–48.

Hepworth, M. (1999b) 'Privacy, security and respectability: the ideal Victorian home', in T. Chapman and J. Hockey (eds), *Ideal Homes? Social Change and Domestic Life*, London: Routledge.

Herlihy, D. (1985) *Medieval Households*, Cambridge, Massachusetts: Harvard University Press.

Hetherington, M. and Hagan, M. (1986) 'Divorced fathers: stress, coping and adjustment', in M. Lamb (ed.), *The Father's Role: Applied Perspectives*, New York: Wiley.

Heubeck, B., Watson, J. and Russell, G. (1986) 'Father involvement and responsibility in family therapy', in M. Lamb (ed.), *The Father's Role: Applied Perspectives*, New York: Wiley.

Hewitt, M. (1999) 'District visiting and the constitution of domestic space in the mid-nineteenth century', in I. Bryden and J. Floyd (eds), *Domestic Space: Reading the Nineteenth Century Interior*, Manchester: Manchester University Press.

Higate, P. (2000) 'Ex-servicemen on the road: travel and homelessness', *Sociological Review*, 48:4, 331–48.

Higgins, J. (1989) 'Homes and institutions', in G. Allan and G. Crow (eds) *Home and Family: Creating the Domestic Sphere*. London: Macmillan.

Higgs, E. (1986) 'Domestic service and household production', in A. John (ed.), *Unequal Opportunities: Women's Employment in England 1980–1918*, Oxford: Basil Blackwell.

Hilbourne, M. (1999) 'Living together full time? Middle class couples approaching retirement', *Ageing and Society*, 19:2, 161–83.

Hilton, B. (1988) *The Age of Atonement – The Influence of Evangelism on Social and Economic Thought, 1785–1865*, Oxford: Clarendon Press.

Hinchcliffe, T. (1992) *North Oxford*: New Haven, Connecticut: Yale University Press.

Hipgrave, T. (1982) 'Lone fatherhood: a problematic status', in L. McKee and M. O'Brien (eds), *The Father Figure*, London: Tavistock.

Hiro, D. (1991) *Black British, White British: A History of Race Relations in Britain*, London: Grafton Books.

Hitchcock, T. and Cohen, M. (eds) (1999) *English Masculinities 1660–1800*, London: Longman.

Hobsbawm, E. (1969) *Industry and Empire: From 1750 to the Present Day*, Harmondsworth: Penguin.

Hochschild, A. (1983) *The Managed Heart: The Commercialization of Human Feeling*, Berkeley, California: University of California Press.

Hochschild, A. (1989) *Second Shift: Working Parents and the Revolution at Home*, Harmondsworth: Viking Penguin.

Hockey, J. (1999) 'The ideal of home: domesticating the institutional space of old age and death', in T. Chapman and J. Hockey (eds), *Ideal Homes? Social Change and Domestic Life*, London: Routledge.

Hood, J. (1993) 'Meanings of housework for single fathers', in J. Hood (ed.), *Men, Work, and Family*, Newbury Park, California: Sage.

hooks, b. (1982) *Ain't I a Woman? Black Women and Feminism*, London: Pluto Press.

Hope, E., Kennedy, M. and De Winter, A. (1976) 'Homeworkers in North London', in D. Barker and S. Allen (eds), *Dependency and Exploitation in Work and Marriage*, London: Longman.

Hostetler, J. (1974) *Hutterite Society*, Baltimore, Maryland: Johns Hopkins University Press.

Houlbrooke, R. (1984) *The English Family 1450–1700*, London: Longman.

Houriet, R. (1973) *Getting Back Together*, London: Routledge.

Howells, J. (1999) *Where to Retire: America's Best and Most Affordable Places*, Oakland, California: Gateway.

Hufton, O. (1984) 'Women without men: widows and spinsters in Britain and France in the eighteenth century', *Journal of Family History*, 9:4, 340–55.

Hughes, E. (1958) *Men and their Work*, Glencoe, Illinois: Free Press.

Humphries, J. (1981) 'Protective legislation, the capitalist state and working class men: the case of the 1842 Mines Act', *Feminist Review*, 7, 1–34.

Hunter, P. and Whitson, D. (1991) 'Women, Leisure and Familism', *Leisure Studies*, 10:2, 219–33.

Hutton, D. (1985) 'Women in fourteenth century Shrewsbury', in L. Charles and L. Duffin (eds), *Women and Work in Pre-industrial England*, London: Croom Helm.

Jackson, N. (1998) 'Lesbian battering: the other closet', in N. Jackson and G. Oates (eds), *Violence in Intimate Relationships: Examining Sociological and Psychological Issues*, Boston, Massachusetts: Butterworth/Heinemann.

Jackson, N. and Oates, G. (eds) (1998) *Violence in Intimate Relationships: Examining Sociological and Psychological Issues*, Boston, Massachusetts: Butterworth/Heinemann.

Jacobson, C. (ed.) (1995) *American Families: Issues in Race and Ethnicity*, New York: Garland.

Jagger, G. and Wright, C. (eds) (1999) *Changing Family Values*, London: Routledge.

James, A. and Prout, A. (1990) *Constructing and Reconstructing Childhood*, London: Falmer Press.

Jenks, C. (ed.) (1982) *The Sociology of Childhood: Essential Readings*, London: Batsford.

Jeremiah, D. (2000) *Architecture and Design for the Family in Britain: 1900–70*, Manchester: Manchester University Press.

Jerome, D. and Wenger, C. (1999) 'Stability and change in late-life friendships', *Ageing and Society*, 19:4, 661–76.

John, A. (ed.) (1986) *Unequal Opportunities: Women's Employment in England 1800–1918*, Oxford: Basil Blackwell.

Johnson, M. (1993) *Housing Culture*, London: University College London Press.

Johnson, M. (1999) *Archaeological Theory: An Introduction*, Oxford: Basil Blackwell.

Johnson, S. (1990) *Staying Power: Long Term Lesbian Couples*, Tallahassee, Florida: Naiad Press.

Jones, J. (1985) *Labour of Love Labour of Sorrow: Black Women, Work, and the Family from Slavery to the Present*, New York: Basic Books.

Jones, V. (ed.) (1990) *Women in the Eighteenth Century: Constructions of Femininity*, London: Routledge.

Jordan, E. (1996) 'The lady clerks at the Prudential: the beginning of vertical segregation by sex in clerical work in nineteenth-century Britain', *Gender and History*, 8:1, 65–81.

Jordan, P. (1995) 'The mother's role in promoting fathering behaviour,' in J. Shapiro, M. Diamond and M. Greenberg (eds) *Becoming a Father: Contemporary, Social Developmental, and Clinical Perspectives*, New York: Springer.

Kahn-Hut, R., Kaplan Daniels, A. and Colvard, R. (1982) *Women and Work: Problems and Perspectives*, New York: Oxford University Press.

Kanter, F. and Halter, M. (1974) 'De-housewifing women, domesticating men: changing sex roles in urban communes', in J. Heiss (ed.), *Family Roles and Interaction: An Anthology*, Chicago, Illinois: Rand McNally (2nd edn).

Kanter, R. (1973) 'Family organisation and sex roles in American communes', in R. Kanter (ed.), *Communes: Creating and Managing the Collective Life*, New York: Harper & Row.

Karn, V. (1977) *Retiring to the Seaside*, London: Routledge.

Katzman, D. (1978) *Seven Days a Week: Women and Domestic Service in Industrialising America*, New York: Oxford University Press.

Keith, P. (1994) 'A typology of orientations toward household and marital roles of older men and women', in E. Thompson (ed.), *Older Men's Lives*, Thousand Oaks, California: Sage.

Kemp, S. and Squires, J. (eds) (1997) *Feminisms*, Oxford: Oxford University Press.

Kennett, P. and Marsh, A. (eds) (1999) *Homelessness: Exploring the New Terrain*, Bristol: Polity Press.

Kent, S. (ed.) (1990) *Domestic Architecture and the Use of Space: An Interdisciplinary Study*, Cambridge: Cambridge University Press.

Kenway, J. and Bullen, E. (2001) *Consuming Children: Education-Entertainment-Advertising*, Buckingham: Open University Press.

Kernahan, S. (1949) 'What housing research means to you', in M. Sherman (ed.), *The Daily Mail Ideal Home Book 1949–50*, London: Daily Mail Ideal Home Publications.

Kerr, R. (1871) *The Gentleman's House; or, How to Plan English Residencies, From the Parsonage to the Palace – With Tables of Accommodation and Cost, and a Series of Selected Plans*, London: John Murray.

Kiernan, K., Land, H. and Lewis, J. (1998) *Lone Motherhood in Twentieth-Century Britain: From Footnote to Front Page*, Oxford: Clarendon Press.

Kimmel, M. (1987a) *Changing Men*, Newbury Park, California: Sage.

Kimmel, M. (1987b) 'The contemporary 'crisis' of masculinity in historical perspective', in H. Brod (ed.), *The Making of Masculinities: The New Men's Studies*, Boston, Massachusetts: Allen & Unwin.

King, R., Warnes, T. and Allan, W. (eds) (2000) *Sunset Lives: British Retirement Migration to the Mediterranean*, Oxford: Oxford International Publications.

Kingdom, E. (1996) 'Cohabitation contracts and the private regulation of time', *Time and Society*, 5:1, 47–60.

Kirshner, J. and Wemple, S. (eds) (1985) *Women in the Medieval World*, Oxford: Basil Blackwell.

Klein, V. (1965) *Britain's Married Women Workers*, London: Routledge.

Kline, S. (1993) *Out of the Garden: Toys, TV and Children's Culture in the Age of Marketing*, New York: Verso.

Knipscheer, C., de jong Gierveld, J., van Tilburg, P. and Dykstra, P. (eds) (1995) *Living Arrangements and Social Networks of Older Adults*, Amsterdam: VU University Press.

Knox, C. (1952) 'Not Enough Leisure', in F. Lake (ed.), *The Daily Mail Ideal Home Book 1952–3*, London: Daily Mail Ideal Home Publications.

Korosec-Serfaty, P. (1984) 'The home from attic to cellar', *Journal of Environmental Psychology*, 4, 303–21.

Korosec-Serfaty, P. (1986) 'Dwelling and the experience of burglary', *Journal of Environmental Psychology*, 6, 329–44.

Koser, K. and Lutz, H. (eds) (1998) *The New Migration in Europe*, London: Macmillan.

Krout, J., Moen, P., Holmes, H. and Bowen, N. (2002) 'Reasons for relocation to a continuing care retirement community', *Journal of Applied Gerontology*, 21:2, 236–56.

Kruk, E. (1983) *Divorce and Disengagement, Patterns of Fatherhood within and Beyond Marriage*, Halifax, Nova Scotia: Fernwood.

Kulik, L. (2002) 'Marital equality and the quality of long-term marriage in later life', *Ageing and Society*, 22:4, 459–81.

Labarge, M. (1986) *Women in Medieval Life*, London: Hamish Hamilton.

Lacey, K. (1985) 'Women and work in fourteenth and fifteenth century London', in L. Charles and L. Duffin (eds), *Women and Work in Pre-industrial England*, London: Croom Helm.

Laing, R. D. (1965) *The Divided Self*, Harmondsworth: Penguin.

Laing, R. D. (1971) *The Politics of the Family and Other Essays*, Harmondsworth: Penguin.

Lamb, M. (ed.) (1986) *The Father's Role: Applied Perspectives*, New York: Wiley.

Lamb, M. (ed.) (1997) *The Role of the Father in Child Development*, New York: Wiley.

Lasch, C. (1977) *A Haven in a Heartless World*, New York: Basic Books.

Lawrence, A. (1994) *Women in England: 1500–1760 – A Social History*, London: Wiedenfeld & Nicolson.

Laws, G. (1997) 'Spatiality and age relations', in A. Jamieson, S. Harper and C. Victor (eds), *Critical Approaches to Ageing and Later Life*, Buckingham: Open University Press.

Layte, R. (1999) *Divided Time: Gender, Paid Employment and Domestic Labour*, Aldershot: Ashgate.

Le Feuvre, N. (1994) 'Leisure, work and gender: a sociological study of women's time in France', *Time and Society*, 3:2, 151–78.

Leclercq, J. (1961) *The Love of Learning and the Desire for God: A Study of Monastic Culture*, New York: Fordham University Press.

Lee, N. (2001) *Childhood and Society*, Buckingham: Open University Press.

Leslie, S. (2000) 'Household specialization and the male marriage wage premium', *Industrial and Labor Relations Review*, 54:1, 78–95.

Levi, P. (1987) *The Frontiers of Paradise: A Study of Monks and Monasteries*, London: Collins Harvill.

Lewis, C. and O'Brien, M. (eds) (1987) *Reassessing Fatherhood: New Observations on Fathers and the Modern Family*, London: Sage.

Lewis, J. (ed.) (1986a) *Labour of Love: Women's Experience of Home and Family, 1850–1940*, Oxford: Basil Blackwell.

Lewis, J. (1986b) 'The working-class wife and mother and state intervention, 1870–1918', in J. Lewis (ed.), *Labour and Love: Women's Experience of Home and Family, 1850–1940*, Oxford: Basil Blackwell.

Lewis, J., Shrimpton, M. and Storey, K. (1988) 'Family members' experience of off-shore oil work in Newfoundland', in J. Lewis and M. Porter (eds), *Women, Work and Family in the British, Canadian and Norwegian Offshore Oilfields*, London: Macmillan.

Lewis, R. and Salt, R. (eds) (1986) *Men in Families*, Beverly Hills, California: Sage.

Lewis, R. and Sussman, M. (eds) (1986) *Men's Changing Roles in the Family*, New York: Haworth Press.

Bibliography

Lewis, S. and Lewis, J. (eds) (1996) *The Work Family Challenge: Rethinking Employment*, London: Sage.

Little, J., Peake, L. and Richardson, P. (eds) (1988) *Women and Cities: Gender and the Urban Environment*, London: Macmillan.

Lockwood, D. ([1966] 1975) 'Sources of variation in working-class images of society', in M. Bulmer (ed.), *Working-Class Images of Society*, London: Routledge.

Lodziak, C. (2002) *The Myth of Consumerism*, London: Pluto.

Logan, S. (ed.) (1996) *The Black Family: Strengths, Self-Help, and Positive Change*, Boulder, Colorado: Westview.

Longino, C., Perzynski, A. and Stoller, E. (2002) 'Pandora's briefcase: unpacking the retirement migration decision', *Research on Aging*, 24:1, 29–49.

Lown, J. (1990) *Women and Industrialization: Gender and Work in Nineteenth Century England*, Cambridge: Polity Press.

Lukes, S. (1974) *Power: A Radical View*, London: Macmillan.

Lummis, T. (1982) 'A historical dimension of fatherhood: a case study 1980–1914', in L. McKee and M. O'Brien (eds), *The Father Figure*, London: Tavistock.

Lund, M. (1987) 'The non-custodial father: common challenges in parenting after divorce', in L. McKee and M. O'Brien (eds), *Reassessing Fatherhood*, London: Sage.

Lupton, D. (1996) *Food, the Body and the Self*, London: Sage.

Lupton, D. and Barclay L. (1997) *Constructing Fatherhood: Discourses and Experiences*, London: Sage.

Lystad, M. (1984) *At Home in America as Seen Through its Books for Children*, Cambridge, Massachusetts: Schenkman.

Mac an Ghaill, M. (1994) *The Making of Men: Masculinities, Sexualities and Schooling*, Buckingham: Open University Press.

Mac an Ghaill, M. (1996) *Understanding Masculinities: Social Relations and Cultural Arenas*, Buckingham: Open University Press.

Macewen, M. (1991) *Housing, Race and Law*, London: Routledge.

MacFarlane, A. (1986) *Marriage and Love in England: Modes of Reproduction 1300–1840*, Oxford: Basil Blackwell.

MacInnes, J. (1998) *The End of Masculinity: The Confusion of Sexual Genesis and Sexual Difference in Modern Society*, Buckingham: Open University Press.

Macmillan, M. (1984) 'Camp followers: a note on wives of the armed services', in H. Callan and S. Ardener (eds), *The Incorporated Wife*, London: Croom Helm.

Malos, E. (1980) *The Politics of Housework*, London: Allison & Busby.

Mapstone, E. (1999) *War of Words: Women and Men Arguing*, London: Vintage.

Marcuse, H. (1964) *One Dimensional Man*, New York: Free Press.

Marsiglio, W. (ed.) (1995) *Fatherhood: Contemporary Theory, Research and Social Policy*, Thousand Oaks, California: Sage.

Marsiglio, W. and Donnelly, D. (1991) 'Sexual relations in later life: a national study of married persons', *Journal of Gerontology*, 46, S338–S344.

Marsiglio, W. and Greer, R. (1994) 'A gender analysis of older men's sexuality', in E. Thompson Jr (ed.), *Older Men's Lives*, Thousand Oaks, California: Sage.

Martin, B. (1984) '"Mother wouldn't like it!"; housework as magic', *Theory, Culture and Society*, 2:2, 19–36.

Martindale, H. (1938) *Women Servants of the State: 1870–1938: A History of Women in the Civil Service*, London: Allen & Unwin.

Mason, D. (2000) *Race and Ethnicity in Modern Britain*, Oxford: Oxford University Press (2nd edn).

Mason, J. (1987) 'A bed of roses? Women, marriage and inequality in later life', in P. Allatt, T. Keil, B. Bytheway and A. Bryman (eds), *Women and the Life Cycle*, London: Macmillan.

Mason, J. (1988) 'No peace for the wicked: older married women and leisure', in M. Talbut and E. Wimbush (eds), *Relative Freedoms*, Milton Keynes: Open University Press.

Mason, J. (1989) 'Reconstructing the public and the private: the home and marriage in later life', in G. Allan and G. Crow (eds), *Home and Family: Creating the Domestic Sphere*, London: Macmillan.

Mason, M. (1995) *The Making of Victorian Sexuality*, Oxford: Oxford University Press.

Mason, P. (1993) *The English Gentleman: The Fall and Rise of an Ideal*, London: Pimlico.

Massey, D. and Denton, A. (1993) *American Apartheid: Segregation and the Making of the Underclass*, Cambridge, Massachussets: Harvard University Press.

Matthews, S. (1994) 'Men's ties to siblings in old age: contributing factors to availability and quality', in E. Thompson Jr (ed.), *Older Men's Lives*, Thousand Oaks, California: Sage.

Mauss, M. (1966 [1927]) *The Gift*, London: Cohen & West.

Mayhew, H. (1851) *London Labour and the London Poor*, London: George Woodfall.

McAdoo, H. (ed.) (1988a) *Black Families*, Newbury Park, California: Sage.

McAdoo, H. (1988b) 'Changing perspectives on the role of the black father' in P. Bronstein and C. Cowan (eds), *Fatherhood Today; Men's Changing Role in the Family*, New York: John Wiley.

McClelland, K. (1991) 'Masculinity and the "representative artisan" in Britain, 1850–90', in M. Roper and J. Tosh (eds), *Manful Assertions: Masculinities in Britain since 1800*, London: Routledge.

McGregor, D. (1966) *Leadership and Motivation*, Cambridge, Massachusetts: MIT Press.

McGuire, B. (1988) *Friendship and Community: The Monastic Experience 350–1250*, Kalamazoo, Michigan: Cistercian.

McKee, L. (1982) 'Father's participation in infant care, a critique', in L. McKee and M. O'Brien (eds), *The Father Figure*, London: Tavistock.

McKee, L. and Bell, C. (1986) 'His unemployment, her problem: the domestic and marital consequences of male unemployment', in S. Allen, A. Waton, K. Purcell and S. Wood (eds), *The Experience of Unemployment*, London: Macmillan.

McKee, L. and O'Brien, M. (eds) (1982) *The Father Figure*, London: Tavistock.

McKee, L. and O'Brien, M. (eds) (1987) *Reassessing Fatherhood*, London: Sage.

McKie, L. Bowlby, S. and Gregory, S. (eds) (1999) *Gender, Power and the Household*, London: Macmillan.

McLeod, H. (1984) *Religion and the Working Class in Nineteenth Century Britain*, London: Macmillan.

McRae, S. (1986) *Cross Class Families: A Study of Wives' Occupational Superiority*, Oxford: Clarendon Press.

McRae, S. (ed.) (1999) *Changing Britain: Families and Households in the 1990s*, Oxford: Oxford University Press.

Meldrum, T. (2000) *Domestic Service and Gender 1660–1750: Life and Work in the London Household*, Harlow: Longman.

Melville, K. (1972) *Communes in the Counter Culture: Origins, Theories, Styles of Life*, New York: William Morrow.

Mennell, S. (1985) *All Manners of Food: Eating and Taste in England and France from the Middle Ages to the Present*, Oxford: Basil Blackwell.

Mertes, K. (1988) *The English Noble Household 1250–1600: Good Governance and Politic Rule*, Oxford: Basil Blackwell.

Middleton, C. (1985) 'Women's labour and the transition to preindustrial capitalism', in L. Charles and L. Duffin (eds), *Women and Work in Pre-industrial England*, London: Croom Helm.

Mignon, S. (1998) 'Husband battering: a review of the debate over a controversial social phenomenon', in N. Jackson and G. Oates (eds), *Violence in Intimate Relationships: Examining Sociological and Psychological Issues*, Boston, Massachusetts: Butterworth/Heinemann.

Milis, L. (1992) *Angelic Monks and Earthly Men*, Woodbridge, Suffolk: The Boydell Press.

Miller, R. (1983) 'The Hoover in the Garden: middle class women and suburbanisation', *Environment and Planning D: Society and Space*, 1:1, 73–84.

Millett, K. ([1970] 1977) *Sexual Politics*, London: Virago.

MINTEL (1999) *Men Living Alone*, London: MINTEL International.

Mitchell, J. (1975) *Sexual Politics*, London: Virago.

Moen, P., Kim, J. and Hofmeister, H. (2001) 'Couples' work/retirement transitions, gender and marital quality', *Social Psychology Quarterly*, 64:1, 55–71.

Morgan, D. (1992) *Discovering Men*, London: Routledge.

Morgan, D. (1996) *Family Connections: An Introduction to Family Studies*, Oxford: Polity.

Morgan, D. (1999) 'Risk and family practices: accounting for change and fluidity in family life', in E. Silva and C. Smart (eds), *The New Family*, London: Sage.

Morris, J. (1986) 'The characteristics of sweating: the late nineteenth century London and Leeds tailoring trade', in A. John (ed.), *Unequal Opportunities: Women's Employment in England 1800–1918*, Oxford: Basil Blackwell.

Myers, M. (1986) 'Angry, abandoned husbands: assessment and treatment', in R. Lewis and M. Sussman (eds), *Men's Changing Roles in the Family*, New York: Haworth Press.

Nakosteen, R. and Zimmer, M. (1997) 'Men, money, and marriage: are high earners more prone than low earners to marry?', *Social Sciences Quarterly*, 78:1, 67–82.

Nardi, P. (ed.) (1992) *Men's Friendships*, London: Sage.

National Federation of Housing Associations (1993) *Accommodating Diversity: The Design of Housing for Minority Ethnic, Religious and Cultural Groups*, London: National Federation of Housing Associations.

New, C. (2001) 'Oppressed and oppressors? The systematic mistreatment of men', *Sociology*, 35:3, 729–48.

Newbolt, P. (1996) *G.A. Henty 1832–1902: A Bibliographical Study*, Aldershot: Scholar Press.

Newman, K. (1988) *Falling from Grace: The Experience of Downward Mobility in the American Middle Class*, New York: Free Press.

Noyes, J. (1973) 'Inquest on New Harmony', in R. Kanter (ed.), *Communes: Creating and Managing the Collective Life*, New York: Harper & Row.

Nutt, D. (1999) 'Women without children: their family and friendship networks', unpublished PhD, University of Lancaster.

Oakley, A. (1974) *Housewife*, Harmondsworth: Penguin.

Oakley, A. (1981) *Subject Women*, London: Fontana.

O'Brien, M. (1987) 'Patterns of kinship and friendship among lone fathers', in L. McKee and M. O'Brien (eds), *Reassessing Fatherhood*, London: Sage.

Oliker, S. (1989) *Best Friends and Marriage: Exchange among Women*, Berkeley, California: University of California Press.

Oliver, P. (1997) *Dwellings: The House Across the World*, Oxford: Phaidon.

Osterud, N. (1986) 'Gender divisions and the organisation of work in the Leicester hosiery industry', in A. John (ed.), *Unequal Opportunities: Women's Employment in England 1800–1918*, Oxford: Basil Blackwell.

Pahl, J. (1983) 'The allocation of money and the structuring of inequality within marriage', *Sociological Review*, 31: 237–62.

Pahl, J. (1988) 'Earning, sharing, spending: married couples and their money', in G. Parker and R. Walker (eds), *Money Matters*, London: Sage.

Pahl, J. (1989) *Money and Marriage*, London: Macmillan.

Pahl, J. (1990) 'Household spending, personal spending and the control of money in marriage', *Sociology*, 24:1, 119–38.

Pahl, R. (1984) *Divisions of Labour*, Oxford: Basil Blackwell.

Palmer, P. (1989) *Domesticity and Dirt: Housewives and Domestic Servants in the United States, 1920–1945*, Philadelphia, Pennsylvania: Temple University Press.

Parke, R. (1996) *Fatherhood*, Cambridge, Massachusetts: Harvard University Press.

Parker, D. and Song, M. (2001) *Rethinking Mixed Race*, London: Pluto.

Parker, S. (1982) *Work and Retirement*, London: Allen & Unwin.

Parnes, H. (1981) *Work and Retirement: A Longitudinal Study*, Cambridge, Massachusetts: MIT Press.

Parnes, H., Crowley, J., Haurin, R., Less, L., Morgan W., Mott, P. and Nestel, G. (1985) *Retirement Among American Men*, New York: Heath.

Parsons, T. (1964) *Essays in Sociological Theory*, New York: Free Press.

Partington, A. (1989) 'The designer housewife in the 1950's', in J. Attfield and P. Kirkham (eds), *A View from the Interior: Feminism, Women and Design*, London: Women's Press.

Payne, G. (1987) *Employment and Opportunity*, London: Macmillan.

Pearson, L. (1988) *The Architectural and Social History of Cooperative Living*, London: Macmillan.

Pennington, S. and Westover, B. (1989) *A Hidden Workforce: Homeworkers in England, 1850–1985*, London: Macmillan.

Peplau, L. and Cochran, S. (1990) 'A relationship perspective in homosexuality', in D. McWhirter, D. Sanders and J. Reinisch (eds), *Homosexuality/Heterosexuality: Concepts of Sexuality*, Oxford: Oxford University Press.

Peplau, L., Cochran, S., Rook, K. and Pandensky, C. (1978) 'Loving women: attachment and autonomy in lesbian relationships', *Journal of Social Issues*, 34:3, 7–28.

Perrot, R. (1990) 'At home', in M. Perrot (ed.), *A History of Private Life. IV – From the Fires of Revolution to the Great War* (trans. A. Goldhammer), Cambridge – Massachusetts: Harvard University Press.

Peterson, M. (1989) *Family, Love and Work in the Lives of Victorian Gentlewoman*, Bloomington, Indiana: Indiana University Press.

Phillips, R. (1923) *The Servantless Home*, London: Country Life Publications.

Pienta, A. and Haywood, M. (2002) 'Who expects to continue working after age 62? The retirement plans of couples', *Journals of Gerontology Series B: Psychological Sciences and Social Sciences*, 57:4, 199–208.

Platt, S. (1986) 'Recent trends in parasuicide ("attempted suicide") and unemployment among men in Edinburgh', in S. Allen, A. Waton, K. Purcell and S. Wood (eds), *The Experience of Unemployment*, London: Macmillan.

Pollock, L. (1983) *Forgotten Children: Parent Child Relationships from 1500 to 1900*, Cambridge: Cambridge University Press.

Power, A. (1993) *Hovels to High Rise: State Housing in Europe Since 1850*, London: Routledge.

Pugh, D. (1983) *Sons of Liberty: The Masculine Mind in Nineteenth-Century America*: Westport, Connecticut: Greenwood.

Qvortrup, J. (1994) 'Childhood matters: an introduction', in J. Qvortrup, M. Bardy, G. Sgritta and H. Wintersberger (eds), *Childhood Matters: Social Theory, Practice and Politics*, Aldershot: Avebury.

Rapoport, A. (1969) *House, Form and Culture*, Englewood Cliffs, New Jersey: Prentice Hall.

Ravenhill, A. (1910) 'Some relations of sanitary science to family life and individual efficiency' in A. Ravenhill and C. Schiff (eds), *Household Administration: Its Place in the Higher Education of Women*, London: Grant Robinson.

Raza, M. (1993) *Islam in Britain: Past, Present and Future*, Leicester: Volcano Press.

Reissman, C. (1990) *Divorce Talk: Women and Men make Sense of Personal Relationships*, New Brunswick, New Jersey: Rutgers University Press.

Rendall, J. (1985) *The Origins of Modern Feminism*, London: Macmillan.

Richards, M. (1987) 'Fatherhood, marriage and sexuality: some speculations on the English middle-class family', in C. Lewis, and M. O'Brien (eds), *Reassessing Fatherhood*, London: Sage.

Richardson, V. (1999) 'Women and retirement', *Journal of Women and Aging*, 11:2–3, 46–66.

Rigby, A. (1974) *Alternative Realities: A Study of Communes and their Members*, London: Routledge.

Riley, D. (1983) '"The free mothers": pronatalism and working women in industry at the end of the last war in Britain', *History Workshop Journal*, 11, 59–118.

Roberts, E. (1949), 'To start you talking', in M. Sherman (ed.), *The Daily Mail Ideal Home Book 1952–3*, London: Daily Mail Ideal Home Publications.

Roberts, M. (1991) *Living in a Man Made World: Gender Assumptions in Modern Housing Design*, London: Routledge.

Robinson, O. and Wallace, J. (1984) *Part-time Employment and Sex Discrimination Legislation in Great Britain*, Department of Employment Research Paper No. 43, London: HMSO.

Rohe, W., Zante, S. and McCarthy, G. (2002) 'Home ownership and access to opportunity', *Housing Studies*, 17:1, 51–61.

Rose, M. (1988) *Industrial Behaviour: Research and Control*, Harmondsworth: Penguin.

Rosenblatt, P. Karis, T. and Powell, R. (1995) *Multiracial Couples: Black and White Voices*, Thousand Oaks, California: Sage.

Russell, G. (1983) *The Changing Role of Fathers*, St Lucia: University of Queensland Press.

Russell, G. (1986) 'Primary care taking and role sharing fathers', in M. Lamb (ed.), *The Father's Role: Applied Perspectives*, New York: Wiley.

Saegert, S. (1980) 'Masculine cites and feminine suburbs: polarized ideas, contradictory realities', *Signs: Journal of Women in Culture and Society*, 5:3, S96–111.

Salaman, G. (1971) 'Two occupational communities: examples of a remarkable convergence of work and non-work', *Sociological Review*, 19, 389–407.

Sambhi, P. (1989) *Sikhism*, Cheltenham: Stanley Thorne.

Sarsby, J. (1985) 'Sexual segregation in the pottery industry', *Feminist Review*, 21, 67–93.

Sarsby, J. (1988) *Missuses and Mouldrunners*, Milton Keynes: Open University Press.

Saunders, P. (1990) *A Nation of Homeowners*, London: Unwin Hyman.

Saunders, P. and Williams, P. (1988) 'The constitution of home: towards a research agenda', *Housing Studies*, 3:2, 81–93.

Savage, M. (1987) *The Dynamics of Working-Class Politics: The Labour Movement in Preston 1880–1940*, London: Routledge.

Savageau, D. (1999) *Retirement Places Rated*, New York: Macmillan Travel.

Scanlon, J. (1995) *Inarticulate Longings: The Ladies Home Journal, Gender, and the Promises of Consumer Culture*, New York: Routledge.

Scase, R. and Goffee, R. (1980) *The Real World of the Small Business Owner*, London: Croom Helm.

Schiff, C. (1910) 'Some relations of sanitary science to family life and individual efficiency', in A. Ravenhill and C. Schiff (eds), *Household Administration: Its Place in the Higher Education of Women*, London: Grant Richards.

Schwartz-Cowan, R. (1989) *More Work for Mother: The Ironies of Household Technology from the Open Hearth to the Microwave*, London: Free Association Books.

Sciama, L. (1984) 'Ambivalence and dedication: academic wives in Cambridge University, 1870–1970', in H. Callan and S. Ardener (eds), *The Incorporated Wife*, London: Croom Helm.

Seidler, V. J. (1991) *Recreating Sexual Politics*, London: Routledge.

Seidler, V. J. (ed.) (1992) *Men, Sex and Relationships*, London: Routledge.

Seiter, E. (1993) *Sold Separately: Parents and Children in Consumer Culture*, New Brunswick, New Jersey: Rutgers University Press.

Shahar, S. (1983) *The Fourth Estate: A History of Women in the Middle Ages*, London: Routledge.

Sharpe, S. (1995) *Just Like a Girl*, Harmondsworth: Penguin.

Shaw, A. (1988) *A Pakistani Community in Britain*, Oxford: Basil Blackwell.

Shaw, A. (2000) *Kinship and Continuity: Pakistani Families in Britain*, Amsterdam: Harwood.

Shaw Sparrow, W. (1908) *The English House: How to Judge its Periods and Styles*, London: Eveleigh Nash.

Sherman, M. (ed.) (1949) *The Daily Mail Ideal Home Book 1949–1950*, London: Daily Mail Ideal Home Publications.

Shoemaker, R. (1998) *Gender in English Society 1650–1850*, London: Longman.

Shorter, E. (1976) 'Women's Work: what difference did capitalism make?', *Theory and Society*, 4, 513–28.

Sibley, D. (1995) 'Families and domestic routines: constructing the boundaries of childhood', in S. Pile and N. Thrift (eds), *Mapping the Subject: Geographies of Cultural Transformation*, London: Routledge.

Silva, E. (2000a) 'The cook, the cooker and the gendering of the kitchen', *Sociological Review*, 48:4, 612–28.

Silva, E. (2000b) 'The politics of consumption @ home: practices and dispositions in the uses of technologies', *Pavis Papers in Social and Cultural Research*, No. 1, Milton Keynes: Open University, Faculty of Social Sciences.

Silva, E. and Smart, C. (eds) (1999) *The New Family*, London: Sage.

Silverstein, M. and Zablotsky, D. (1996) *Journal of Gerontology Series B: Psychological Sciences and Social Sciences*, 51:3, S150–S156.

Simon, B. (1987) *Never Married Women*, Philadelphia, Pennsylvania: Temple University Press.

Simpson, B. (1999) *Changing Families: An Ethnographic Approach to Divorce and Separation*, Oxford: Berg.

Singh Ghuman, P. (1999) *Asian Adolescents in the West*, London: British Psychological Society Books.

Sinha, R. (1998) *The Cultural Adjustment of Asian Lone Mothers Living in London*, Aldershot: Ashgate.

Skellington, R. and Morris, P. (1992) *Race in Britain Today*, London: Sage.

Smart, C. and Neale, B. (1999) *Family Fragments*, Cambridge: Polity Press.

Smith, H. (1982) *Reasons's Disciples: Seventeenth Century English Feminists*, Urbana, Illinois: Illinois University Press.

Smith, M. (1986) 'Pluralism, race and ethnicity in selected African countries', in J. Rex and D. Mason (eds), *Theories of Race and Ethnic Relations*, Cambridge: Cambridge University Press.

Solheim, J. (1988) 'Coming home to work: men, women and marriage in the Norwegian offshore oil industry', in J. Lewis and M. Porter (eds), *Women, Work and Family in the British, Canadian and Norwegian Offshore Oilfields*, London: Macmillan.

Solomon, K. and Szwabo, P. (1994) 'The work-oriented culture', in E. Thompson Jr (ed.), *Older Men's Lives*, Thousand Oaks, California: Sage.

Somerville, J. (2000) *Feminism and the Family: Politics and Society in the UK and the USA*, Basingstoke: Palgrave.

Somerville, P. (1989) 'Home sweet home: a critical comment on Saunders and Williams', *Housing Studies*, 4:2, 113–18.

Somerville, P. (2000) 'The meaning of home for African-Caribbean-British people', in F. Boal (ed.), *Ethnicity and Housing*, Aldershot: Ashgate.

Sonnenfeld, J. (1988) *The Hero's Farewell: What Happens when CEOs Retire*, New York: Oxford University Press.

Spencer, A. and Podmore, D. (1983a) 'Life on the periphery of a profession: the experience of women lawyers', British Sociological Association Annual Conference, Cardiff (mimeo).

Spencer, A. and Podmore, D. (1983b) 'Women lawyers: marginal members of a male dominated profession', in A. Spencer and D. Podmore (eds), *In a Man's World: Essays on Women in Male-Dominated Professions*, London: Tavistock.

Stacey, J. (1991) *Brave New Families: Stories of Domestic Upheaval in Late Twentieth Century America*, New York: Basic Books.

Staples, R. (ed.) (1999) *The Black Family: Essays and Studies*, Belmont, California: Wadsworth (6th edn).

Steedman, C. (1999) 'What a rag rug means', in I. Bryden and J. Floyd (eds), *Domestic Space: Reading the Nineteenth Century Interior*, Manchester: Manchester University Press.

Stein, S. (1992) *The Shaker Experience in America: A History of the United Society of Believers*, New Haven, Connecticut: Yale University Press.

Stone, L. (1979) *Family, Sex and Marriage in England 1500–1800*, Harmondsworth: Penguin.

Stone, L. (1992) *Uncertain Unions: Marriage in England 1660–1753*, Oxford: Oxford University Press.

Stoneall, L. (1979) 'The Women of Hidden Valley', in R. Shon le Cavan and M. Singh Das (eds), *Communes: Historical and Contemporary*, New Delhi: Vikas.

Stopes-Roe, M. and Cochrane, R. (1989) 'Traditionalism in the family: a comparison between Asian and British cultures and between generations', *Journal of Comparative Family Studies*, 20:1, 141–58.

Strauss, M. (1999) 'The controversy over domestic violence by women: a methodological, theoretical and sociology of science analysis', in X. Arriga and S. Oskamp (eds), *Violence in Intimate Relationships*, Thousand Oaks, California: Sage.

Stromberg, A. and Harkess, S. (1988) *Working Women: Theories and Facts in Perspective*, Mountain View, California: Mayfield.

Sullivan, O. (2000) 'The division of domestic labour: twenty years of change?', *Sociology*, 34:3, 437–56.

Szinovacz, M., DeViney, S. and Davey, A. (2001) 'Influence of family obligations and relationships on retirement: variations by gender, race and marital status', *Journals of Gerontology Series B: Psychological Sciences and Social Sciences*, 56:1, 20–7.

Taylor, F. (1917) *The Principles of Scientific Management*, New York: Harper Brothers.

Thompson, E. Jr (ed.) (1994) *Older Men's Lives*, Thousand Oaks, California: Sage.

Thompson, E. P. (1968) *The Making of the English Working Class*, Harmondsworth: Penguin.

Thompson, F. (1988) *The Rise of Respectable Society: A Social History of Victorian Britain 1830–1900*, London: Fontana.

Thompson, M. (1979) *Rubbish Theory: The Creation and Destruction of Value*, Oxford: Oxford Press.

Thompson, P., Itzin, C. and Abendstern, M. (1990) *I Don't Feel Old: The Experience of Later Life*, Oxford: Oxford University Press.

Toliver, S. (1998) *Black Families in Corporate America*, Thousand Oaks, California: Sage.

Tomlinson, A. (1990) 'Home fixtures: doing it yourself in a privatised world', in A. Tomlinson (ed.), *Consumption, Identity and Style: Marketing, Meanings, and the Packaging of Pleasure*, London: Routledge.

Tosh, J. (1991) 'Domesticity and manliness in the Victorian middle class', in M. Roper and J. Tosh (eds), *Manful Assertions: Masculinities in Britain since 1800*, London: Routledge.

Tosh, J. (1999) *A Man's Place: Masculinity and the Middle-Class Home in Victorian England*, New Haven, Connecticut: Yale University Press.

Trumbach, R. (1978) *The Rise of the Egalitarian Family*, New York: Academy Press.

Tunstall, J. (1962) *The Fishermen: The Sociology of an Extreme Profession*, London: MacGibbon & Kee.

Turner, B. and Rennell, T. (1996) *When Daddy Came Home: How Family Life Changed Forever in 1945*, London: Pimlico.

Turner, J. (1981) *Hard up Husband: James Turner's Diary, Halifax 1881/2*, Orwell: Ellisons.

Turner, V. (1987) 'Betwixt and between: the liminal period in rites of passage', in L. Mahdi (ed.), *Betwixt and Between: Masculine and Feminine Patterns of Initiation*, La Salle, Illinois: Open Court.

Vanek, J. (1980) 'Time spent in housework', in A. Amsden (ed.), *The Economics of Women and Work*, Harmondsworth: Penguin.

Valentine, G. (1999) 'Oh please, Mum. Oh please, Dad: negotiating children's spatial boundaries', in L. McKie, S. Bowlby and S. Gregory (eds) *Gender, Power and the Household*, London: Macmillan.

Vartanian, T. and McNamara, J. (2002) 'Older women in poverty: impact of midlife factors', *Journal of Marriage and the Family*, 64 (May), 532–48.

Veblen, T. (1934) *The Theory of the Leisure Class*, New York: Modern Library.

Vicinus, M. (1985) *Independent Women: Work and Community for Single Women 1850–1920*, London: Virago.

Vogler, C. (1998) 'Money in the household: some underlying issues of power', *Sociological Review*, 46:4, 687–713.

Vogler, C, and Pahl, J. (1994) 'Money, power and inequality within marriage', *Sociological Review*, 42:2, 263–88.

Waehler, C. (1999) *Bachelors: The Psychology of Men Who Haven't Married*, Westport, Connecticut: Praeger.

Wagner, J. (1979) 'Male Supremacy: its role in a contemporary commune and its structural alternatives', in R. Shon le Cavan and M. Singh Das (eds), *Communes: Historical and Contemporary*, New Delhi: Vikas.

Wagner, P. (1984) 'Suburban landscapes for nuclear families: the case of greenbelt towns in the United States', *Built Environment*, 10:1, 35–41.

Walby, S. (1986) *Patriarchy at Work*, Cambridge: Polity Press.

Walters, W. (2002a) 'Later-life migration in the United States: a review of recent research', *Journal of Planning Literature*, 17:1, 37–66.

Walters, W. (2002b) 'Place characteristics and later life migration', *Research on Aging*, 24:2, 243–77.

Wardhaugh, J. (1999) 'The unaccommodated woman: home, homelessness and identity', *Sociological Review*, 47:1, 91–109.

Warr, P. (1987) *Work, Unemployment and Mental Health*, Oxford: Clarendon Press.

Warren, T., Rowlingson, K. and Whyley, C. (2001) 'Female finances: gender wage gaps and gender asset gaps', *Work Employment and Society*, 15:3, 465–88.

Waters, M. (1989) 'Patriarchy and virarchy: an exploration and reconstruction of concepts of masculine domination', *Sociology*, 23:2, 193–211.

Watkins, S. (1984) 'Spinsters', *Journal of Family History*, 9:4, 310–25.

Wearing, B. and Wearing, S. (1988) 'All in a day's leisure: gender and the concept of leisure', *Leisure Studies*, 7:1, 111–23.

Weber, M. ([1922] 1978) *Economy and Society: An Outline of Interpretive Sociology*, Berkeley, California: University of California Press.

Webster, W. (1998) *Imagining Home: Gender Race and Identity, 1945–1964*, London: UCL Press.

Weeks, J., Heaphy, B. and Donovan, C. (1999) 'Partnership rites; commitment and ritual in non-heterosexual relationships', in J. Seymour and P. Bagguley (eds), *Relating Intimacies: Power and Resistance*, London: Macmillan.

Weeks, J., Heaphy, B. and Donovan, C. (2001) *Same Sex Intimacies: Families of Choice and other Life Experiments*, London: Routledge.

Wekerle, G., Peterson, R. and Morley, D. (eds) (1980) *New Space for Women*, Boulder, Colorado: Westview.

Werbner, P. (1988) 'Taking and giving: working women and family bonds in a Pakistani immigrant neighbourhood', in S. Westwood and P. Bhachu (eds), *Enterprising Women: Ethnicity, Economy and Gender Relations*, London: Routledge.

West, J. (1982) *Women, Work and the Labour Market*, London: Routledge.

Western, J. (1992) *A Passage to England: Barbadian Londoners Speak of Home*, London: UCL Press.

Wheelock, J. (1990) *Husbands at Home: The Domestic Economy in a Post Industrial Society*, London: Routledge.

Whyte, W. (1957) *The Organisation Man*, Harmondsworth: Penguin.

Wilkin, D. and Hughes, B. (1987) 'Residential care of elderly people: the consumer's view', *Ageing and Society*, 7:1, 175–201.

Willcocks, D., Peace, S. and Kellaher, L. (1987) *Private Lives in Public Places*, London: Tavistock.

Wilson, A. (1997) *The Strange Ride of Rudyard Kipling: His Life and Works*, London: Secker & Warburg.

Wilson, D. and Johnson, C. (1995) 'White attitudes towards black and white interracial marriage', in C. Jacobson (ed.), *American Families: Issues in Race and Ethnicity*, New York: Garland.

Wilson, E. (1980) *Only Halfway to Paradise: Women in Postwar Britain: 1945–1968*, London: Tavistock.

Wilson, J. (1990) *Single Fathers: Australian Men Take on a New Role*, Melbourne: Sun Books.

Winn, D. (1986) *Men on Divorce: Conversations with Denise Winn*, London: Piatkus.

Woloch, N. (1996) *Women and the American Experience: A Concise History*, New York: McGraw-Hill.

Woollacott, J. (1980) 'Dirty and defiant work', in G. Esland and G. Salaman (eds), *The Politics of Work and Occupations*, Milton Keynes: Open University Press.

Worden, S. (1989) 'Powerful women: electricity in the home 1919–40', in J. Attfield and P. Kirkham (eds), *A View from the Interior: Feminism, Women and Design*, London: Women's Press.

Yaswen, G. (1973) 'Sunrise Hill Community: post-mortem', in R. Kanter (ed.), *Communes: Creating and Managing the Collective Life*, New York: Harper & Row.

Young, M. (1984) 'Police wives: a reflection of police concepts of order and control', in H. Callan and S. Ardener (eds), *The Incorporated Wife*, London: Croom Helm.

Young, M. and Willmott, P. (1957) *Family and Kinship in East London*: Harmondsworth: Penguin.

Young, M. and Willmott, P. (1975) *The Symmetrical Family*, Harmondsworth: Penguin.

Zelizer, V. (1989) 'The social meaning of money: "special moneys"', *American Journal of Sociology*, 95:2, 342–77.

Zimmeck, M. (1986) 'Jobs for the girls: the expansion of clerical work for women, 1850–1914', in A. John (ed.) *Unequal Opportunities: Women's Employment in England 1800–1918*, Oxford: Basil Blackwell.

Zimmerman, L., Mitchell, B., Wister, A. and Gutman, G. (2000) 'Unanticipated consequences: a comparison of expected and actual retirement timing among older women', *Journal of Women and Aging*, 12:1–2, 109–28.

Zweig, F. (1952) *The British Worker*, Harmondsworth: Penguin.

Index